Fundamental Modeling Concepts

Fundamental Modeling Concepts

Effective Communication of IT Systems

Andreas Knöpfel, Bernhard Gröne, Peter Tabeling

John Wiley & Sons, Ltd

Copyright © 2005   John Wiley & Sons Ltd, The Atrium, Southern Gate, Chichester, West Sussex PO19 8SQ, England

Telephone (+44) 1243 779777

Email (for orders and customer service enquiries): cs-books@wiley.co.uk

Visit our Home Page on www.wiley.com

This publication is designed to provide accurate and authoritative information in regard to the subject matter covered. It is sold on the understanding that the Publisher is not engaged in rendering professional services. If professional advice or other expert assistance is required, the services of a competent professional should be sought.

Other Wiley Editorial Offices

John Wiley & Sons Inc., 111 River Street, Hoboken, NJ 07030, USA

Jossey-Bass, 989 Market Street, San Francisco, CA 94103-1741, USA

Wiley-VCH Verlag GmbH, Boschstr. 12, D-69469 Weinheim, Germany

John Wiley & Sons Australia Ltd, 42 McDougall Street, Milton, Queensland 4064, Australia

John Wiley & Sons (Asia) Pte Ltd, 2 Clementi Loop #02-01, Jin Xing Distripark, Singapore 129809

John Wiley & Sons Canada Ltd, 22 Worcester Road, Etobicoke, Ontario, Canada M9W 1L1

Wiley also publishes its books in a variety of electronic formats. Some content that appears in print may not be available in electronic books.

Library of Congress Cataloging-in-Publication Data

Knöpfel, Andreas.
  Fundamental modeling concepts : Effective Communication of IT Systems / Andreas Knöpfel, Bernhard Gröne, Peter Tabeling.
     p. cm.
Includes bibliographical references and index.
ISBN-13: 978-0-470-02710-3
ISBN-10: 0-470-02710-X (pbk. : alk. paper)
1.   Management information systems. 2.   Computer architecture. 3.   System design – Methodology. I. Title: Communicating the architecture of information systems. II. Gröne, Bernhard. III. Tabeling, Peter. IV. Title.
  T58.6.K594 2006
  658.4′038011 – dc22

                   2005034998

British Library Cataloguing in Publication Data

A catalogue record for this book is available from the British Library
ISBN-13: 978-0-470-02710-3
ISBN-10: 0-470-02710-X

Typeset in 11/13.5 Palatino by Laserwords Private Limited, Chennai, India
Printed and bound in Great Britain by Bell & Bain, Glasgow
This book is printed on acid-free paper responsibly manufactured from sustainable forestry in which at least two trees are planted for each one used for paper production.

For Dieter, Vera and Olaf
— Andreas

For Ruth and Eva
— Bernhard

For my parents
— Peter

Contents

Foreword

At the end of my education in electrical engineering, 40 years ago, I actually didn't care much about software – I thought it to be rather trivial. But ten years later, a friend of mine at Siemens Corp. got me involved in the analysis of a software system which had been developed with an effort of over 100 man years. From that day on, the problem of mastering informational complexity has dominated my professional life. At that time, it was quite clear to me and many others that hardware capabilities such as storage capacity, channel bandwidth and processor speed would continue to grow exponentially for many years, and that as a consequence of this, the size and complexity of software systems would grow exponentially, too. Today, the code base of large software companies, such as SAP, has already passed beyond many hundreds millions of lines of code.

While new programming languages and tools helped developers implement more functionality in shorter times, understanding the resulting software turned out to be one of the biggest challenges. Preventing a software system from collapsing under its own complexity cannot be achieved by technology alone. Large development organizations need to think, design and communicate very efficiently and at a much higher level than in the early days. In 1990, Hasso Plattner, one of the founders of SAP, became aware that identifying and documenting the core system structures was a crucial part of mastering the complexity of their evolving R/3 system. He saw the need to grasp and express the valuable knowledge and ideas of the leading developers. In order to build on it, they had to preserve this intangible asset and make it available to the company. As if it had been planned, at that point in time we met again after not having had any contact since he had written his Masters thesis 22 years ago. From then on, we cooperated closely.

Together with my research group, I had developed a method for modeling and describing large software systems, later known as FMC (Fundamental Modeling Concepts). My engineering background helped me to avoid the idea that software and hardware should be viewed as two completely separate categories which had nothing in common. On the contrary, I was convinced from the very beginning that the complexity of digital hardware and the complexity of software originated from the same phenomenon. In both cases, the implementation is only a formal structure which does not show the ideas behind it. These ideas must be described separately. In order to guarantee that such descriptions can easily be understood, modeling concepts should be used which are equally capable of describing systems of cooperating people. This is the philosophy behind FMC.

Using FMC for modeling the R/3 platform provided convincing proof of quality – both of R/3 and of FMC. We built up a comprehensive library of compact yet precise technical reports. Writing all these documents was a remarkable undertaking, but Hasso Plattner is convinced that the effort paid off in the long term. The reports allowed new personnel to become acquainted with the system architecture much faster and established a foundation for more efficient development.

Today, software engineering is considered as important as the other, established engineering disciplines. However, it has not yet reached the same level of maturity. When it comes to architectural design, software projects suffer from insufficient abstractions, cumbersome modeling techniques and fuzzy terminology. This book tackles this unsatisfactory situation.

For a retiring academic teacher, nothing is more gratifying than to see how his students take over and cultivate the results of his lifelong efforts. The three authors of this book once were my PhD students, and it made me very proud when I first read this excellent manuscript. This book will be of much help to everyone who is in charge of managing complex software projects.

Potsdam, December 7th, 2005
Siegfried Wendt

Preface

The very beginning of FMC dates back to a workshop initiated by Siegfried Wendt in the Lüneburger Heide, Germany, in 1974. The participants identified the field of human communication as the main source of problems in software engineering, namely intransparency of descriptions (discrepancy over what is meant and what is expressed) and information monopoly (information not being shared). During the next three decades, scientific research and cooperation with different industrial partners shaped a set of modeling principles which have proved to address the identified problems efficiently.

Today most people agree about the huge impact of effective and efficient communication on the software development process. There is also a consensus that the creation of large and complex systems requires clarity concerning the concepts before proceeding to dive into implementation. While the advent of UML has significantly improved the state-of-the-art methods of representing structures at code-level, communication at the conceptual level often misses a high–level standard.

This book is a comprehensive description of FMC's concepts, notation and its application in practice. A few typical, familiar scenarios where FMC can be used to improve the development process provide the starting point. Chapters 2–5 explain how to read FMC diagrams and how to understand the main concepts of FMC. The remaining chapters delve into the concepts of developing and refining FMC models and explain the application of FMC in the development process. They provide the link between conceptual models and implementation structures and illustrate how FMC supports the daily work of software engineering and how it supplements the existing approaches.

FMC provides both a mental framework to identify useful abstractions, and a simple notation to illustrate them. Finding the right abstractions and developing useful models and representations is very important. Since this is not always easy, is rarely formal and depends on the intended purpose, the concepts and notations of FMC are illustrated by means of many examples. Completing the exercises will also give you the first idea of how to apply the concepts in practice.

Even though we participated in the development of FMC, we did not invent it. First of all, our thanks go to Siegfried Wendt for his vision and his enduring effort in making software systems more understandable. We would like to thank everyone who contributed to the development of FMC, to learn about its application in real–life projects and to realize this book. We owe a large debt of thanks to the Hasso Plattner Institute for Software Systems Engineering, especially to Hasso Plattner, for providing vital support in the accomplishment of this endeavor. Thanks to Rémy Apfelbacher and his fellows for contributing the reference sheets and the glossary and also for developing the FMC Visio™ stencils. Our thanks to Robert Mitschke, Jan Karstens, Konrad Hübner, Thimo Langbehn for their reviews and constructive criticism. Also our thanks go to all the reviewers supporting our proposal. Finally, we would like to thank the people of Wiley, especially Benjamin Devey, Drew Kennerly and Sally Tickner, for their professional and friendly assistance in the publication of this work.

Chapter 1

Introduction

"But the business of software building isn't really high-tech at all. It's most of all a business of *talking to each other and writing things down*. Those who were making major contributions to the field were more likely to be its best communicators than its best technicians." – Tom DeMarco [DeM95]

1.1 The need for communication

1.1.1 Software and people

Developing software is a hard task. Many approaches have been followed in order to implement more functionality in less code statements and to support coding with powerful tools. Unfortunately, software projects are still hard to handle. One reason is that the 'human factor' becomes more and more important, as:

- software is being developed in teams;

- many projects require an integration of third-party products or other existing software which have to be understood; and

- coding only takes a small fraction of the total time to develop a software product, as collecting requirements, organizing teamwork and discussing concepts becomes more and more important.

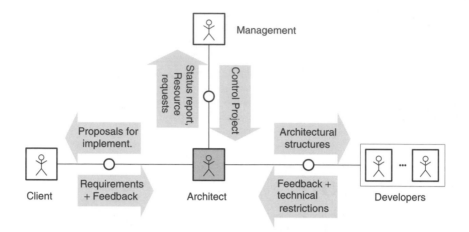

Figure 1.1:   Stakeholders have to communicate

In a nutshell: being able to understand, describe, and communicate technical information becomes an increasingly important skill required by architects, developers and project managers.

Figure 1.1 shows a typical project set-up from the communication point of view. The architect communicates with the client, the management and the team of developers. For each of them, he or she has to focus on different aspects and use different levels of technical detail.

This chapter outlines the communication tasks of an architect which will be addressed in this book.

1.1.2   Structure information to prepare communication

"Take a look at the product XY and tell us if we can build on it in our project."

There are so many systems, platforms and technologies that you have to understand before you can write a single line of code. By learning a technology, or analyzing an existing system, you need to build a model of it in your mind.

Modeling

A *model* is an abstraction of an existing or planned system which comprises only those aspects which are relevant to its purpose. A system model can be used, for example, to communicate, construct or analyze.

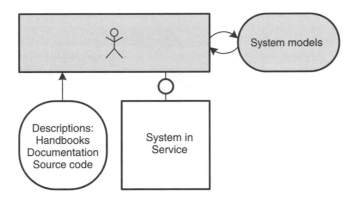

Figure 1.2: Structure information about a system

Modeling describes the process of creating a model, which includes choosing the most important facts and leaving out others. This *abstraction* heavily depends on the purpose of the model and its addressees.

By jotting down the models, you are able to recall this knowledge later on. Furthermore, you can use them to communicate this information to other people.

There are many modeling techniques and notations which address various purposes. This book will present the Fundamental Modeling Concepts (FMC) which were developed to support communication about technical systems.

The FMC block diagram in Figure 1.2 shows a person who reads system descriptions, such as handbooks, documentation or the source code, observes and uses the system in service, to work out a new set of system models. In this case, the architect or developer uses modeling to structure information about a system, to abstract from too many details, or to obtain an overview.

FMC Block Diagrams

A *block diagram* shows the compositional structure of a system. The building blocks are *agents* (rectangular nodes) which process information, and *locations* (round nodes) which are used to store or transport information. Lines or arrows connect agents and locations and depict which agent can access which location, including the direction of information flow. Block diagrams are introduced in Chapter 2. A notation summary can be found on page 300.

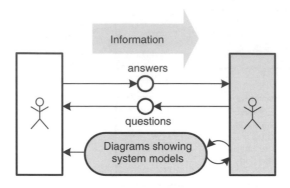

Figure 1.3:   Retrieve system information from people

1.1.3   Retrieve system information from people

"You must have missed this topic in the list of requirements!"

"Ask someone from department X to explain their module, we need to integrate it into our product. Unfortunately, they are very busy at the moment."

It is not unusual that important system knowledge can only be found in the heads of their developers and architects. Even worse, sometimes it is spread over many people but no one has a complete picture.

This scenario is similar to the previous Section 1.1.2, but in this case you need to interview humans to obtain technical information. Many factors can affect efficient communication. Even assuming that all interviewees are willing to share their knowledge, there is still the danger of talking at cross–purposes or of focusing on unimportant details.

You can support interviews with diagrams, as shown in Figure 1.3, because you can show the interviewee what you have understood so far, and establish a common terminology. Furthermore, working with graphics to grasp abstract structures makes communication more effective – there is something to 'point at' while discussing.

Iterative Modeling

Instead of creating an accurate model after you have collected all the facts, it is often better to start with an incomplete or potentially wrong model which shows what you have understood so far, and let the knowledge bearers correct you. Prepare diagrams which serve as starting points for subsequent interviews.

The same applies to creating a system architecture. Allow for iterations of the system model, give every team member the opportunity to consider their aspects and the consequences for the architecture.

Another scenario also deals with obtaining information from people: finding out the customer's requirements. A typical problem of requirements engineering are requirements which come up after the development has already begun. It is simply not realistic for a customer to think of every requirement before he or she has seen or even touched a solution, usually a prototype.

Mental Prototypes can support the process of finding and formulating requirements. A *mental protoype* is a model of a system which outlines a potential system solution. It describes functionality, but leaves open most of the implementation details. The customers can imagine how the system works, check if their requirements are met and whether they are happy with this solution.

Mental prototyping only works if customers can understand the model easily and can execute the model in their mind.

Mental Prototype

System model showing an abstract solution to the customer's requirements. Serves to get feedback from the customer and to refine or discuss requirements. See Section 8.3.1.

1.1.4 Communicate system information to people

"I will write this program for the customer, but please don't ask me to explain it to them."

"Don't annoy me with those marketing diagrams. I want more substantial information, but no source code, please!"

"Can you please explain . . ."

Sharing knowledge is a crucial task when working in a team. Communication becomes more complex if you have to address more than one or two people, and if they have different knowledge and expectations.

In this scenario, you need to consider didactical issues, as you need to transport your knowledge to other people in an efficient way. As Figure 1.4 shows, diagrams of system models can support this process, assuming that the addressees understand them quickly.

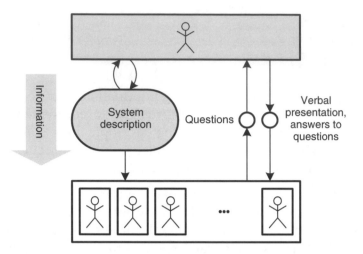

Figure 1.4:   Communicate information about a system

Didactical Modeling

Use diagrams of the system model to transport information to other people. Focus on these diagrams while explaining the system. Get feedback from the attendees about comprehensibility, apply their suggestions to your final report. See Section 8.4.2.

1.1.5   Support communication

"I don't think we're talking about the same subject."

It is not unusual for people to talk at cross–purposes, so use the same words even though they may have a different meaning to them, or do not contain the same level of detail.

If the discussion is about technical issues, you can avoid this situation by using system models to focus the discussion (see Figure 1.5). Use pencil and paper or the whiteboard to point out what you have understood so far and ask if everyone agrees with that. The discussion will usually focus on your diagrams. Invite participants to modify them to show their point of view. Section 8.4.1 introduces some steps to support meetings.

Figure 1.5 shows five people communicating via a common channel at the bottom. They also use system models to support communication (three modify them, two only read them).

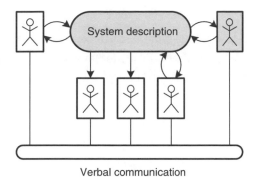

Figure 1.5: Support communication about a system

Ad Hoc Modeling

Modeling a system which is currently discussed using no other tool than a pen and
a whiteboard or paper to support communication. Ad hoc modeling serves to obtain
agreement on a common terminology and a common level of detail and helps to focus
the discussion.

1.1.6 Structure teamwork

"I need to know who's working on which topic."

"You too? I thought it was my task to design this interface!"

"My colleague is ill and I have no clue what he's been doing for the last months."

Managing a team of developers requires a great deal of communication. The
project manager has to know who is working on which part of the system and
has to make sure that the parts will later work together. It is therefore useful if
the project manager can map the tasks of each developer to the elements of the
system architecture whenever possible.

The architecture of the system to be developed should be known to everyone
who is working on it. Developers should know the purpose of the components
on which they are working, their future interaction with other components and
the names of those who work on them.

A good means of mapping tasks to architectural elements is the *System Map*. It
is a diagram showing a detailed model of the system and its architecture. After
being developed by architects, it serves as a basis for discussion about details
and should be known by all team members.

System Map

A Model showing the complete system at a reasonable level of detail. It depicts what every team member must know about the system and allows them to locate their work and their responsibility. See Section 8.3.2.

1.2 The FMC Idea

1.2.1 Requirements for a modeling technique supporting communication

Using system models to support communication among people sets some requirements for the modeling technique and its notation:

- **Abstraction**. The ability to describe the conceptual architecture on many different levels of abstraction is of major importance.

- **Simplicity**. A description technique should be restricted to a few elementary concepts and notational elements.

- **Universality**. Although being simple, a description technique should also offer enough expressive power to cover a wide range of system types without being bound to a specific paradigm.

- **Separation of concerns**. The description of complex systems has to include different conceptual aspects. It is important for an architectural description technique to support the separation of these aspects by offering comprehensive means for their illustration.

- **Aesthetics and secondary notation**. The notational elements of an architectural description technique should support proper layout including the easy formation of graphical patterns.

1.2.2 FMC

The Fundamental Modeling Concepts (FMC) presented in this book are examples of a modeling technique created especially to support the communication about information processing systems. FMC uses a simple notation which can be used easily for ad–hoc creation of models in meetings. FMC is not tied to a programming paradigm, and can even be used for information processing systems which are implemented with a hardware / software mix.

FMC has been created and refined by Siegfried Wendt and his group in many industrial projects. FMC is based on established concepts such as Petri nets and Entity / Relationship modeling, and has been consequently tailored to support communication.

1.2.3   Three aspects – Three diagram types

Three fundamental aspects

FMC separates three fundamental aspects of an information processing system:

- *Compositional Structure* describes the structure of the system in terms of active and passive components. Agents are active and process information, while storages and channels are passive components which keep or transport information. With the help of this structure, we can see which agent can access which storages and communicate with other agents via channels or storages.

- *Behavior* of agents that operate on data, and respond to requests which they receive via channels.

- *Data / value structure* describe the structure of information which can be found in storages or is sent via channels, as well as the relationships between data in different storages.

One diagram type per aspect

For each of the three fundamental aspects, FMC provides one diagram type, as depicted in Figure 1.6 which shows block diagrams for the compositional structure, Petri Nets for the behavior, and Entity / Relationship diagrams (E/R diagrams) for data / value structure. This figure also shows which questions are answered by which diagram type.

Relationship between the diagram types

The compositional structure provided by a block diagram is the cornerstone of an FMC model. Petri nets then describe the behavior of an agent or a set of agents that can be found in the block diagram. Entity/Relationship diagrams are needed if the structure of data and their relationships require a more abstract description. Nevertheless, this data can be located in storages and channels of

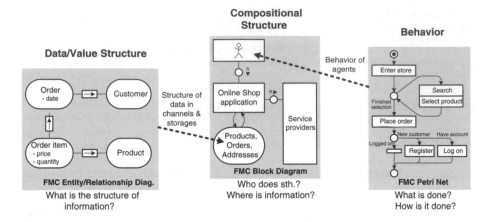

Figure 1.6: Three aspects of an FMC model and their corresponding diagram types

the block diagram. Figure 1.6 shows the relationship between the three FMC diagram types.

Take a look at Section 6.1 to learn more about the FMC meta model describing the elements of the diagram types and their relationships.

1.3   Outline of this book

Chapters 2 to 5 deal with the introduction of the three FMC diagram types: Block diagrams for compositional structures, FMC Petri Nets for dynamic structures, and Entity/Relationship diagrams for value structures. These chapters also provide exercises to help you recapitulate what you have learned so far.

Chapter 6 goes into greater detail of FMC modeling. It introduces the FMC meta model and advanced modeling concepts, such as structure variance, abstraction and refinement, or non–hierarchical transformations.

As most information processing systems are implemented using software, mapping the system structures of FMC models to implementation is an important aspect which is discussed in Chapter 7.

Chapter 8 focuses on ways of applying FMC in your daily work. The scenarios described there originate from the authors' experience, but the list is not exhaustive. Most of them deal with communication.

The intention of FMC modeling is to support communication. This makes high demands on comprehensibility of diagrams, which depends on various factors that are the subject of Chapter 9.

Chapter 10 discusses FMC's relationship to other modeling approaches such as Structured Analysis (SA) and the Unified Modeling Language (UML).

The pattern language for request processing servers in Chapter 11 is one of the results of the analysis of various server systems and shows how FMC diagrams can be used to describe server concepts in a compact and concise way.

The appendix of this book provides, among other things, reference sheets for the notation of the three FMC diagram types, and a glossary of important FMC terms.

Chapter 2

Compositional Structures

2.1 An example: The travel agency

2.1.1 The scenario

Imagine a small, fictitious travel agency called World Tours Unlimited – WTU. In Figure 2.1, we see Mr. Smith, an employee of this agency, talking with Laura Jones. Ms. Jones is planning a trip to Japan and asks for some proposals. Mr. Smith prepares a compilation of proposals from different travel organizations and presents the alternatives to Ms. Jones. She decides to take flight LH417 from Rome to Tokyo on February 18, 2005. Mr. Smith checks the availability and reserves the flight at the corresponding travel organization. Then, he issues the invoice and the ticket to Ms. Jones, who in turn issues the payment. They mutually acknowledge receipt and Ms. Jones leaves the office.

2.1.2 A dynamic system

What we observed is a small dynamic system of two active components: One is Ms. Jones, the customer, the other is Mr. Smith, who represents the travel agency; they are the active components, the *agents* of this simple system. As Figure 2.2 illustrates, they use different *channels* for interaction. Channels allow agents to communicate, i.e., to exchange messages.

A dynamic system is a physical entity that shows observable behavior which results from the interaction of its different system components. Examples of dynamic systems are: a chemical plant, a TV station, a typewriter, a watch, etc.

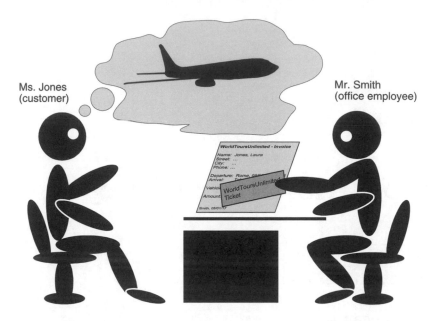

Figure 2.1:   Travel agency. Sketch of a sales scenario

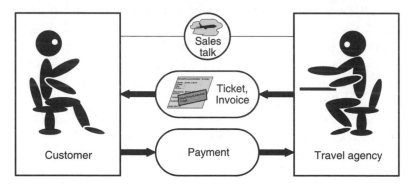

Figure 2.2:   Illustrative block diagram of the sales scenario

Locations are passive components of a system, which may be observed by agents and are used to store, transport or manipulate entities in that location. Locations for information may be very concrete, like the mailbox in some front garden, or more abstract, like the archive of some Internet library or a counter variable. These locations are the passive components of any IT system.

In FMC compositional structures, two types of locations can be distinguished:

Storages are used by agents to store information.

Channels are used for communication between agents.

In our example, the ability to see, talk and hear, which enables Ms. Jones and Mr. Smith to conduct their sales talk in the office of the travel agency, constitutes a bi-directional channel for verbal communication and gestures. The counter is used for the exchange of ticket, invoice and payment.

> *Agents* are responsible for the dynamics in an IT system. They read, write or modify information in the different locations to provide the functionality of the system. They are responsible for any action which can be observed. A weather forecast system may send emails to certain subscribers by writing to their inboxes. A subscriber may read the information from the inbox and then clear the inbox.

2.1.3 An information-processing system

Now, let us focus solely on the informational aspect of the scenario. We abstract from the exchange of physical goods or any other materials. It does not matter how Ms. Jones actually performs the payment, or how Mr. Smith creates a ticket to Tokyo. The physical form of the information does not matter on that level.

> *Information* may be stored, read, modified, sent or received. Information is passive, it does not perform activities. Examples of information are a reservation entry of the travel agency, a picture of a sunset, a storm warning or a notice of receipt. Each information is bound to a certain carrier, i.e., a shape or symbol that encodes the information. As information is bound to a carrier, it is bound to the location of its carrier. A storm warning may be a sign at a certain place on the beach, an email in someone's mailbox or an electric signal on a telephone line.

This abstraction does not affect the idea of agents which communicate via channels. Yet, the identification of system components is no longer based on a primarily one-to-one mapping to physical entities. Now, identification of system components refers to the informational tasks that are performed within the system. Agents, storages and channels are identified with regard to a well-defined purpose – the storage, transportation or provision of specific information. *Block diagrams* represent these abstractions.

> An *Information Processing System*, an IT system, is a dynamic system that may only be understood by interpretation of its state and interface variables. By assigning a meaning to the state and interface variables of an IT system, physical values are turned into information. The electrical charges in some circuit may encode a cookie recipe, the red light emitted from a traffic control means 'stop'. The travel agency, a database system, a computer game console, etc., are information processing systems.

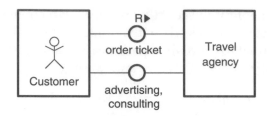

Figure 2.3:   Focusing on informational aspects. FMC block diagram

2.1.4   A block diagram showing the system

In the travel agency example, there are two tasks to be solved. Customers make use of consulting services to do their travel planning and they order tickets for specific tours. They do this by communicating with the travel agency. The compositional structure of this model is shown in Figure 2.3. With regard to the informational aspect, there is no difference whether a customer communicates directly with an office employee or uses some technical device which provides access to the services of the travel agency. Mr. Smith becomes exchangeable. Abstracting from implementation, the resulting model is valid for different travel agencies using different ways of providing their services to different customers.

The block diagram shows a separate channel for each task. These channels may not be directly mapped to different physical media. Yet, this model may ease system comprehension or contribute to the development of a system which supports the work of a travel agency. Discussion about the interaction process for ordering a ticket is separated from the discussion about the process of advertising and consulting.

Nevertheless, this model provides little help in explaining the functioning of a travel agency. Several important questions are not answered:

- What kind of information is required by the travel agency in order to provide its services?

- What kind of information does it provide to the customer?

- At which locations is the information stored?

- Do other agents access these locations?

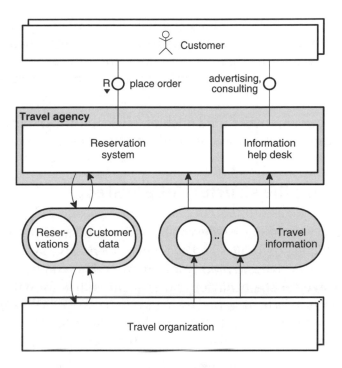

Figure 2.4:   The travel agency system

2.1.5   A refined model

Probably, a travel agency needs to exchange data with travel organizations to do consulting, and to manage reservations. Figure 2.4 shows the compositional structure of a model which allows us to answer these questions.

In this case, the travel agency is composed of two different agents. The information help desk, on the one hand, selects and prepares data from the travel information storage for advertising and consulting. Various travel organizations provide this data. The reservation system, on the other hand, processes orders from the customers. A shared storage, probably implemented on top of some database system, is used by both the travel agency and the travel organizations to check availability and manage reservations and customer data.

This compositional structure is the stage which confines the possible behavior of the system. Any data we talk about is tied to a certain location. Any operation on data, i.e., reading, writing or modifying information, is caused by a specific agent. Arcs between agent symbols and location symbols specify whether an agent can read, write or modify the referred storage resp. channel. The direction of an arc refers to the direction of information transfer. For instance, the travel organizations provide travel information which in turn is read by the travel agency.

Because block diagrams play a fundamental role in the understanding of system, we will take a closer look at their semantics and notation.

2.2   Modeling the structure of a system

Any information processing system can be understood in terms of active system components which use storages and channels, i.e., passive system components, to exchange, store, derive and modify information. This compositional structure provides the stage for the behavior and sequences of information that can be observed. So each information processing system can be described by a model that integrates a compositional structure, a corresponding dynamic structure and a set of observable value structures, i.e., the observable information.

Often, such a model represents an abstraction from physical hardware and software structures. Mail boxes in some electronic mail systems are virtual storages with a complex mapping to data structures and perhaps some even more complex mapping to a distributed database. So the model may be called an *equivalent model*. Yet, those models allow us to understand, specify or predict the intended system behavior. Various patterns provide a bridge between high-level models and typical implementations by programming multi-purpose processor systems.

2.3   Agents accessing storages

Storages are locations within a system which are used by agents to store values for future access. Conceptually, a value that is written to a storage persists until this information is overwritten by an agent. Typical implementations of storages are hard-disks, memory chips, variables, object attributes, memory cells, databases, or simply blackboards.

Storages can also be rather abstract locations, like the order queue in an enterprise resource planning (ERP) system. Probably, a closer look at the implementation of the ERP system will reveal that the order queue is spread over several computer systems. Nevertheless, the idea of one order queue in one

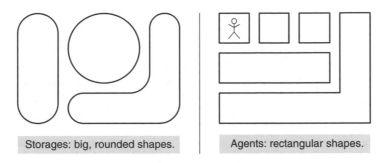

Storages: big, rounded shapes.

Agents: rectangular shapes.

Figure 2.5: Storages and agents. FMC notation

location may help to understand how orders are processed in that ERP system. In that case, it is a useful abstraction.

Agents access storages whenever they read, write or modify information. Arcs connecting agents and storages illustrate the possibility of an agent to access a certain storage. Typical implementations of agents are controller chips, a CPU executing program code, a subroutine, an object and its methods, a web service, an ERP system or simply a human being.

The FMC notation for storages and agents is shown in Figure 2.5. Some dots between two storages or agents, as shown in Figure 2.4, indicate an undetermined number of components.

2.3.1   Read access

To show that an agent can read a storage, use a directed arc from the storage symbol to the agent symbol (see Figure 2.6). The arrow symbolizes the direction of information flow. Reading a storage does not remove the content – the information is still available for future use. In the travel agency example, both the information help desk and the reservation system may read the travel information storage. Obviously, this information should not be removed by just reading it. There is nothing exciting about this fact, but it distinguishes *information flow* from *material flow*. If material goods are taken for input, they are removed from their original location. To make this difference visible, thick arcs were used in Figure 2.2 to emphasise material flow for ticket transfer and payment.

At any time, a storage in an IT systems contains exactly one informational value. This value may be an elementary value, like a boolean, or a structured

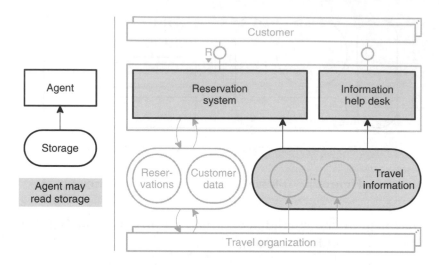

Figure 2.6: Read access

value like the payroll of a large company. However, an agent performing a read access conceptually reads the entire storage at once, in one indivisible step. This abstraction provides a concise definition of read access and allows us to focus on the purpose of the access. In practice, the agent may focus on certain components of a structured value. We may look at the implementation details, but we are not required to do so. For instance, with regard to its purpose, there is no need to know how the help desk of the travel agency reads the travel information. It is sufficient to know that the help desk may access this data.

2.3.2 Write access

A directed arc pointing from the agent symbol to the storage symbol shows that an agent can write to a storage (see Figure 2.7). Again, the arrow symbolizes the direction of information flow. Without being able to read the previous content, an agent writes a new value to a storage. This means the entire content of this storage is replaced in one step – any previous content is overwritten.

In the travel agency example, each travel organization has its own storage to provide the help desk with information. If a travel organization releases new travel information, it performs a write access. The old content, whether it differs or not, is overwritten.

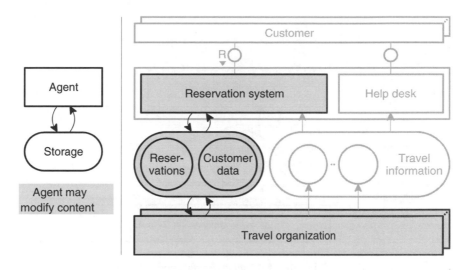

Figure 2.7:   Write access

2.3.3   Modifying access

Often, the new value of a storage depends on the old value of the storage. A very simple example is a counter, which increments a register storage each time it is triggered. To do so, the counter reads the register, increments the value and writes back the new value. Even though the storage is accessed for read and write, the incrementation, conceptually, is one indivisible operation. This logical unit is called *modifying access*.

The ability of an agent to perform modifying accesses to a storage is visualized by the symbol of *modifying arcs*. This symbol is composed of a reading and a writing arc, which are slightly bent toward each other at both ends and which connect an agent with a storage (see Figure 2.8).

Incremental changes of structured information may easily be explained by the concept of modifying access. Again, let us consider the travel agency example. If a customer orders a ticket, a reservation has to be made. The reservation has to be registered in the storage for reservations and customer data, in the travel agency example. This storage already contains the registrations of other customers. The new registration is added to the existing entries. Conceptually, it is a modifying access, because the new value immediately depends on the old value – the database is changed.

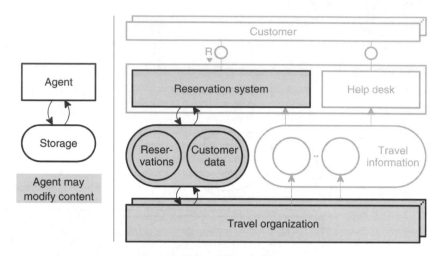

Figure 2.8: Modifying access

2.3.4 Concurrent use of storages

In general, agents may act concurrently with each other. Exclusive activity is only obliged by domain specific algorithms or protocols. Whenever multiple agents have access to the same storage, there is a potential conflict. It occurs when one of them writes to the storage while at the same time another agent tries to read or write to the storage, too. In such a situation, the outcome is not defined.

Imagine the reservation system changing a telephone number in the customer data storage. During the *transition interval*, a travel organization reads the storage to inform the customer that the flight has been cancelled because of a strike. Chances are high that the access fails–perhaps a wrong number is determined, and a wrong person is notified instead of the customer. At least, after the transition interval, a valid value is stored in the storage.

The situation becomes worse when two agents write to a storage at the same time. What happens if one agent tries to write '3' to a storage, while another one tries to write '5' to a storage? The outcome is not defined. Information processing systems are *directed systems* – i.e., at a single point in time, only one agent may write to a specific location.

These conflicts must be solved by using additional means to assure the proper use of storages (or channels), such as a mutex. For instance, an additional agent providing a semaphore service might offer a solution. Often a management agent encapsulates access to the storage. An example for that solution is a database management system that encapsulates the access to the database towards its clients. Nevertheless, a conceptual model may abstract from the details of access management to reduce complexity. It is sufficient to remember that the details have to be specified at implementation level.

2.4 Agents communicate via channels

2.4.1 Channels

Channels are locations by which agents communicate. They are symbolized by small circles. In contrast to a storage, the values on a channel are conceptually transient. If a sender uses a channel to send a message to a receiver, the receiver may notice and memorize this message on receipt. If the receiver misses or forgets the message, it cannot be restored by re-reading the value from the channel unless the sender resends the message.

Examples of channel implementation are: a processor bus, a TCP connection, a method or procedure call, a semaphor or mutex, an event, sending messages such as e-mails, calling a web service, or a telephone connection.

A typical example for communication via channels is speaking. Whether a telephone or air is used to transport the words, the information is transient. In the travel agency example, there is a channel between the customer and the reservation system. When the customer places an order, for instance during a personal sales talk or via the Internet, the customer is in the role of a sender. If the reservation system being in the role of the receiver misses the order, the customer needs to repeat it. Typically, a channel is used to trigger the receiver of the message to perform some action.

2.4.2 Communication scenarios

Simplex connection

The most elementary communication scenario is a directed point-to-point connection, a *simplex connection*. Figure 2.9 shows further variants of point-to-point communication.

Duplex connection

A *duplex connection* combines two simplex connections. Each agent may send messages while simultaneously receiving messages from its communication

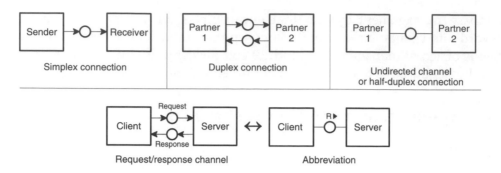

Figure 2.9: Common variants of point-to-point communication

partner. As an example, consider two people communicating via a chat system. Each of them may write messages while at the same time receiving replies from their counterpart.

Half-duplex connection

Often messages refer to each other as in a sequence of questions and answers. Then agents alternately exchange messages. In this case a *half-duplex* connection will work. In a *half-duplex* connection, one *undirected channel* connects both communication partners. Each partner may send and receive messages, but at a single point in time, only one communication partner may send a message.

Consider a simple TCP socket-connection which connects two applications on different computer systems. The socket-connection allows both application agents to send and receive concurrently. With regard to the application model, we experience a duplex connection. Yet, the physical layer may be implemented using an old Ethernet connection which was designed to support only half-duplex. The operation system layer on both computer systems simulates a duplex connection by buffering and sequencing the messages which are incoming and outgoing from the applications concurrently. Both the duplex and the half-duplex model are correct. Again, this is a question for the appropriate model.

Undirected channels as 'wildcards'

The notation of undirected channels is also used for scenarios that are *undefined* with regard to a specific protocol. An example for this purpose is the channel between the customers and the information help desk in Figure 2.4. It is unclear whether a customer or the help desk initiates the communication. It is even unclear whether both agents strictly alternate in communication or if messages may be exchanged concurrently.

Request–response communication

Many channels are used in *client-server scenarios*, i.e., for request–response communication. The client sends its request to the server and waits until the server has processed the request and sent a response. Much of the communication in IT systems is based on that interaction pattern. For this reason, a short notation was introduced. As Figure 2.9 shows, a *request–response channel* is symbolized in the same way as an undirected channel, but with a small triangle or arrow which points into the direction of the request.

For instance, the customer and the reservation system in the travel agency example are connected by a request–response channel. Abstracting from details of the sales talk, a customer requests a reservation. The response from the reservation system contains an acknowledgment and details about reservation, i.e., the ticket, or a problem description.

In programmed systems, agents commonly are implemented by one or more hardware processors which process the instructions of a software package that describes the behavior of the agent. For instance, the registration system of the travel agency might be implemented by a computer system which was programmed appropriately. So a request–response dialog between agents often maps to a simple procedure call with some return value from one software package into another or from one object to another. We will discuss possible mappings in detail in Chapter 7.

2.4.3 Broadcast communication

Of course channels are not restricted to one-to-one communication. Broadcast communication is a common scenario where multiple receivers are listening to the same channel. They all receive the same messages from one sender, for example, a television broadcast. This scenario should not be confused with a publish–subscriber scenario. In that case, agents may subscribe for messages from a certain sender. Only subscribers will receive messages from the sender. Typical examples are newspaper subscriptions or e-mail newsletters. Two exercises at the end of this chapter will deal with these scenarios.

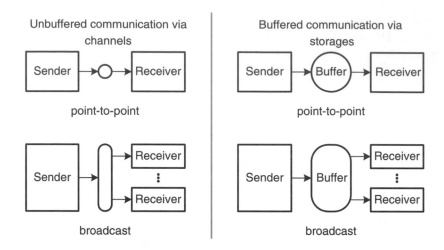

Figure 2.10: Channels versus storages

2.4.4 Using storages for communication

As Figure 2.10 illustrates, even storages may be exclusively used for communication. This is the case if one agent writes values to the storage and another agent reads these values. In contrast to using a channel, the sender's values are buffered. Now it is the receiver's decision when to read the message. It may be necessary to prevent the receiver from reading information which the sender is currently updating and which may be inconsistent. This requires additional means for buffered communication, as shown in Section 7.3.2.

By writing on a blackboard or a sheet of paper, you can communicate with others who will not miss the information even if they are not attentive for a while. Another more technical example is microprocessor which may write a value to the register of some attached hardware device. Additional wiring implements the channel for the handshake protocol which ensures that the device can properly read the value. In this model, the register works as a storage. With regard to its purpose, we may have another model: The register combined with the handshake logic conceptually implements a channel between the processor and the attached device.[1]

---

[1] Both models are valid. It is not a decision between right or wrong. The question is, which model is appropriate to explain a specific aspect of the system. This seems to be of less help. But in the end, it is this freedom that is necessary for describing systems in a comprehensible way. There is no dedicated procedure to find the right abstraction, but the different examples and exercises throughout the whole book should create the idea of a useful model.

2.5 Summary

Information processing systems contain elements which are either:

- *active components* which process information; or

- *passive components* which persistently store information (storages) or transport transient information (channels).

The classification depends on the level of abstraction and reflects the purpose of a model. With regard to the travel agency example, a model which explains the application domain may show a storage for registrations, i.e., a passive component. A model which explains the implementation of that storage probably reveals a database management system, i.e., an active component, which manages the registration database.

To communicate about a system, we need to agree on a compositional structure, which is appropriate to explain the behavior of the considered system with regard to its purpose. The following questions provide a basic framework for solving this task.

- Identify agents: What has to be done in the system and who is responsible?

- Identify storages: Where do agents store (operational) data?

- Identify access to storages: Which agents need to read, write or modify the contents of which storage?

- Identify channels: Which agents need to communicate with each other?

The following question is a criterion to decide whether the resulting model might be useful or not:

Can you give each system component a proper name?

An agent should carry a name that concisely refers to its role in the system. The name of a storage usually refers to its contents. Channels should also be labeled. Usually one or two words suffice to identify the purpose of communication or to identify the protocol being used.

If it is impossible to find an appropriate name, it may be a sign that the role of this agent, storage or channel is ambiguous, misty or non-specific. In that case, review the model, check responsibilities, reassign tasks and apply appropriate modifications.

Agent and storage nodes may be nested to express refinement. The interpretation of nesting in block diagrams is presented in detail in Section 6.3 of this book.

2.6   Exercises

Exercise 2.1 Basic communication scenarios 1

Imagine a scenario of TV receivers that may receive transmissions from a single TV station only. Draw a simple block diagram representing this scenario.

Exercise 2.2 Basic communication scenarios 2

Imagine a scenario of some clients which may subscribe and unscribe for a wake-up service.

Draw a block diagram representing this scenario. Hint: How does the wake-up service know which client to call?

Exercise 2.3 Newspaper with Web access

Online readers of the newspaper can read articles via WWW using their Web browser. The publisher uses a standard HTTP server which has direct access to static content like images or style-sheets. Articles are stored in XML format and have to be accessed via a formatter converting XML to HTML. This formatter needs style information from the static content. The HTTP server uses the fastCGI protocol to access the formatter.

Draw a block diagram showing the compositional structure of this system.

Exercise 2.4 Newspaper: Editorial department

The articles are written by the editorial department of the print version of the newspaper. They use a desktop publishing (DTP) tool and store the articles in the DTP format. The editorial department of the online version modifies static content like styles or images using a web editor tool. To obtain article content from the print version, they trigger a converter which reads the articles in DTP format and creates copies in XML format.

Extend the block diagram of the previous exercise to show the new components of the system.

Chapter 3

Dynamic Structures

In the previous chapter, you learned about a travel agency which acts as a broker for travel organizations. The agency was introduced by a verbal description of a specific scenario that might have happened in the agency, i.e., Ms. Jones bought a ticket to Tokyo. Then we focused on the informational aspect and identified the compositional structure of that system. This structure is static and does not express what happens between Ms. Jones and Mr. Smith.

The compositional structure provides the scenery, the stage, for any behavior which may be observed. Any observable activity is related to the agents, channels and storages of the system. Agents communicate with others, given that they are connected via channels, and read, write or modify the contents of storages which they can access. These *actions* happen in a certain *temporal order*. It is a *partial order*, because agents can act concurrently. The sequence of actions depends on the state of the system and follows certain system-specific rules. Knowing these rules – the system's *causal order* – and the current state, you can predict the behavior of the system.

3.1 Petri nets: Basic principles

Petri nets are an appropriate means of describing the sequence (more precisely the partial order) of actions or events. Petri nets may be used to represent the causal order as well as the control state[1] of the system. For instance, Figure 3.1

---

[1]The distinction between operational state and control state depends on the purpose of the state values. See Section 6.2 for more details.

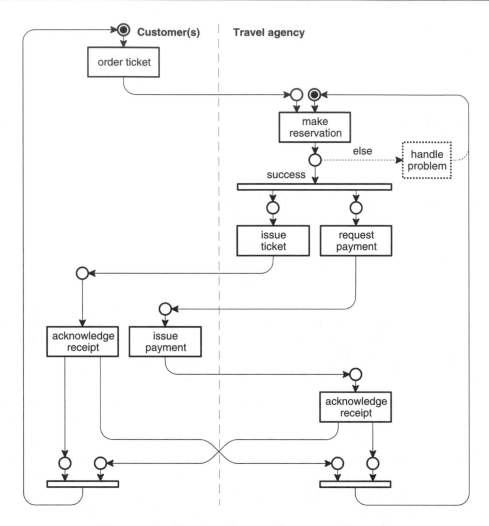

Figure 3.1: Petri net for travel agency, ticket sale

specifies the different possibilities of buying a ticket at the travel agency. This process starts by ordering a ticket, continues with the reservation and so on. To explain what happens in detail, let us use a Petri net.

A Petri net is a directed, bipartite[2] graph of transitions and places which serves as a scheme to generate any kind of partial order by applying a well-defined set

---

[2]In a bipartite graph, only two types of nodes exist. Connections (arcs) between two nodes are only allowed if the types of nodes differ. In case of the Petri net, transitions can only be connected with places and vice versa—a direct connection between two transitions or two places is prohibited.

of rules – in the case of a behavior description, this partial order represents the causal order of actions in time.

When it is being used to describe the behavior of a dynamic system, a transition represents a type of action that may be observed in the system. Each time the transition fires, a corresponding operation may be observed in the system. A transition is symbolized by a rectangle. A label refers to the associated type of operation. In the example in Figure 3.1, typical actions are 'make reservation' or 'issue payment'.

Transitions are connected via directed arcs (arrows) to circular nodes which are called the places of the Petri net. A place can be empty or marked by a token which is symbolized by a small black dot. Input places of a particular transition are all places with arcs ending at that transition. Output places of a transition are all places which are endpoints of arcs starting at that transition. Most output places are input places for other transitions.

A transition fires if:

- all its input places are marked and

- all its output places are unmarked.

After firing,

- the operation associated with the transition has been performed;

- all input places of the transition are empty; and

- all its output places are marked;

as depicted in Figure 3.2.

Small unlabeled rectangles represent NOP (No OPeration) transitions. A NOP transition is not associated with any operation. Apart from this, it is treated like any other transition. So firing a NOP transition will not cause any visible operation in the system. Yet it changes the control state represented in the marking of the Petri net which determines the future operations.

By itself, a Petri net does nothing. When you are reading a Petri net, you have to become a Petri net processor and apply the firing rules. So let us start with the Petri net in Figure 3.1. At the beginning, only the transition labeled 'order ticket' is ready to fire. Firing this transition means that a ticket was ordered and that the marking of the connected places was changed. Afterwards the next

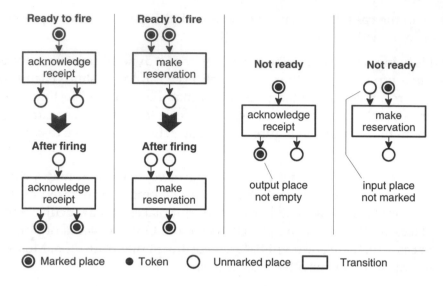

Figure 3.2: Examples of basic firing rules

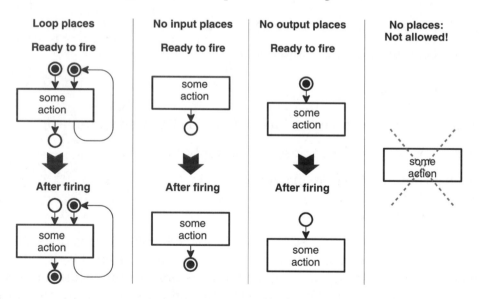

Figure 3.3: Special cases for firing rules

transition which is ready to fire is 'make reservation'. Try to continue with the next transitions to get a better idea of the concept.

Figure 3.3 illustrates three special cases of transitions which are ready to fire. The left case shows a transition which is connected with a place that is an input and output place at the same time. We call it a loop place. If such a place is marked, the corresponding transition may fire, even though this does not strictly comply with the previous firing rules. Firing the transition takes the mark from the loop place and immediately places a new token to the released place. If such a place is not marked, the transition cannot fire. This pattern can be used to activate and deactivate certain parts of a Petri net. Removing the token from the loop place deactivates the transition, placing the token activates the transition.

A transition that has no input places, as shown in the second scenario, may fire whenever its output places are empty. A transition that has no output places may fire whenever its input places are marked. Transitions which are not connected with any place are principally possible but should be avoided.

3.2 Conflicts and conditions

After firing the transition 'make reservation', only one place is marked in the Petri net. This place is the input place of two transitions which are both ready to fire. From the context of the application domain, it is obvious that either the reservation succeeds or a problem has occurred which needs to be handled. However, what happens if multiple transitions which are ready to fire share one or more input places?

Probably the travel agency, which is simulated by the Petri net, does not work with tokens in reality. Yet, to process the Petri net, you can use the idea of tokens, indivisible physical marks which are consumed (taken from input places) and produced (put to output places) when a transition fires. This metaphor leads to the following solution.

Since a token cannot be shared, only one transition can get the token and fire. But which transition will be the lucky winner? Someone has to make a decision and resolve the conflict. In a real system, a system component will perform this task. Simulating the behavior by processing a Petri net, then it is up to the Petri net processor, e.g., you as a reader, to come to a decision.

The decision for one specific alternative may depend on a specific condition, a *predicate*, to be true. Otherwise conflict resolution occurs at random and the behavior of the system is undetermined. If the firing of a transition depends on a predicate, this predicate is written next to the arc that connects the input place with the corresponding transition. A predicate is a statement about the

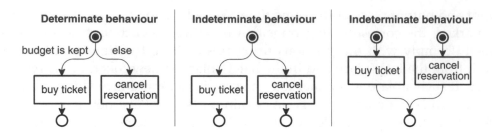

Figure 3.4:   Examples of firing conflicts

operational state of the system[3]. It is either true or false and refers to one or multiple values of the system which may be observed on the different storages and channels. For that reason, the system component being responsible for the decision needs access to the corresponding locations.

Figure 3.4 illustrates the concept. Each of the three Petri nets shows a conflict – either a ticket is bought or the reservation is canceled. The rightmost Petri net in Figure 3.4 illustrates the fact that output places may also be a subject of conflict. The capacity of the output place is limited – only one token may be placed on the output place at a certain point in time. For that reason, only one transition may fire and mark the output place. However, only the Petri net to the left produces a determined behavior. The predicates on the conflicting arcs determine that if and only if the budget is kept, then a ticket is bought, or else the reservation is canceled.

Whenever it is possible to specify a predicate making a conflict determinable, it should be made visible in the Petri net.

3.3   Basic patterns

The network of transitions and places will be different for most Petri nets. Yet there are a few basic patterns that occur very often. The description of any type of behavior may be exclusively composed of sequences of actions, conditional actions, repeated actions and concurrent actions (even though this is not always appropriate). Figure 3.5 illustrates the Petri net representation of these four patterns:

- *Sequence*. Actions are performed one after another.

---

[3]The distinction between control and operational state and its relation to the description of behavior using Petri nets is described in detail in Section 6.2.

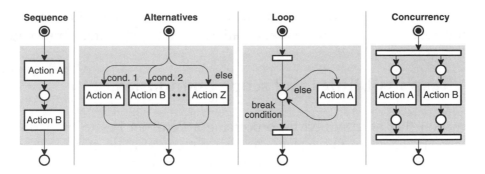

Figure 3.5: Basis patterns of behavior

- *Alternatives.* One action is selected from a repertoire of alternatives. A predicate for each alternative specifies which action to take. Usually, predicates are mutually exclusive. It is a special, but common, case of a conflict scenario.

- *Loop.* A certain action is performed or repeated resp., if or until resp., the break condition of the loop is true. It is another example of a conflict scenario. Only endless loops will have no break condition. For instance, the behavior of most reactive systems has no dedicated end. Also the travel agency will probably sell tickets as long as there are enough customers (see Figure 3.1).

- *Concurrency.* If actions may be performed concurrently, there is no immediate causal relationship between these actions. The actions may be performed simultaneously and in any possible order. Consider the example in Figure 3.5. The NOP transition preceding A and B forks the activity. So A and B may fire simultaneously, A may fire before B, or B may fire before A. Afterwards, the NOP transition following A and B synchronizes the concurrent activities.

In Petri nets, concurrent threads of activity which were forked once by firing a common transition, do not need to synchronize later. Also, synchronization is not limited to those threads which originate from a common activity. For instance, in the travel agency example, after the reservation is made, ticket transfer and payment are handled concurrently. Yet, there is no single complementing transition for synchronization representing the end of the transaction.

Finally, let us explain the gray shading in Figure 3.5. Each shading confines a sub-net of a Petri net that is bordered by transitions and only excludes the start and end place of each Petri net. In anticipation of the concept of refinement, these sub-nets represents the four basic alternatives for refining a single transition.

3.4   Responsibilities and scope boundaries

Each action that is identified by processing a Petri net has to be performed by a specific agent of the system. A Petri net contains no statements about the compositional structure. Yet, in FMC each Petri net refers to a specific compositional structure. For each transition, there is usually exactly one agent which is responsible for performing the associated action. Consider the Petri net of the travel agency example in Figure 3.1. Each action is performed either by the customer or the reservation system.

Considering this relation, a Petri net is partitioned into distinct areas of responsibility. Each area is a sub-net that is in the scope of a certain agent. Scope boundaries, i.e., thin dashed lines, may delimit these areas – which are called swimlanes in these cases – from each other. A caption on each area refers to the corresponding agent. An appropriate arrangement of places and nodes enhances clarity.

Each sub-net is a little Petri net on its own. The marking of such a sub-net represents the control state of the associated agent. Transitions and conditions refer to the operational state, i.e., the channels and storages that may be accessed by the corresponding agent. For agents acting concurrently, transitions in the associated sub-nets will independently fire from each other. Yet most sub-nets are coupled by one or more arcs crossing the scope boundary.

An arc crossing a scope boundary represents the possibility of one agent triggering an action of another agent. Figure 3.6 illustrates a scenario of three agents interacting with each other. Figure 3.7 shows the compositional structure associated with this Petri net. Agent A repeatedly calls B, which performs some action and delegates a subtask to A or C, before returning control to A. Every time action A.2 is performed, a token is passed from the sub-net describing agent A to the one of B. This action triggers agent B to perform either B.1 or B.2. In that special case, control is also passed from A to B, because agent A needs to wait for a response or a sub-request (to perform some action of type A.3) from B. With regard to the type of agents, the meaning of a token crossing a scope boundary might be anything from a web client sending an HTTP request to a web server, to the release of a semaphore, a trigger signal on a wire, or a procedure call.

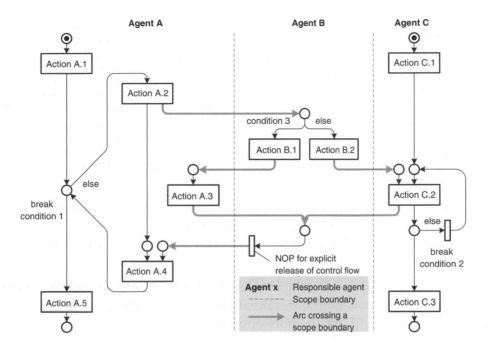

Figure 3.6: Petri nets and scope boundaries

Figure 3.7: Block diagram associated with Figure 3.6

Now consider the NOP transition in the sub-net of B. With regard to the structure and firing rules of Petri nets the NOP transition is not necessary. If the NOP is omitted, the lower place in sub-net B would be directly connected with a transition in the sub-net of A. With that modification, agent A could perform step A.4 as soon as the lower place is marked, without waiting for agent B to explicitly release control.

Usually, it is in the scope of each single agent to decide when to release control or pass control respectively, to another agent. This decision is an activity of that single agent. So it has to be represented by a transition of the sub-net which is associated with the agent. Often, this activity is combined with a preceding operation. So in the Petri net, there is one transition representing this preceding operation and the release of control. The transitions labeled B.1 and B.2 in

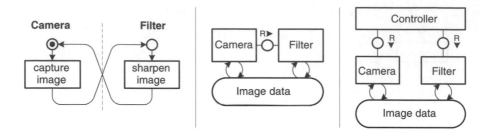

Figure 3.8:   Different compositional structures with the same behavior

Figure 3.6 are examples of the common case. Nevertheless, if nothing has to be done other than just to release control, a label would not provide any additional information – so a NOP transition in the sub-net of the releaser has the same meaning.

Exceptions to the rule that any agent decides for itself when to release control, are interrupt scenarios or the deactivation of system components. However, Petri nets describing these are more complex anyway, so we will discuss them later.

Coming to the end of this section, let us take a closer look at the relationship between Petri nets and the associated compositional structure of a system. What does it mean that the activity of one agent can trigger an activity of another agent? Such a dependency could be realized by a channel between these two agents which is used to pass the necessary information. Instead of a direct connection, an additional agent in the role of a controller might also ensure the sequence of actions. The Petri net is valid for both compositional structures. Figure 3.8 shows an example. You will learn more about this subject in Section 6.2.4 which introduces the concept of 'discrete control loops'.

3.5   Summary

The behavior of an information processing system consists of the entirety of operations that may be observed in the system. Each operation is the result of one or more agents performing some actions. These actions happen in a specific temporal order that follows system-specific rules and depends on the control state of the agents and on the operational data in the storages and channels throughout the system.

Petri nets are a means of representing the causal structure and control state of the system. Applying so-called firing rules, they may be used to produce a partial ordering of events that correspond to the behavior of the actual system. Transitions represent the possible types of action. The marking of the different places represents the control state of the system. Firing a Petri net transition represents the execution of the associated action and a state transition of the described system to the subsequent control state.

By assigning each transition to a single agent, a Petri net may be partitioned into multiple subsets. Each subset represents the dynamic structure and the control state of a single agent. Usually, the arcs and the tokens, respectively, crossing the boundaries between the sub-nets represent communication. A Petri net comprising several sub-nets defines the protocol for this communication.

Here are a few guidelines for creating a Petri net:

- Identify transitions: What actions will occur in the system?

- Identify causal structure: What happens successively, repeatedly, alternatively, concurrently?

- Identify sub-nets (only if necessary): Which agent is responsible for which action?

- Layout: Readability is increased if the arrangement of nodes follows certain patterns – for instance, transitions representing successive actions are usually arranged top-down.

The following checklist may help to decide whether or not the resulting Petri net might be useful:

- Can you give each transition a label that concisely describes the associated activity?

- Can you name the conditions for each determinable conflict?

Because transitions represent types of action, the label of a transition may be a single verb. For a concise labeling, generic words should be avoided as well as complete sentences. Very often, up to five words will be enough. If this is impossible, it may be a sign that multiple actions are intermingled.

3.6   Exercises

Exercise 3.1 The publisher/subscriber pattern

In applications which are based on the Model View Controller (MVC) framework, a model is used to store and modify abstract pieces of information. One or more views may be used to represent the information of a model on the screen. Whenever one of the model's attributes is changed, the corresponding representation on the screen is changed. The coupling between model and views is based on the publisher/subscriber pattern:

A model, acting in the role of the publisher, maintains a list of subscribers, i.e., its views. Whenever an attribute of the model has been changed, the changed method of the model has to be carried out and an update request is sent to all the subscribers of the model. Each subscriber examines the information of the model and updates its display accordingly.

Create a Petri net that shows the interaction between a model and its views for this scenario.

Exercise 3.2 Reading the newspaper with a web browser

This exercise picks up the example of the online newspaper:

To access an article of the newspaper, a reader enters a URL or clicks some link in his web browser to specify the requested article. The web browser uses this input to create an HTTP request and sends it to the Web server of the publisher. If the web server finds that the requested resource belongs to a restricted section of the newspaper, it performs an authority check. This means, that it looks for any authorization data contained in the HTTP request. If this information is provided and matches the registry information of the provider, the authentication is successful. In that case, the web server delivers the requested resource, which is then rendered by the web browser. Otherwise, the web server responds with a '401 unauthorized' HTTP message. A web browser receiving such a message will prompt the user to enter their username and password for the requested resource. The web browser will store this information and create a further HTTP request. This request is largely identical with the previous one, but now contains the new authentication data. In fact, because the web browser buffers this information, it does not have to prompt the user each time a restricted resource is requested. Whenever the reader requests a resource, the browser will include associated authentication data with the request, if it is available.

Create a Petri net with swim lanes showing the interaction between the agents.

Chapter 4

Value Structures and Mind Maps

First, block diagrams were introduced to describe the compositional structure of information processing systems. Agents having access to channels and storages are supposed to read, write or modify the content for the purpose of communication, calculation or storage. Then, Petri nets were introduced to describe the behavior of the different agent, i.e., the protocols and algorithms that define the sequences of values on the different channels and storages throughout the system. Now, we focus on the information or the data which is the subject of any activity in any information processing system. For instance, each channel or storage has only one purpose: to provide a location to read or write data.

A channel or storage is characterized by the kind of values and the kind of information that is written on it. The purpose of each channel or storage defines the repertoire of values that may be written to that location. For instance, a storage for travel reservations will probably not contain information about pollution statistics.

To understand an information processing system, we need to understand and specify the types of information that may occur at the different locations in the system. An information is a statement or request about objects, their attributes and the relationships between them. An object can be anything that constitutes an individual entity, whether it is a concrete item or an abstract concept. In this context, the term 'object' is not confined to the instances of a class in a programmed system.

If the repertoire of information, i.e., the possible statements or requests, is small, we may explicitly itemize this repertoire. For instance, the state of a switch might be either 'open' or 'closed'. Even if the repertoire is large, if the structure of information is simple, it may be enough to name two or three examples of the repertoire to understand its meaning. For instance, a storage for the background color of some HTML document might hold an RGB value like this one: red = 180, green = 200, blue = 255, which encodes a light blue.

Complex informational values are structured chunks of information that refer to objects of different type, different attributes and different relations. Often, the associated terminology is specific to the concepts of a certain domain area. Before dealing with single values, you have to understand these concepts. Entity/Relationship diagrams (E/R diagrams) are used to visualize different types of objects, attributes and relationships. Hence, they are an appropriate means:

- to illustrate the repertoire of complex values which a channel or storage may take;

- to provide a mind map into unknown domains.

They are usually not appropriate when the subject is the specific structure of a single value.

4.1   Entity sets and relationships

An Entity Relationship diagram (E/R diagram) represents *entity sets* and the types of relations, the *relationships*, that relate the different entities to each other. Entities of the same type have the same attributes and may participate in the same types of relations. They belong to the same class. In this context, a *class* is nothing but a set of entities of the same *type*. Conceptually, the term is not restricted to programming structures. Of course, we may classify objects in a programmed system, but we will come to that later.

For instance, the upper diagram in Figure 4.1 illustrates a set of employees and a set of rooms. An ellipse surrounds instances of the same type. John, Susan, Mary, Richard, Frank and Barbara are instances of the type of employee. All of them work for the same company. We know their names as well as the rooms of the company in which they are working. While each entity has a typical set of attributes which is inherently part of the entity, relationships may be established and detached without challenging the existence of the affected entities. So a name is an attribute that belongs to each employee. But the

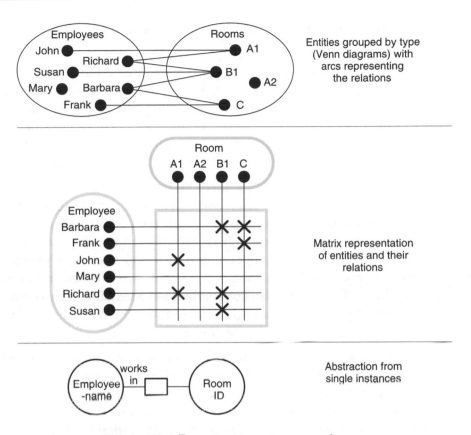

Figure 4.1: From instances to sets and types

existence of rooms and employees is not bound to a special assignment of both. Mary, being a teleworker, has no special room in the company. The rooms do exist independently of the employees. The relationship connecting employees with the rooms is the fact that certain employees are working in certain rooms.

The individual relations between members of the different sets are represented by straight lines connecting the participating instances. For complex structures, a matrix representation of such a relationship can be less confusing. An example representing the room assignment is shown in the middle of Figure 4.1.

An E/R diagram represents an abstraction from specific instances and relations, i.e., from a specific structure. It defines a type of structure for a certain domain. So, an E/R diagram represents any possible structure of a certain domain, that is admissible, ever. That is why we may say that an E/R diagram specifies the range of value structures, i.e., the repertoire of actual values for a certain domain.

A set in an E/R diagram comprises all entities of one certain type. Sets are represented as rounded nodes. A label refers to the corresponding type. In some cases, a list of attributes is specified. Generally, specific instances are not shown. With regard to the rectangular shape of the matrix representation of a relationship, the relationship, i.e., the set of relations of a certain type, is represented as a rectangle which is connected to the associated entity nodes.

The very simple E/R diagram at the bottom of Figure 4.1 reads as follows. There are employees and there are rooms. Each employee has an attribute which is its name and each room has an ID. Employees and rooms are related in a way in that employees work in certain rooms. It is a binary relationship because two entities participate in each relationship: an employee and a room. An employee who sometimes works in different rooms, participates in different relations of the same type. The E/R diagram also covers the case when an employee works at home. In this example no statements are made about the number of relations in which entities of a certain type may be engaged.

The E/R diagram in Figure 4.2 refers to the travel agency example. Customers may reserve seats for a certain tour. The recorded information is stored in the reservation storage which can be accessed by the travel agency and the different travel organizations (Figure 2.4). Here is the link between compositional structure and the *range of value structures*. The E/R diagram defines the repertoire of informational values which are admissible for a certain storage or channel in the system. Since we are talking about information, in the strict sense, the labeling in the E/R diagram should have been 'customer data', 'tour data', etc.

The reservation example also demonstrates that E/R diagrams are not restricted to binary relationships. Conceptually, any number of entities may participate

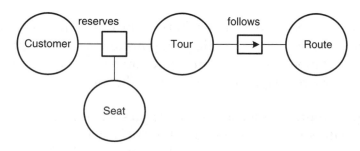

Figure 4.2:   Entity relationship diagram for travel agency reservations

in a relation, although in practice most relations involve only two entities. Complex structures arise from the fact that many entities are involved in relations of different type. For instance, a tour does not only refer to customers reserving seats, it also refers to a certain route.

The notation is based on the proposal of Chen [Che76]. The decision to vary the original notation by representing entity nodes as circles and relationship nodes as rectangles, was made to allow more layout options and for didactic reasons. As Figure 4.1 suggests, it should be easier to associate circles with sets and rectangles with relationship matrices rather than vice versa. For instance, most people are familiar with the circle notation of Venn diagrams, even though the name is probably less popular.

4.2 Cardinalities

Often, a reader of an E/R diagram might be interested in the number of relations of a certain type, which an entity might be engaged in. For instance, each tour follows one specific route. Conversely, a certain route may be used for no, one, or many tours. These ranges are called the cardinalities of a relationship. Arrows or small numbers attributing the relationship nodes represent the range of cardinality. This expresses the number of relations of a certain type in which one entity may participate.

Figure 4.3 illustrates the idea. An arrow on the relationship node represents a functional relationship between two sets. Each element of a domain set is related to exactly one element of the image set. For instance, the relations of the left and the middle structure in Figure 4.3 represent functions. The relationship between

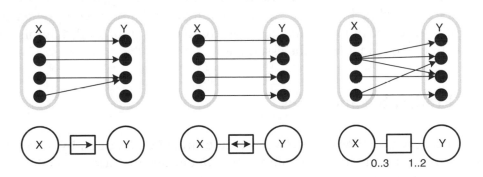

Figure 4.3: Cardinalities

Figure 4.4: Example of an advantage of the min/max notation

'Tours' and 'Routes' in Figure 4.2 is another example of that kind of relationship. If the function is a one-to-one relationship, as in the middle structure, this is symbolizes by a bi-directional arrow on the relationship node.

An empty relationship node makes no statement about cardinalities. In that case, entities of both sets may be connected by an arbitrary number of the other set. A number or a range of numbers attached to an arc which connects an entity node with a relationship node may be used to denote the cardinality in more detail. For instance, the numbers in the right E/R diagram of Figure 4.3 read as follows: An element of X may participate in 0, 1, 2 or 3 relations which refer to elements of Y. An element of Y may participate in 1 or 2 relations which refer to elements of X. This notation follows the min/max notation. It must not be confused with an entity-oriented notation as is used in UML. The advantage of the min/max notation is that its meaning is not limited to binary relationships. An example for a ternary relationship is shown in Figure 4.4.

Not every structural restriction may be sufficiently expressed using cardinality numbers. In certain cases, additional predicates are required to completely declare a restriction. However, remember that FMC diagrams are no substitute for formal specifications. Their intention is to increase human comprehension and easy communication about information processing systems. Cardinality numbers are useful, but often are not required for human comprehension. Generally, cardinal numbers increase the complexity of an E/R diagram and may distract the reader from the essentials.

4.3 Predicates and roles

In practice, each relationship between entities may be described by a *predicate*. This predicate is true for each combination of entities that are associated with each other by a relation of that type. It is wrong for any other combination of entities. For instance, the relationship between 'Tours' and 'Route' in Figure 4.2

is characterized by the predicate 'T follows R'. If the variables 'T' and 'R' are substituted by a specific tour and a specific route, the predicate becomes a statement which will be either true or false.

Generally, it is useful to write the predicate of some relationship next to the corresponding relationship node. Sometimes, though, the meaning of a relationship node is obvious and needs no description. Yet an unambiguous predicate often conceals more than it reveals. Appropriate abbreviations are easier to read and prevent from overburden than an E/R diagram with text.

For instance, the simple annotation 'follows' represents the complete and correct, but daunting predicate 'T follows R with T being a member of Tours and R being a member of Routes'. Few people would really like to read this.

Usually, a very short sentence associating different entities in different roles is sufficient. Based on this idea, the following survey shows a few useful abbreviations to characterize a relationship, and Figure 4.5 shows an example for each case:

- A single verb, sometimes combined with an adverb, characterizes most relationships. To clarify which side plays which role in the relation, the expression may be shifted toward the side that takes the role of the subject (in a grammatical sense). This type of notation works especially well for binary relationships.

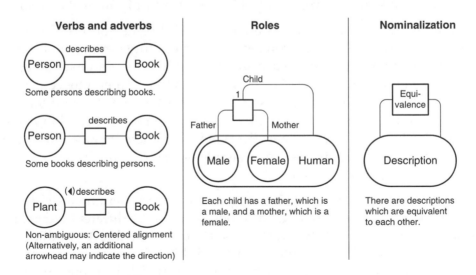

Figure 4.5:   Alternative ways to characterize the meaning of a relationship

- Nouns referring to the roles of the different entities in the relationship may be written next to the corresponding arcs.

- A single noun may characterize the type of relationship independent of any roles (nominalization). This is often useful to characterize quadratic relationships like trees or equivalence relationships.

4.4 Partitions

Perhaps you were wondering a little about the notation of Figure 4.5 when writing entity nodes inside other entity nodes. Obviously, there are humans which are male and those which are female.

Graphical containment of entity nodes represents containment of entity sets. If an entity node 'A' contains another entity node 'B', the set of 'A' contains the set of 'B'. The type associated with entity node 'B' is a subtype of the one associated with 'A'. The concept of graphical containment is used to itemize sets of different types which share a common super-type. Generally, an entity node containing several sub-nodes illustrates a *partition*. This means that the different sub-nodes represent subsets which are pairwise disjunctive – each entity belongs to one specific subset and the enclosed entity nodes do not overlap. The only exception to this rule results from the overlapping of surrounding entity nodes. So it is easily possible to illustrate relations between sets of different type in a type hierarchy. The child-relationship of Figure 4.5 is a typical application of that concept.

A set containing several subsets is the union of all of its subsets. There is no meaning in some entity node containing another single entity node. If it is impossible to explicitly itemize each subset, the 'dot' notation may be used to indicate further subsets. Figure 4.6 shows an example. An employee may be a manager, an engineer or a sales person, but the dots give us the hint that there may also be other types of employee. We also could omit the three dots and add another subset node labeled 'Other'. To avoid a complete itemization, the 'dot' notation seems appropriate. Yet, the example on the right in Figure 4.6 would not work with the 'dot' notation.

Graphical containment is a very intuitive means of representing a single partition or perhaps a few hierarchical partitions. Visualizing different independent partitions of the same entity, creates visual confusion due to multiple containment nodes crossing each other. To avoid this effect, additional partitions are illustrated using a dedicated *partition symbol*, which is a longish triangle. Figure 4.7 shows an example.

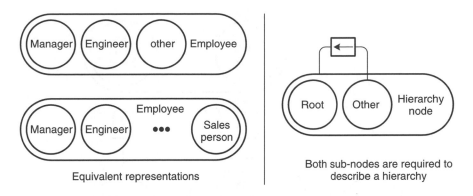

Figure 4.6:   Disjunctive sets and the 'dot' notation

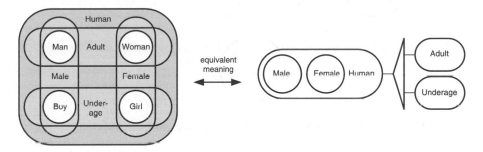

Figure 4.7:   Orthogonal partitions

4.5   Reification

Sometimes, the elements of a relationship may constitute the nucleus for a new entity type that may participate in other relations that have attributes by themselves.

Let us consider Figure 4.8, which shows an E/R diagram representing informations which are stored in the reservation storage of the travel agency example. A customer may reserve a seat for a certain tour. A ternary relationship exists between customers, tours and seats. At the same time, this relationship represents the set of reservations, which are booked by the travel agency or other travel organizations.

In this case, each element of the relationship represents both the relating link and the derived entity. Those derived entities may have no direct physical counterpart. They are the *reification* of some concrete fact, a statement about the relation among some given entities. It is a type of meta-information capturing,

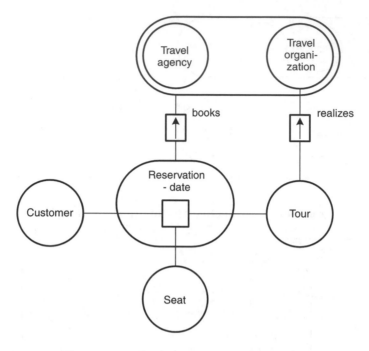

Figure 4.8:   Reification: tour reservations

for instance, when or where a certain relation was established. In the example, each 'Reservation' has a 'date', which denotes when a reservation was booked. The reification of a certain relationship is represented by surrounding the corresponding relationship node with an entity node.

Usually, the nominalization of the relationship predicate emphasises the reification. So in Figure 4.8, the reified 'reserves' relation is now labeled 'Reservation'. It is important to distinguish between links to the constituting relationship and the reified entity set. For instance, travel agencies do not participate in the 'reserves' relationship, but do participate in the 'books' relationship with reservations.

4.6 Summary

FMC E/R diagrams are used to describe the range of value structures, which may be observed on the storages and channels of a dynamic system. They are also used to describe the terminology of a certain domain (topic map).

Representing structures, entity relationship diagrams are composed of entity nodes and relationship nodes:

- *An entity node* is a rounded node, which represents a set of entities which are of the same type, i.e., they constitute a class. Usually, an entity node wears a label which refers to the associated type. Additionally, attributes may be listed.

- *A relationship node* has the form of a rectangle, which represents a set of relations which are of the same type, i.e., a relationship. The predicate of a relationship defines a criteria, which is true for any entity tuple that participates in that relationship. A labeling on the relationship node or the connecting arcs may refer to that predicate as well as to the range of cardinalities.

Usually, you will not create an E/R diagram for every storage or channel throughout the system. Only the vital or complex structures need to be visualized. Here are a few guidelines for creating an E/R diagram:

- Identify entities. What kind of information, which chunks of data, are required and produced while solving a certain task in the given domain? Often, the domain-specific terminology provides a good starting point for identifying the vital entities. Carefully distinguish between instances and types, or subjects and their descriptions, respectively. For instance, explicitly determine whether you are talking about cars or certain types of car descriptions, or both.

- Identify relations. How are the informations structured? How do the entities refer to each other? If restricted to the description of data structures, typical relationships are 'contains', 'refers to' or 'describes'. But arbitrary relationships may be identified.

The following question is a criterion to decide whether or not the resulting model might be useful:

Can you give each entity node a proper name? Can you label the relationship nodes appropriately?

Cardinality numbers or symbols are often useful, even though not always required for human comprehension. Often, the declaration may be restricted to the specification of functional relationships.

4.7   Exercises

Exercise 4.1 Data stored in the newspaper system

The newspaper is composed of several sections. Each article in the newspaper is assigned to a specific section with regard to its subject. The publisher employs several authors that may act in the role of a writer or an editor. As a writer, he or she creates articles. Editors are responsible for the content of a complete section. Taking advantage of the possibilities of the Web, the newspaper has public sections and restricted sections. After authentication, registered readers of the newspaper have access to the restricted sections.

Most of these issues are stored in the newspaper system. Create an E/R diagram which represents the range of value structures.

Exercise 4.2 Min/max notation

The E/R diagram in the middle of Figure 4.5 illustrates the relationship between father, mother and child.

Explain the cardinality number of '1' beside the role of the child.

Exercise 4.3 Cardinality number

Figure 4.3 introduced the notation of small uni-directed and bi-directional arrows to represent the range of cardinality for a relationship.

Specify the range of cardinality for a relationship node which is labeled by a uni-directed arrow and for a relationship node which is labeled by a bi-directed arrow.

Chapter 5

FMC Basics: Summary

System modeling with FMC relies on a few, but very fundamental, concepts. They form the foundation for describing a wide range of systems, namely, the class of information processing systems.

An information processing system is a special type of dynamic system. Like any dynamic system, it is composed of a set of system components, that interact with each other. The observable behavior of the system is the result of these interactions. Considering information processing systems, we focus on the informational aspects of the system. Anything that may be observed in such a system is a discrete information, that is processed, communicated or stored.

Describing those systems means *representing models* of the systems. The models capture the relevant system structures that may be observed during the lifetime of the system. Three categories of system structures need to be considered in order to create a complete FMC model of an arbitrary information processing system.

The category of compositional structures arises from the definition of dynamic systems. Each compositional structure defines a set of system components and their connections. At hardware level, this could be a structure of logical gates and registers, which directly maps to physical structures. Looking at a programmed system, we face instead conceptual components such as an editor or a spell checker. With regard to physical realization, such models are illustrative models. Yet, in representing the purpose of the physical structure, those models are a pre-requisite for system analysis and development. Looking at compositional structures of information processing systems, we distinguish active and passive components, i.e., agents and storages, resp., channels.

The discrete values which may be observed on the channels and storages of an information processing system are pieces of information. The domain and purpose of the system define the type of information. So, we find anything from elementary values such as boolean or integers, to complex structures like tables or trees. Like any structure, a value structure is composed of entities (with certain attributes) which are linked by relationships. A repertoire of admissible values, resp., value structures, may be defined for each location in the system. This is the second category of structures.

A snapshot of a dynamic system made at a single point in time may be sufficient to identify its compositional structure and current value structures. By extending the scope of observation over a certain period of time, the behavior becomes visible. The third category of structures are dynamic structures, which are defined by the causal relationship of events or operations, i.e., the activities.

> The model of any information processing system combines a compositional structure, a dynamic structure and a range of value structures. Even though all these structures refer to each other, they represent the fundamental aspects of each dynamic system and should be distinguished from each other.

Figure 5.1 illustrates this threefold character of a system model and subsumes the basic questions to identify the associated structures.

With regard to the three fundamental categories of system structures, FMC provides three types of diagram to describe these structures. These are block

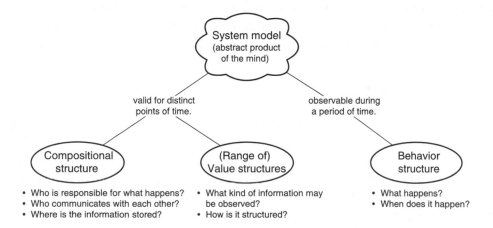

Figure 5.1:   The three fundamental aspects of each FMC model

	Compositional structures Block diagrams	Behavior structures Petri nets	Range of value structures Entity relationship diagrams
Rectangular nodes	Active components Agents	Types of activity Transitions	Relationships
Rounded nodes	Passive components Storages, Channels	Control state and conditions Places and Marks	Entity sets
Arcs	Read or write access (directed)	Causal relationship (directed)	Participation in a relationship (undirected)

Figure 5.2:   FMC diagrams. Three types of bipartite graphs

diagrams, Petri nets and Entity relationship diagrams. All FMC diagrams are *bipartite graphs*. This means that each diagram contains nodes of two different types, whereas nodes of one type may be connected only with nodes of the other one and vice versa. Nodes of the one type have a rounded shape, while nodes of the other have a rectangular shape. Figure 5.2 defines the semantics for each type of FMC diagram.

The notation is the result of a further development of existing standards. Block diagrams are based on the German industrial standard DIN66200 [DIN92]. While the concept of Petri nets had already been introduced by Carl Adam Petri in 1961 [Pet61], the bipartite notation of these nets was later introduced by Anatol Holt [HC70]. Finally, the concept of E/R diagrams is based on a publication by Peter Pin-Shan Chen [Che76].

The diagrams in Figure 5.3 constitute the complete model of a system composed of two chess player playing a game of chess. The set of possible chess positions spawns the range of value structures. Obviously, the Petri net represents a pretty high abstraction of the behavior for someone being familiar with the rules of this game. Yet, this may be an appropriate model.

The FMC approach is not restricted to programmed systems. Conceptually, any type of information processing system may be described, for instance, pure hardware systems without any software processing unit or non-technical systems like an enterprise or a council office. In fact, looking at the chess

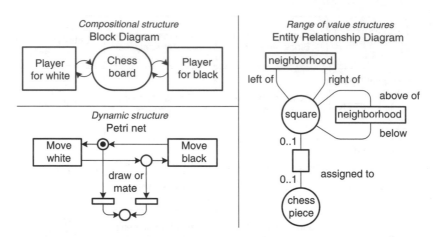

Figure 5.3:   Complete model represented by FMC diagrams, following [Wen01]. Published with permission from S. Wendt

scenario of Figure 5.3, this model is valid for human players as well as for a computer-based chess simulation. This integrative view enables the seamless description of systems that are realized partially by hardware and partially by software – something which is required especially in the design of embedded systems.

FMC is primarily a consistent and coherent way of thinking and talking about dynamic systems. It was developed to enable people to communicate the concepts and structures of complex information processing systems in an efficient way, between the different types of stakeholders. By employing a human agent metaphor, block diagrams may be easily mapped to a network of human beings exchanging information. Even though it may not be in an appropriate context (with regard to speed, accuracy, shape, etc.) this metaphor can increase system comprehension for people with a non-technical background.

Chapter 6

Reinforcing the Concepts

6.1   The meta model: A mind map to FMC

In the previous part of the book, different terms belonging to the domain of compositional structures, dynamic structure and range of value structures were introduced. These terms represent the different types of entities and relations that spawn the fundamental concepts behind any kind of information processing system. They provide a language with which to talk about information processing systems while abstracting from a specific domain: agents, operations, values, etc. The different sets of abstract entities and their relationships are integrated in the FMC meta model. It is a model that does not represent a specific system. It captures the structure of any FMC model. It is a model about models. This is why it is called a meta model. Because it refers to sets and relationships, it can be represented by an E/R diagram as shown in Figure 6.1.

The diagram is partitioned into three distinct areas corresponding to the three types of system structures. Arcs crossing the different areas refer to the relationships between the different structures. Let us begin the discussion with the ternary relationship between locations and points in time. Each element of this relation defines an observation window for a certain location and a certain interval in time. Each interval starts at a certain point in time and ends some time later. The value which is observable within such a window is constant. Whenever a value of some location is changed, this is called an *event*. It is the result of a write access to that location caused by a certain operation. *Operations* are elemental *activities*,

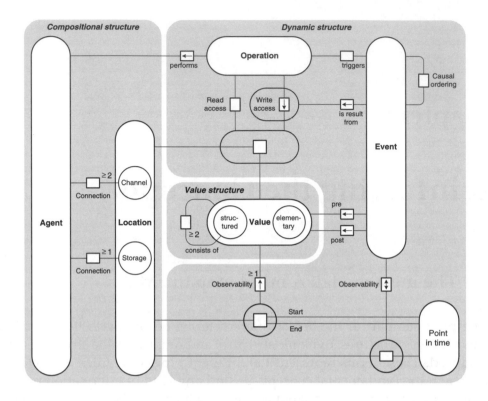

Figure 6.1:   FMC meta model

which are performed by agents to store, transfer or process information. Each operation includes exactly one write access, but may require multiple read accesses.

The meta model does not define any notation as, for instance, the symbols for agents or read access. It provides the fundamental concepts for thinking and talking about information processing systems. The terminology of the FMC meta model might be compared with the terminology of classical physics, which defines the foundations of how to think and talk about mechanical engineering. As the notions of force, mass, velocity, energy, etc., provide the mental framework for describing mechanical systems or models, the notions of agent, storage, operation, event, etc., provide the mental framework which is used to describe information processing systems. The terminology is called 'fundamental', because all terms directly or indirectly refer to each other and none of the terms can be deduced from the others.

6.2 Operational versus control state[1]

6.2.1 Introduction

System theory describes the relationship between input X and output Y, that is, between influence and reaction. Information processing systems are discrete systems which means that X and Y are elements of discrete sets, in this case sets of information. The output of many systems not only depends on the actual input value, but on something that is called the *state* Z of the system. The state integrates all the information which affects the future behavior of the system and which is stored on the different internal channels and storages of the system.

Regarding complex systems, X, Y and Z are usually structured – there are vectors of structured information. We can also distinguish two different types of information processing system:

- sequential machines;

- concurrently working systems.

A sequential machine which shows a deterministic behavior can be described by a *state machine model (automaton model)*. In that case, the relationship between some current input $X(n)$, the current state $Z(n)$, the generated output $Y(n)$ and the consecutive state $Z(n + 1)$ can be written as:

$$Y(n) = \omega[Z(n), X(n)]$$
$$Z(n + 1) = \delta[Z(n), X(n)]$$

A concurrently working system is a system which is composed of multiple components or subsystems which are working concurrently. The components usually communicate with each other. Synchronization is achieved by connecting input and output variables of the different components via channels. Each subsystem may be composed of either single sequential machines or multiple concurrently working subsystems.

So when describing the behavior of information processing systems, we may focus on the description of state machines and their synchronization [Hoa78].

Conceptually, there are three different approaches used to describe the behavior of a state machine:

---

[1]This section closely refers to two technical reports of Siegfried Wendt [Wen98a, Wen98b]. Some passages have been directly adopted by permission of the author.

- graphs such as Petri nets or State charts representing the set of possible states and transitions;

- tables, itemizing $Y(n), Z(n + 1)$ for each valid combination of $Z(n), X(n)$;

- algebraic formulas describing $\omega[Z(n), X(n)]$ and $\delta[Z(n), X(n)]$.

6.2.2   Problem and solution

Often the input, output and state are composed of different variables, so we are describing vectors of information. Any state variable stores a piece of information which is expected to be required some time later. The number of possible states for systems with many state variables and large domain sets is enormous. For instance, the behavior of the travel agency system depends on the state of negotiation as well as on the content of the reservations, the customer data and the travel information storage. Even though the set of states is finite, it is impossible to itemize each possible state explicitly. So the question is:

> *What is the concept which is used to describe the behavior of systems with a large set of states in a comprehensive way?*

For a complex system, it is virtually impossible to represent each possible state explicitly as a node in a Petri net or State chart or as a table entry. Also, the closed definition of the state transition function and the output function is hardly possible. A representation which is manageable by a human reader is achieved by an appropriate combination of graphical and textual notation and a *smart partitioning of the state space*. A typical application of this partitioning approach is the well-known distinction between program variables and the program counter.

> *The concept is based on the distinction between variables of the control state and variables of the operational state.*

The benefit of this distinction in the management of large state sets has already been described in publications about sequential circuit theory and automaton theory almost forty years ago [Glu65, Wen70].

> *Whether a state variable is to be classified as an operational variable or a control variable, depends on how the domain of that variable is defined.*

There is no mathematical criterion for distinction, it is based on semantics; the purpose of the variables. We will now consider a number of examples which illustrate the difference and provide a foundation to specify a strict and universal definition for both types of variables.

6.2.3   Criteria of distinction

Operational state

Figure 6.2 shows the compositional structure of a simple ticket machine. A customer may buy tickets of a single type. The machine shows the behavior of a strictly sequential machine, i.e., an automaton. It can only be triggered by inserting coins. With regard to the state of the automaton, the user receives a ticket with or without some change or nothing. It is appropriate, to separate three components of state in order to predict the behavior of the automaton.

The first state component corresponds to the contents of the ticket container. The capacity of this container is limited. By selling enough tickets, the container may become empty. Obviously in this case, the ticket machine behaves differently than it would if tickets were available.

The second state component corresponds to the cash deposit. Whenever a ticket is sold, the income for the ticket is added to this deposit. The deposit represents a state component, because its value influences the behavior of the ticket machine. Normally, the deposit provides the change, whenever the amount that was paid exceeds the price of a ticket. But the machine cannot provide the change in cases when the required coins are missing or when it blocks further input, because the deposit is full.

The third state component corresponds to the contents of the transaction buffer. This buffer contains the coins which are collected, until the machine issues the

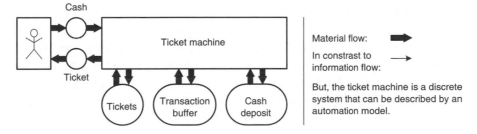

Figure 6.2:   Ticket machine example of compositional structure

ticket and transfers the paid amount to the deposit. This is probably the most obvious state component of the ticket machine.

In this example, all of the three state variables meet the criteria for a typical operational variable:

> *The domain of an operational variable can be specified without itemizing each transition between the possible values, explicitly.*

Often, but not always, there is no need to explicitly itemize each value of the domain. In the example of the ticket machine, there is no need to explicitly itemize each possible allocation of the ticket container, the cash deposit or the transaction buffer. This might be different for a flight simulator referring to an operational variable with a domain like this: {*'beginner','advanced','expert'*} which may be set by a user before starting.

Looking at operational variables, i.e., storages for operational values, we ask for possible allocations and the resulting consequences of operating the system. With regard to the ticket machine, we may find:

- The contents of the ticket container determines the number of tickets that may be sold without replenishing.

- The contents of the cash deposit determines the number of different coins that are available for change and the amount of money that belongs to the selling company.

- The contents of the cash deposit determines the amount of money the customer has already paid and the type of coins that were used.

Whenever there is no need to itemize the elements of the domain explicitly, the extreme extension of the domain becomes easy. The appropriate means of representation for these cases are E/R diagrams or algebraic notation. For instance, consider two different variants of the ticket machine. For simplicity, the machine accepts 10 cent coins only. If one ticket cost 1 dollar, then the domain of values for the transaction buffer contains ten values. If one ticket costs 100 dollars, then the domain of values for the transaction buffer already contains a thousand values. Despite this large number, the second case is as easily understood as the first one. In any case, the behavior – i.e., the transitions between the possible values – may be described by the same algebraic formula:

$$\begin{pmatrix} Y(n) \\ Z(n+1) \end{pmatrix} = \begin{cases} \begin{pmatrix} nothing \\ Z(n) + 10\,cents \end{pmatrix} & if\ (Z(n) + 10\,cents) < TICKETPRICE \\ \begin{pmatrix} ticket \\ 0\,cents \end{pmatrix} & else \end{cases}$$

There would be less reason to describe these variants using different Petri nets. A different Petri net would be required for each different price. With increasing prices, the Petri nets would become larger. Apart from the physical limitations in rendering large diagrams, both aspects are likely to interfere with human understanding.

Control state

Variables that do not meet the criteria for an operational variable are control variables:

> *The domain of a control variable can only be specified by explicitly itemizing each value and each permissible transition between those values. The appropriate means of representation is a graph.*

Figure 6.3 shows the compositional structure of a system which automatically processes workpieces of two different types. The control of this system is a component that operates a belt drive to convey the workpieces, a clamp to hold them during work and a machine tool to drill, polish and chamfer them. It also receives input from a detector for the type and temperature of the workpieces. The behavior of the control depends on its input and some internal state. I/O interpreters perform the mapping between the discrete world of information and the continuous world of physics in the environment of the control.

The workpieces are thick metal plates, which are delivered on a conveyor belt which is powered by the belt drive. A run activates and a stop signal deactivates the drive, which responds with an acknowledge signal. If the belt delivers a workpiece of type A or B (see Figure 6.4), the workpiece detection informs the control. To process the workpiece the belt is stopped and the clamp is closed. Afterwards the machine tool is used to perform the metalworking specific to the type of the workpiece. To prevent overheating of the workpieces or the tools the process is interrupted whenever a certain temperature is exceeded. After cooling down the process is resumed. An infrared sensor in the workpiece detector provides the control with the necessary signals.

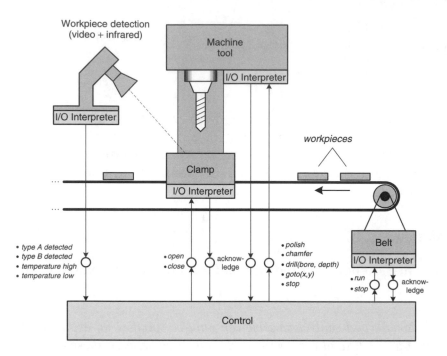

Figure 6.3:   Line production example showing compositional structure

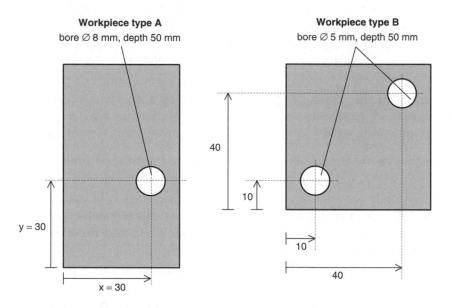

Figure 6.4:   Line production example showing two types of workpiece

Workpieces of type A obtain one bore of 8mm in diameter and 50mm depth. Workpieces of type B obtain two bores of 5mm in diameter and 10mm depth. All bores will be chamfered. Additionally, workpieces of type A will be polished.

The Petri net in Figure 6.5 specifies the behavior of the control which is managing the production process. Each transition refers to a specific type of command, which is sent to one of the different actuators, i.e., the belt drive, the clamp and the tool machine. For reasons of simplicity, we assume that the tool machine exchanges its tooling inserts, whenever necessary, on its own. Each actuator responds with an acknowledge signal after execution of one command. These signals and the messages from the workpiece detector trigger the control to proceed one step. There are three wait states, in which a 'temperature high' warning may be detected before the drilling is finished. In that case the machine tool is stopped and the control waits for the temperature to fall below a certain level. In theory, there may be a conflict between temperature signals and acknowledge signals from the machine tool. In practice, this is no problem and it has no influence on the example. Predicates attached to the arcs of the Petri net represent the corresponding firing conditions.

The control is a typical example of a system that has a control state only. The set of possible states can only be defined by explicitly itemizing all possible states and transitions that are necessary to process the workpieces. In this example, there are 18 different states and 22 possible transitions. The Petri net represents each of them. A Petri net describing a state machine requires only one mark traversing the net. The place being marked represents the current state of the machine.

According to the previous definition, the Petri net explicitly itemizes each value, i.e., each control state, and each permissible transition between those values, i.e., each permissible state transition. Obviously, the dynamic structure could have been also described using a tabular representation or an algebraic notation, but the graph representation has a higher perceivability for control flow.

As in Figure 6.3, there are few block diagrams explicitly showing storages for the control state. We may consider such a storage to be some integral part of the corresponding control. Explicitly showing the storage would not contribute any information that is not already obvious – such as a control requiring a location to store the control state, but it would increase the visual complexity of the diagram and may distract the reader from other components which are relevant to the understanding of the system.

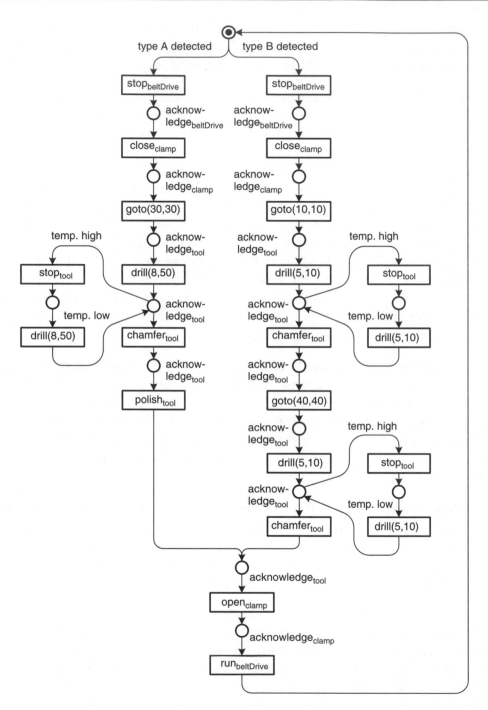

Figure 6.5: Line production example showing control flow

Systems with operational and control state

The previous examples were systems with either an operational or control state, only. In practice, the state of many systems is composed of some operational and some control states. Normally, they are stored in different locations in the system. Each transition from one state to another may affect the control state and the operational state. To represent the dynamic structure of those systems, the Petri net representation for control flow is combined with algebraic representations describing operational behavior. In the strict sense, this is an extension of the original Petri net concept. Transition nodes and arc predicates refer to the operational state of the system. The marking represents the control state.

Figures 6.6 and 6.7 illustrate a simple example. A sorter receives unsorted arrays of numbers from its environment and creates a corresponding sequence of sorted arrays. An unsorted array is provided in one step and triggers the sorting operation. New input is not accepted until the sorter has released the result. Implementing the bubblesort algorithm, the sorter requires one location to store the array, one to remember the position up to that the array which is already sorted, and one that refers to the current position for comparing two adjacent entries. The operational state is composed of different operational variables. Usually, different variables are stored in different storages of the system. In the example, it is neither possible nor necessary to itemize explicitly each possible element of the domain for each of these variables.

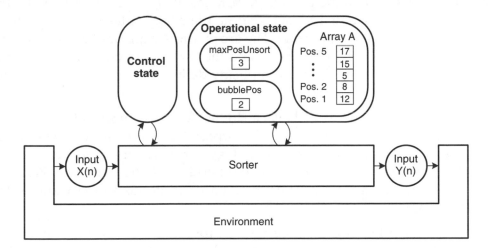

Figure 6.6:   Block diagram for a sorter (in the middle of sorting an array)

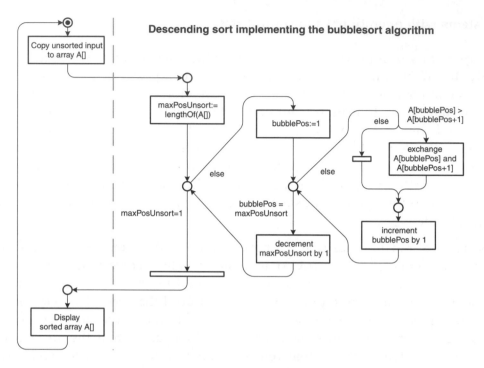

Figure 6.7: Petri net of a sorter

The Petri net describes the behavior of the sorter. The structure of the Petri net explicitly identifies the possible control states, which are represented by the different places, and the possible transitions, which are represented by the different transition nodes. The labels of the transitions refer to the operations that are necessary to sort the array. The arc predicates are predicates about the operational state, i.e., about the array and the two array pointers. Referring to the operational state, the Petri net implicitly defines the operational state and also its transitions.

Exceptionally, Figure 6.6 also shows a storage for the control state. The sorter could be implemented using a general purpose processor for Petri nets which was configured with the Petri net in Figure 6.7. In this case, the storage for the control state would contain the marking of the Petri net. With regard to programmed systems, this marking corresponds to the value of the program counter.

As storages may be used to store the control state or the operational state, channels may also be used to communicate operational values or control information and often we find a mix of both. For instance, in the sorter example, whenever the environment provides a new unsorted array, i.e., an operational value, this also triggers the sorter. This is a mix of *value* and *event communication*.

Systems showing concurrent activities may also be described using Petri nets (see Chapter 3). Such a Petri net can be partitioned into different, interconnected sub-nets, each describing the strict sequential behavior of a subsystem with its own control state. In contrast, locations storing operational variables may be the subject of common access. The storage for reservations in the travel agency scenario in Chapter 2 is an example of this case.

6.2.4   Discrete control loop

The idea of separating the control state from the operational state may also guide the overall design of the compositional structure of the system. It may be appropriate to split the system into a control unit and an operational unit. The resulting structure, shown in Figure 6.8, is called a *discrete control loop* ('Steuerkreis' in German) according to [Wen98a, Wen70].

The operational unit is responsible for input and output operations as well as for operations on the operational state of the system. Nevertheless, each activity of the operational unit requires a request from the control unit. So, the operational unit defines the repertoire of operation which may be performed by the system. The control unit is responsible for commanding the right sequence which depends on the current control state $Z_{Ctrl}(n)$ and the predicates about the operational state $Z_{Op}(n)$ and the input $X(n)$ from the environment.

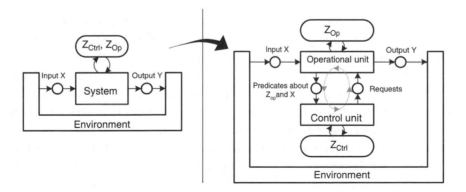

Figure 6.8:   Discrete control loop

If a Petri net represents the dynamic structure of a system in such a manner that its marking represents the control state and the transitions refer to operations on the operational state, then the discrete control loop model can be used for a straightforward implementation. The *control unit* implements the state machine, which is defined by the graph of the Petri net, while the *operational unit* implements the agents, which are necessary to perform the operations being identified by the transition labels. The operational unit also determines the predicates based on the input from the environment and the operational state which constitutes the input for the control unit.

For instance, the sorter shown in Figure 6.6, might be implemented using the discrete control loop model. Then the operational unit would have to provide services to initialize, increase and decrease the two position counters, to exchange any two entries of the array and to compare array positions and counters.

If possible, with regard to the intended behavior, the control unit and the components of the operational unit may even work concurrently with each other and synchronize only when necessary. The discrete control loop pattern may also be applied hierarchically as components of the operational unit may be very complex. The internal compositional structure of those components could follow the same pattern. For instance, in a business processing system, the upper control unit might be implemented by a work flow engine. The operational unit would contain components to support order acquisition, shipment, billing, etc. There is a good chance that an order acquisition component could also be composed of a control unit and operational components for entering and checking order information.

Historically, this approach originates from hardware design and it is related to the control and data path pattern, but it is not confined to that domain. Also, in the development of programmed systems, it facilitates the identification of understandable models. Assigning the responsibility of causal dependencies to a single component in the compositional structure can simplify complex networks of arbitrary control channels between agents. However, a strict hierarchical approach is not appropriate for any system or on any abstraction level. In some systems, the compositional structure may become even clearer, if not following the discrete control loop pattern (see Figure 3.8). Also, a single control or a control hierarchy may constitute a single point of failure or a bottleneck. In these cases, a direct mapping of this model to implementation structures is not recommended.

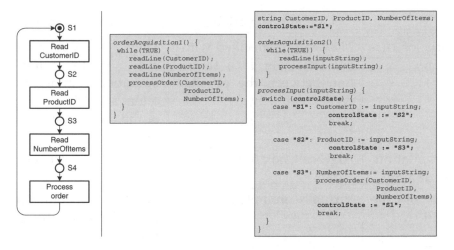

Figure 6.9: An example describing the behavior of a control unit at program level

Also this approach does not anticipate any software structures. Figure 6.9 illustrates this statement by presenting two equivalent alternatives for describing the behavior of a control unit for a very simple order acquisition system at program level. Processing the left program, the control state can be determined by observing the values of the program counter and the execution stack of the processor. In contrast, the right solution explicitly refers to a variable which stores the control state. This would be the typical approach for a system with an event-driven user-interface. A third solution (which is not shown here) could represent the state machine model of the controller using a table-based approach. Even though any of these solutions has a different structure, their behavior is the same and complies with the abstract model. With these considerations in mind, the Discrete Control Loop pattern provides a powerful approach for the identification of models which are useful for human communication about information processing systems without cementing the implementation.

6.2.5 Summary

Table 6.1 summarizes the different characters of operational and control variables. Sometimes, it may be hard to decide whether a state variable is to be classified as an operational or a control variable. In these cases, try to answer the following question: Which of the two views is more likely to be understood in communicating the purpose of that variable?

	Operational variables	Control variables
Criteria of distinction	They can be specified without itemizing each transition between the possible values, explicitly.	They are variables that do not meet the criteria for operational variables – very often, a specific itemization of the domain is not necessary.
Representation of the domain	Algebraic notation, E/R diagram	Graphs like Petri nets
Power of the domain	Virtually unlimited	Limited by the human need to understand the control flow
Extensibility of the domain	Easy: for instance, extending the domain of some counter variable	Difficult: extensions are modifications of the control flow
Naming the variable's domain	Meaningful labels are always possible: for instance, 'sorting-position' or 'reservations'	Labeling has no meaning: only single states have a dedicated meaning

Table 6.1:   Comparing operational and control variables

6.3   Block diagrams: Advanced concepts

In Chapter 2, block diagrams were introduced to describe the compositional structure of information processing systems. Active components are represented by rectangular nodes, passive components are represented by rounded nodes. Only nodes of different types may be connected with each other. An arc connecting an agent node with a storage or a channel node represents the possibility of this agent to read, write or modify the content. Now, we consider the meaning of nested nodes and some means to describe structure variant systems.

6.3.1   Nested nodes: Different views versus layout

Basically, it is important to distinguish visual containment caused by:

- representing different views of the system's compositional structure in one diagram;
- grouping multiple nodes for layout reasons.

In the first case, visual containment represents a *consists of* or *contains* relationship. The enclosing node is a system component that is composed of the inner nodes. For instance, Figure 6.10 shows the model of an image processing pipeline as it is used in many digital cameras to transform the raw sensor image data into image data suitable for viewing. The diagram identifies the pipeline as a single component. A refined model shows the internal structure of that pipeline as being composed of four filters and three internal storages. The lower diagram integrates the two different views. Visual containment is used as a natural approach to illustrate this structural relationship. The enclosed structure is called a *refinement* of the enclosing node.

By nesting, different views of the compositional structure are represented in the same diagram. However, the clear separation of different aspects of a system is very important in order to reduce the complexity in the development of large systems. So how do we explain this obvious contradiction?

There may be situations when the representation of a different aspect in one representation, enhances system comprehension. Nesting may be used to illustrate the purpose of a system component. In the image processing example, it may be useful to identify the pipeline *and* to communicate an idea of its purpose by showing the filter chain. Nesting can be used to illustrate how different aspects of the system are related to each other. In contrast to software modules, modularization, flexibility and re-use – a major motivation for separation of concerns [Par72] – is no great issue in the creation of FMC diagrams.

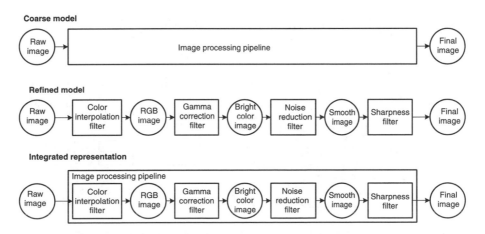

Figure 6.10: Image processing example for the refinement of agents

The notation of nested nodes is easy to understand. However, some attention is required in order to distinguish those arcs that are attached to an enclosing node and those that are attached to an enclosed node. If an arc connects a channel with an enclosing agent, this represents a channel to each agent which is enclosed. If it is connected to an enclosed agent, this represents a connection to this agent only. Equally, an arc may be attached to an enclosing or an enclosed storage, which has an analogous meaning. Figure 6.11 illustrates the idea since both diagrams are representations of the same compositional structure.

Containment may also be the result of layout considerations. Figure 6.12 shows two block diagrams. Again, both diagrams are representations of the same compositional structure. In this case, a news server system is described which is composed of one master server for load balancing and several workers processing requests from different web clients. The left diagram is likely to

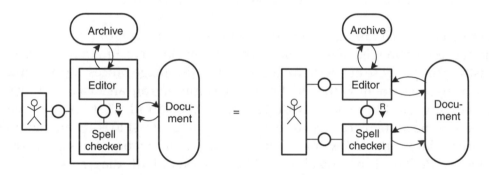

Figure 6.11:   An editor example of nested nodes and read/write arcs

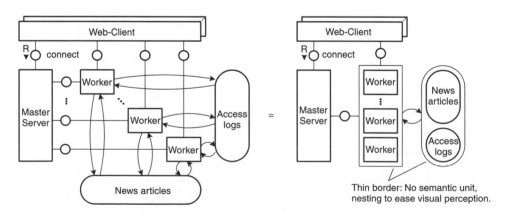

Figure 6.12:   A news server example showing nesting to ease perception

cause some confusion because of the many crossing arcs. Nesting eliminates these crossings.

As district from the previous examples, the enclosing nodes constitute no semantic unit. No meaningful name could be given to the node enclosing news articles and access logs. For that reason, a node which was introduced for layout reasons only, is nothing but a notational means of easing the layout. Those nodes have a thin border to distinguish them from real agents or storages, which have a thick border.

6.3.2 From conceptual to implementation structures

Whenever nesting is used to represent different views of the system's compositional structure in one diagram, these views refer to different layers of abstraction. For higher levels of abstraction, the focus is on conceptual structures, while the implementation or design decisions that are shown on lower levels are hidden.

The identification of lower level system structures is based on the same principles as the identification of higher level system structures. We ask the same questions that were presented in the first part of this book. But, as Figures 6.13 and 6.14 illustrate, the consideration of implementation structures may take two different directions:

- the refinement of active and passive components;

- the assignment of responsibilities or roles to platform structures.

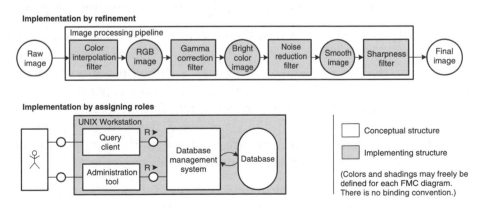

Figure 6.13: Two directions of implementation using agents as an example

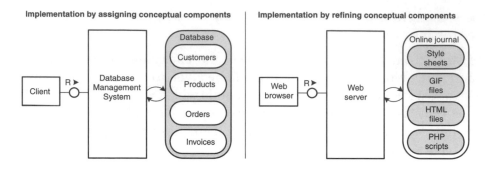

Figure 6.14: Two directions of implementation using storages as an example

When refining a model, the focus is on the inner structure of single components. Instead of asking what is to be done in the system, we ask what is to be done in the system component. This principle is called *functional decomposition* or *hierarchical decomposition* and may be applied recursively. There are no rules as to whether the refined structure is shown on a separate diagram or as an integral part of the entire higher level structure. In any case, the relationship between models of different resolution should be made visible by naming and nesting.

The structure of a conceptual system model can be quite different from the structure of the implementing platform or the physical structure of an information processing system. Often, a one-to-one mapping between conceptual components and the building blocks of the implementation platform is not possible. So the question 'Who is responsible?' can be answered differently, if we move the focus from conceptual system components to platform components. With regard to implementation, the conceptual model provides the roles that are implemented on top of an appropriate configuration of platform components.

For instance, the second diagram in Figure 6.13 shows a user who can use a query client and an administration tool to access a database system. A UNIX workstation is used to implement the query client, the administration tool and the database system. Alternately, processing the corresponding programs, the workstation plays different roles in multiplex. The enclosing component is the result of a design decision. In the strict sense, the term refinement is not appropriate in this context. The refinement of a generic Unix workstation is definitely different from the conceptual model, in this example.

With regard to implementation structures, conceptual models are often *equivalent* or *illustrative models*, whose structure is difficult to map to the actual physical structure. Yet, equivalent or illustrative models are necessary in order to understand and predict the behavior of complex systems [BMW94]. The conceptual model of a company may identify components for order processing, manufacturing, shipment and billing. In a very small company, these conceptual components may be virtual and represent only the roles of a single person. With regard to this implementation, the conceptual model is an equivalent or illustrative model. However, it is a valid model, because it allows the behavior of the company to be predicted.

The idea of equivalent models is very popular. It is not restricted to information processing or FMC, nor does it imply a vague and fuzzy representation of the system. For instance, in the field of electrical engineering, equivalent networks are universally accepted to describe the behavior of transistors, power supply lines and other electrical components. The equivalent model of a transistor includes an ideal current supply – something you probably will not find when dissecting a real transistor. Yet such a model allows you to calculate precisely the electrical behavior of a transistor.

Different systems may require a different number of model layers in order to illustrate the transition from conceptual structures to implementation structures. For instance, different conceptual storages may be mapped to one database system which is mapped to different virtual machines which are mapped to a heterogeneous cluster of workstations. FMC is special due to the fact that there is no need change the way we think about systems in terms of agents, storages and channels. In consequence, there is no need to introduce a different notation for each layer of abstraction.

6.3.3   Syntax and meaning of refinement

As mentioned in Chapter 5, a block diagram, like any other FMC diagram, is a bipartite graph where each diagram contains nodes of two different types, whereas nodes of one type may be connected only with nodes of the other one and vice versa. Nodes of the one type have a rounded shape, while nodes of the other have a rectangular shape.

There is only one simple rule that must be followed when refining a block diagram. The derived block diagram has to be a bipartite graph as well. Figure 6.15 illustrates the resulting possibilities when refining an agent, storage or channel.

Any refinement of an agent constitutes an *agent-bordered* sub-net of a block diagram. Only agents of that sub-net can be connected with the channels and

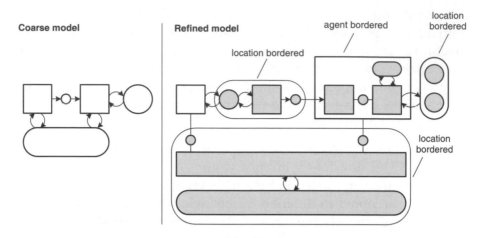

Figure 6.15:   Bipartite refinement using a block diagram example

storages in the environment. Apart from that, the refinement may have any structure which complies with the syntax of block diagrams. Any refinement of a location, storage or channel, constitutes a *location-bordered* sub-net of a block diagram. Only locations of that sub-net can be connected with the agents in the environment. Any connection between an agent and some location in the abstract model has to be mapped to one or more connections in the refined model.

The meaning of refinement appears to be intuitive, but nevertheless needs some discussion. The refinement of an agent still has the character of an active system component, i.e., an agent. One possible refinement of a storage is a simple set of different locations. Such a structure has preserved the character of a passive system component. The environment is not affected by those transformations. With regard to the borders of those sub-nets, the behavior remains the same. This type of simple refinement is called *strict hierarchical refinement*.

Very often, storages for the common access of different agents are realized by an access manager which encapsulates the actual location to store the information. Read and write arcs are replaced by channels. Immediate access is replaced by communication. Despite the passive character of the storage, the implementation structure has an active character. With regard to the borders of such a sub-net, the behavior has changed. Consequently, any component in the immediate environment is affected by this non-trivial transformation. The semantic layer defining the abstractions of the model is changed.

The same applies to the refinement of channels. A channel is a single location. Whenever an agent writes a value to some channel, any agent listening to that channel immediately receives this information. Following this model, information cannot be lost by mistake – a channel provides an ideal medium for non-buffered communication. Attached agents do not need to worry about delays and timeouts or measures for error correction, etc., but the implementation of channels often reveals mediating agents or even negotiation with communication services. Consequently, the refinement of channels also constitutes a non-trivial transformation.

Channels and storages can be powerful abstractions encapsulating complex protocols and the behavior of implementation structures. Bipartite refinement provides a smart approach to handle syntactically non-trivial transformations between abstract high-level structures and mappings to lower-level implementation structures.

Figure 6.16 illustrates the applicability and usefulness of this concept by comparing two block diagrams of the travel agency system introduced in Chapter 2. The left diagram shows the compositional structure of the travel agency on the non-technical level of business processes where the domain of value structures covers information such as traveling advertisements, consulting dialogs and contracts, etc. The right diagram shows an implementation of the information help desk and its environment.

The storage for travel information is implemented by a variety of different communication and storage systems providing different interfaces to its users. The passive storage – a useful abstraction at the business layer – reveals a network of active and passive components at the implementation layer. The help desk gathers information from these data providers: Adapters convert the information into a unique format. The core component of the help desk is the document builder. It provides the documents assembled from the collected information and from a set of predefined templates to a HTTP server. People interested in travel agency services can read the documents from this web server using a web browser.

The domain of value structures in this model covers information like DB and XML schemes, protocols like HTTP, IMAP or HTTP. Even though formally the model is a bipartite refinement (ignoring the fact that the reservation system no longer directly accesses the travel information), the interfaces of the agents are very different. Therefore, the model is not a strict hierarchical refinement of the abstract model – it shows a different *semantic layer*. This powerful concept of FMC is discussed in more detail in Section 6.5. We could continue to describe the

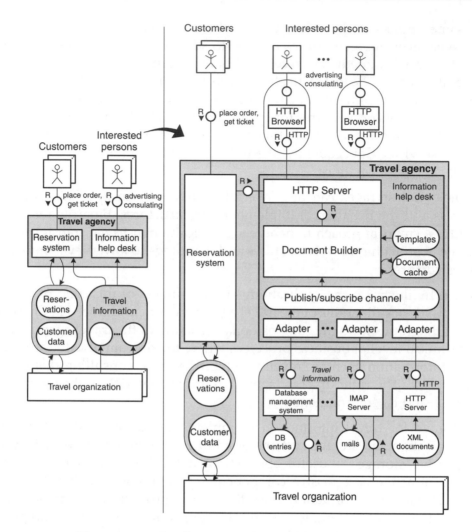

Figure 6.16: Implementing the Travel agency system

dynamics and value structures for this new model, and then refine or introduce new aspects one more time, and so on. However, we will not do this here, but hopefully this example will give you an idea of how to close the gap between abstract models and structures which are relevant for implementation.

6.3.4 Structure variant systems

Sometimes, the compositional structure of a system is also referred to as the static structure of the system in contrast to its dynamic structure, which refers to the system behavior. However, the compositional structure of certain systems may also vary over time.

A computer may be connected to or disconnected from a network. New hardware or software modules may be added or activated, others may be deactivated or removed. A new database for recording orders and invoices may be installed. A web server may be activated by the computer's operating system loading the corresponding program into memory and scheduling a new process. In object-oriented systems, objects are created and removed. In each of these cases, we may have an idea of the creation or removal of agents, storages or channels.

Whenever the modification of a system should be considered to be part of the intended or planned system behavior (in contrast to some exceptional damage), there is a need for modeling structure variance. As presented so far, a single block diagram of a structure variant system may only refer to the interval between two modifications, when the compositional structure is static. A separate block diagram could be created for each possible compositional structure, but the transition from one model to another remains invisible using this approach.

Considering the question, 'Who is responsible?', for each modification of the compositional structure, there must be some agent who is responsible for performing that particular operation. As for any other operation, making a structural alteration refers to a certain location in the system. The only difference is in the range of values. Normally, a location stores some value which represents a piece of information. In this special case, the value is some part of the system structure, which is composed of agents, storages or channels, with connections to the environment of this workplace. Such a special location is called a *structure variance storage*.

Figure 6.17 illustrates the idea. Agent A can modify the compositional structure inside the structure variance storage. The special role of this storage is emphasized by the dashed border of the corresponding node in the diagram. In this example, agent A has created the structure, which is composed of B, C and D. It has also established the link of B and D with their environment. After completing this structure variance operation, the components of the environment can interact with the components inside the structure variance storage, as with any other system component.

A block diagram only identifies the parts of the system that are affected by structure variance and the agents responsible for these operations. The dynamic structure determines the details and conditions of these modifications. A Petri

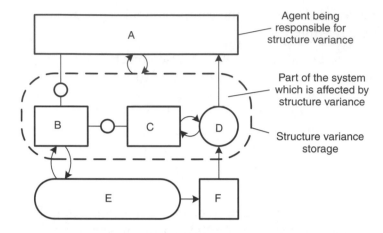

Figure 6.17:   The concepts of the structure variant system

net, describing the behavior of an agent which can modify the system structure, may contain transitions with labels like 'create agent . . .', 'fork process . . .', 'shutdown system . . .', 'delete object xy', etc.

With regard to object-oriented systems, we have to anticipate that only some objects should be considered to represent agents, storages or channels. The concept of structure variance is not applicable for the many objects which only represent values. In Section 7.4, the various mappings between FMC models and object-oriented systems are discussed in more detail.

Conceptually, the content of a structure variance storage may be modified permanently during the lifetime of the system. So what is the benefit of using a block diagram to represent a single arbitrary structure?

In many systems, structure variance is only relevant when activating or deactivating the entire system. Often, the structure to be activated is already defined by design. Also, in a complex system environment, there is often no need to illustrate each possible assignment of the structure variance storage, but it can be important to understand the concepts of activating or deactivating components. A separate infrastructure may be required to control this process. Dependencies between components have to be considered.

For instance, consider the HTTP server example in Figure 6.18. Clients such as web browsers may connect to the communication service of the HTTP server. Several workers are processing requests from the clients, while other workers may be idle. The mutex is used to avoid conflicts when a new client is trying to establish a new connection via the communication service. So, at any time

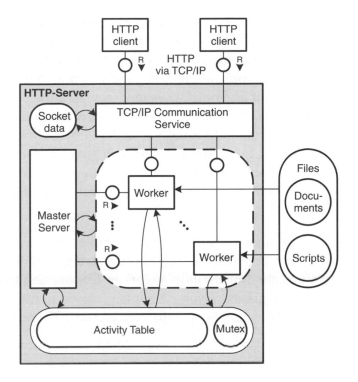

Figure 6.18:   Web server: a structure variant system

only one worker can be waiting to accept an incoming connection request. The number of workers can be varied by the master server in order to optimize the processor load and the performance of the system. Each worker reports its work status to the activity table which is monitored by the master server. Depending on the number of client requests, the master server creates new workers, removes idle workers or instructs a worker to finish after processing its current request.

However, structure variance is not the only reason for a system to change its behavior. Conceptually, we may distinguish two alternatives whenever a system starts or stops providing a certain service:

- the *creation or removal* of agents, storages or channels;

- a *parameterization* of existing system components.

Consider a person using a laptop computer to read news, captures notes and create drawings on the screen. For each purpose, this person has a separate

application. At a single point in time, only one application is active, which
consumes the entire space on the screen. When the user finishes reading the
news and starts creating a drawing, they may have the idea that the news reader
is replaced by the drawing application. But, they also may have another idea.
By parameterizing the input and output system, they are now connected to the
drawing component, while the news reader is still present in the background.
Both models are valid – their individual value depends on their purpose. In
the context of a user trying to understand the switching between applications,
structure variance is probably not the appropriate means of explanation. This
model might be useful for an engineer designing a desktop manager.

Figure 6.19 illustrates another example. Again, we have two models of the same
system. The model on the left shows the conceptual structure of the system. Different clients communicate directly with a worker. Information transfer comes
without delays and transmission errors. A switch is used to establish separate
channels, each connecting one client with one worker. This model shows a
structure variant system.

The model on the right shows a possible implementation. Clients and workers
are connected to a communication service provider. The communication is
mediated and buffered. The service provider has to guarantee the quality of
service, so the assertions of the conceptual model remain valid. In this model,
the compositional structure is static.

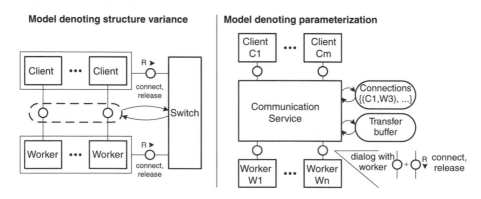

Figure 6.19:   An example of structure variance versus parameterization

6.4 Petri nets: Advanced concepts

6.4.1 Transition–bordered and transition–like sub-nets

Petri nets are used in FMC to describe the dynamic structure of information processing systems. Transitions, which refer to activity types, are represented by rectangular nodes. Places and tokens, which refer to the control state, are represented by circles and marks. Often, a higher-level Petri net contains nodes which are refined in further Petri nets. As Petri nets are bipartite graphs, the concepts of bipartite refinement and simplification may also be applied.

There is only one simple, syntactic rule that must be followed when refining or simplifying a Petri net. The derived Petri net must also be a bipartite graph. Refining a Petri net means refining behavior. From that point of view, the primary focus is on refining transitions, not places. The result of refining a transition is a special type of a *transition–bordered* sub-net – a *transition–like* sub-net.

Figure 6.20 illustrates the two terms. A sub-net of a Petri net is transition–bordered, if any node which belongs to the sub-net and which is connected with a node in the environment of the sub-net is a transition. So any node in the environment which is connected with a node inside the transition–bordered sub-net can only be a place. Typically, a rectangular border is used to delimit a transition–bordered sub-net. N1, N2, N3 and N4 in Figure 6.20 are examples of transition–bordered sub-nets.

Conceptually, a transition–bordered sub-net may be any arbitrary selection of a Petri net that meets the criteria above. Transition–like sub-nets are transition–bordered sub-nets such that we may think of describing the refinement of a determined, indivisible operation – an operation which may be represented by a single transition.

In Figure 6.20, sub-nets N1 and N4 meet the criteria. We may have the idea of N1 or N4 firing and processing the contained sub-net in one indivisible step. The tokens are removed from any input place and tokens are placed on each output place. N2 and N3 do not meet the criteria since processing N2 involves different tokens being exchanged with the environment, consecutively. Processing N3 may be considered to be done in one indivisible step, but only one of its two output places will be marked.

Simple transition–bordered sub-nets are delimited using a dashed border. Transition–like sub-nets are delimited by a continuous line like the border of a normal

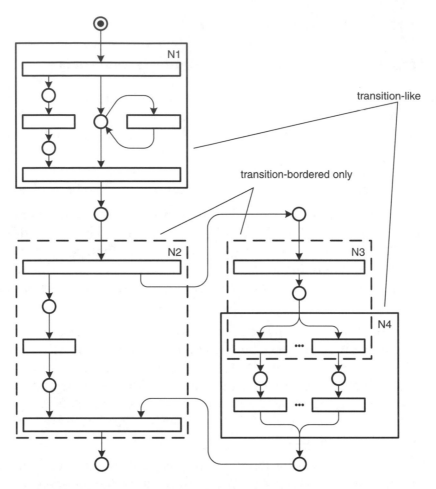

Figure 6.20:   Transition−bordered and transition−like sub-nets

transition. As for transitions, transition−bordered and transition−like sub-nets should be given a meaningful label. In general, delimiting sub-nets facilitate the visualization of relationships between models of different abstraction. Figure 6.21 shows an example of the use of a transition−bordered sub-net as placeholder for a rather complex dynamic structure. By repeating the border and the label of the sub-net in the right diagram, a reference to the left Petri net is established.

6.4.2   Safe Petri nets

Some marking of a Petri net is *safe*, if for any marking that may be reached by applying the firing rules, the following statement is true:

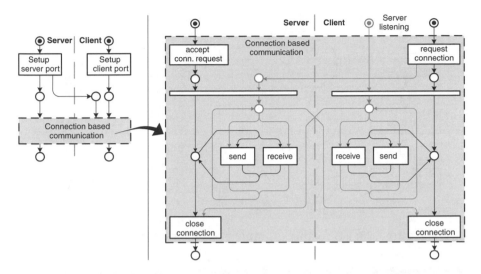

Figure 6.21: An example of transition–bordered sub-nets serving as placeholders

If every input place of some transition is marked, then all output places of this transition are empty and the transition may fire.

A Petri net with a safe marking is called *safe* or *safely marked*. Generally, reading a safe Petri net is easier than reading an equivalent, but unsafe, Petri net describing the same dynamic structure. Checking whether or not a transition may fire no longer requires checking the output places. Scenarios with a transition, which is prevented from firing because of the marking of output places, are forbidden. Also, in a safe Petri net, only input places may be a subject of firing conflicts. Scenarios as shown in the right Petri net of Figure 6.22 are not allowed.

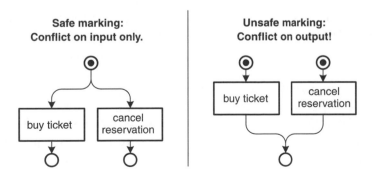

Figure 6.22: An example of safe versus unsafe marking

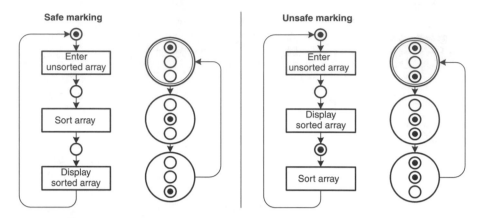

Figure 6.23:   A further example of safe versus unsafe marking

Figure 6.23 shows two Petri nets which are defining the same simple sequence of actions: enter an unsorted array, sort the array, finally display the sorted array and repeat the sequence. The safe Petri net lists these steps just in the order in which the operations are performed. There is a single token representing the current control state. Reading the right Petri net may be confusing, at least at first glance. The direction which is defined by arcs connecting places and transitions does not correspond to the order of firing, because the two tokens constitute an unsafe marking. The reachability graph, on the right, illustrates how the flow of tokens is changed. In most cases, safe Petri nets are easier to understand.

Conceptually, the dynamic structure of each sequential machine can easily be represented by a Petri net which contains only one token representing the current control state. This token is passed from transition to transition, each having exactly one input and one output place. The simple Petri nets, which are called State Machines, are equivalent to State Transition Diagrams. Many Petri nets describing the behavior of information processing systems are of this type.

Systems with concurrent behavior are often composed of different sequential machines. The behavior of each single sequential machine is described by a safe Petri net. The dynamic structure of the overall behavior can be described by connecting the different safe sub-nets. Usually the resulting Petri net is no longer safe. In many situations the resulting Petri net is still simple enough to be understood very easily. However, in complicated scenarios, synchronization and deadlock problems may feature.

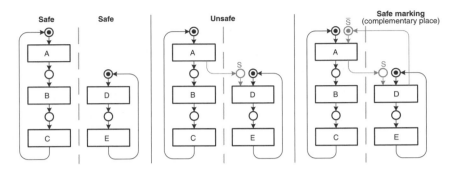

Figure 6.24:   Synchronizing Petri nets

Figure 6.24 illustrates the problem. There are two safe Petri nets to the left. In the middle, the graphs are connected so only after firing transition A, may transition D fire. Even so, the marking is unsafe because if A, B and C have fired without firing D then the input place of A is marked, but so is S which prevents A from firing. Introducing a *complementary place* between D and A the Petri net is transformed into an equivalent, but safe, Petri net.

The concept of adding complementary places may be useful to avoid problems adherent to the refinement of unsafe Petri nets. Whenever a transition belonging to a safe Petri is refined by applying one of the four basic patterns (see Figure 3.5) then the resulting Petri net is also safe. The dynamic structures described by these Petri nets are compatible with each other. This may be different when refining unsafe nets.

6.4.3   Multitoken places

Until now, places have had a boolean character, i.e., they were either marked with a token or empty. For certain domains, it can be useful to have a different number of tokens which a place may store, called its *capacity*, and a different number of tokens which an arc transports, known as *the arc weight*.

Capacity   The capacity of a particular place is defined by a natural number. It denotes the maximum number of tokens which one place may store at the same time. In some cases, an unlimited capacity can be defined.

Arc weight   This denotes the number of tokens that are delivered or removed by the arc when firing.

With these definitions, the firing rules have to be extended as follows.

A transition may fire if:

- each input place contains at least as many tokens as are required to be removed according to the arc weight;

- each output place contains free space to store at least as many tokens as are to be delivered according to the arc weight. If the output place is also an input place, removed tokens result in additional free space which has to be taken into account.

After firing:

- the operation associated with the transition has been performed;

- the number of tokens on each input place is reduced according to the corresponding arc weight;

- the number of tokens on each output place is increased according to the corresponding arc weight.

Multitoken places are often used to describe the dynamic structure of producer/consumer scenarios. In this context, Petri nets are also popular for describing material flow systems, which are beyond the focus of this book. In these models, places represent buffers for materials or even individuals, which are processed or moved when firing a transition. Arc weights denote the number of entities being handled or produced. But, multitoken places are also useful in the context of information processing systems. Queues or semaphore sets may be easily represented by multitoken places. Figure 6.25 shows an example of both applications.

6.4.4   Recursive Petri nets

Recursion, denotes a common approach in the definition of functions and algorithms which can be applied to solve those problems which may either be solved very easily or which may be systematically reduced to this trivial case. Popular applications can be found in parsers, route-planning systems or sorting algorithms. A very simple example is the recursive definition of the factorial of an integer.

$$factorial(n) = \begin{cases} 1 & if\ n = 1 \\ n * factorial(n - 1) & else \end{cases}, n \in N$$

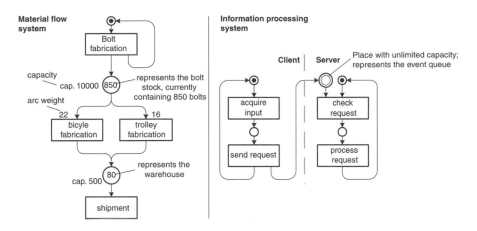

Figure 6.25: Modeling producer/consumer scenarios using multi–token places

This definition is used as a starting point to illustrate how Petri nets may be used to describe recursive behavior. Recursion is certainly not the most efficient way to calculate a factorial, but it is a very simple example which can be used to introduce the concept. Imagine a person who passes an integer, for instance 4, to a service provider in order to calculate the corresponding factorial. The service provider knows only the answer for the trivial case – if the integer was 1, the answer is 1. In our case, it reduces the argument, i.e., decreases the integer to 3, and passes it to a helper who knows how to solve the reduced task. With the result of the reduced task, i.e., 6, the service provider finishes the computation: $4 * 6 = 24$ and returns the result.

The left Petri net in Figure 6.26 illustrates the dynamic structure of this simple example. It is an abstraction from the actual problem of computing a factorial, but focuses on the idea of recursive behavior in general. The reduced argument defines the subsequent task of a similar type: computing a factorial. This task has to be performed before the original task can be finished. Conceptually, both tasks rely on the same dynamic structure. Introducing recursion, the service provider becomes its own helper. This corresponds to the transition in the right Petri net. The arcs which were formerly connected with the input and output of the helper transition are now connected with the start and end place of the service provider's sub-net.

Whenever the argument is reduced, a new token is put at the upper place of the recursion net. After finishing a task, the *return place* is marked. After finishing the entire task, the token has to be passed back to the client. Otherwise the ongoing task has to be finished by re-entering the recursive sub-net. With

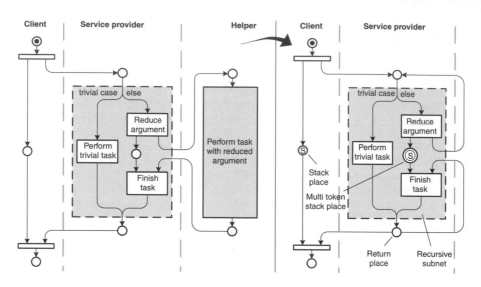

Figure 6.26:   Deriving the pattern of recursive Petri nets

regard to the firing rules of Petri nets, a token on the return place is a subject of an undetermined conflict. Nevertheless, the conflict is determined with regard to the 'call hierarchy'.

The concept of *stack places* was introduced to solve this problem [Wen80]. Tokens on a stack place have a *time-stamp* denoting the time when the token was put on that place. Transition pairs embracing the call of a sub-net which describes a recursive behavior are connected by a stack place or a multitoken stack place, respectively. So each finishing transition of such a pair has two input places: one stack place and the *return place*. An *additional firing rule* which refers to the time-stamp on the stack tokens, is used to resolve the conflict previously described: observe the time-stamps of the tokens on the stack places leading to the conflicting transitions. The stack place with the newest token refers to the transition which fires next by consuming the corresponding stack token and the token on the return place. Recursive argument reduction requires stack places inside the recursive sub-net to provide unlimited capacity for tokens. The time-stamps define the order between these tokens.

This sounds quite complicated and sometimes it helps to play around a little with a recursive Petri net in order to understand the concept. This is the focus of an exercise at the end of this chapter. But, the good news is that you do not really have to do recursive processing of recursive Petri nets in order to understand their meaning. The following example is used to illustrate this statement.

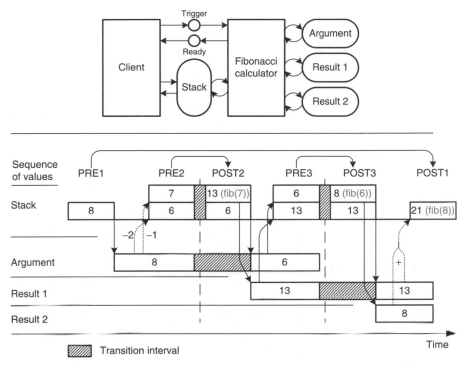

Storages and the sequences of assigned values when calculating the Fibonacci of 8.

Figure 6.27: Block diagram for recursive calculation of Fibonacci numbers

Figure 6.27 shows the compositional structure of a very simple system. A client can use a calculator to compute the Fibonacci number of a given positive integer. Even though in practice, there are probably more interesting applications of recursion than the Fibonacci function, this function provides the ideal complexity to illustrate the idea of a system performing a recursively defined task. The Fibonacci function is based on the following recursive definition.

$$fibonacci(n) = \begin{cases} 1 & \text{if } n = 1 \text{ or } n = 2 \\ fibonacci(n-1) + fibonacci(n-2) & \text{else} \end{cases} \quad , n \in N$$

To calculate the Fibonacci number of 8, we need to know the Fibonacci numbers of 6 and 7. The Fibonacci calculator represented in the block diagram uses a stack and three additional storages to perform the computation. The associated behavior is defined by the Petri net in Figure 6.28.

The client puts a certain number, in this case 8, on top of the stack. Then it triggers the Fibonacci calculator to start the computation. For the trivial case,

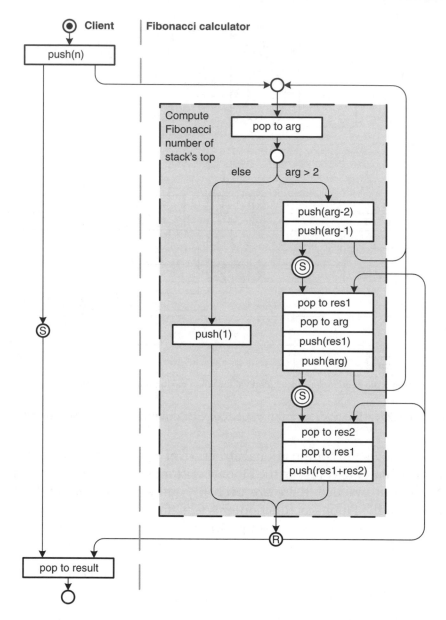

Figure 6.28:　Petri net for the recursive calculation of Fibonacci numbers

the top element is replaced by 1. Otherwise, the top element of is replaced by 6 and 7, denoting two subsequent tasks. The Petri net illustrates the recursive computation of these tasks by re-entering the sub-net describing the Fibonacci algorithm. However, we may continue directly with the result of performing the first subtask, because we know the purpose of this operation. In this case, the result is the stack with the top element 7 being replaced by the Fibonacci number of 7, which is 13. With this approach, reading and understanding a recursive Petri net can be restricted to a single flat level.

The Fibonacci computation continues by exchanging the two uppermost elements of the stack. So the result of *Fibonacci*($n - 1$) is saved, while $n - 2$ is placed on the top. Then the Fibonacci number for the stack's top element is recursively calculated. Again, we take the result for granted, and do not bother to re-enter the recursive sub-net. Now the stack contains the results of *Fibonacci*($n - 1$) and *Fibonacci*($n - 2$) which are transferred to the local storages of the calculator (called Result1 and Result2). The sum of these two values represent the final result which is put on the stack.

There are two important points about this example:

- Reading a recursive Petri net is not difficult, as long as we resist recursively re-entering recursive sub-nets. To support this approach, the recursive sub-net should be visually emphasized by a dashed border and furnished with a meaningful label.

- The recursive definition of a function may not refer to state or storages. However, a system designed to compute the values of a function recursively will need a storage, appropriately a stack, to keep track of subtasks and intermediate results. Depending on the depth of recursion, this storage needs to be very large. If not for operational values, at least the marking of the stack places needs a representation in the control-state storage. In a programmed system, these storages are typically implemented by the processor stack.

6.4.5 Timing constraints

Firing a transition does not take any time because tokens are either present at places or not. Removing a token from an input place or placing a token on an output place does not consume any time. As presented so far, a Petri net is a schema for generating possible sequences of activities. Originally, no statements about time are being made. But, operations do take time and we also may wait any time we want for a transition to fire. Many approaches have been published to extend Petri nets by introducing timing constraints. This section focuses on the very basic concepts in this domain and illustrates how FMC integrates with real-time modeling. Readers who are interested in timed Petri nets in general, analysis methods and simulation may take a look into the secondary literature covering the topic in more detail [Mur89].

Conceptually, there are two different types of statement about time, when considering the dynamic structure of a system:

- *delay* denotes the time it takes before a certain activity is to be performed;

- *duration* denotes the time it takes to perform a certain operation.

Figure 6.29 shows a small example illustrating the behavior of a system that captures images from different input sources. If a user selects a certain input source, the system immediately captures an image from that source. The process of capturing an image has a duration of something between 50 and 100ms. Before capturing the next image, a delay of five seconds will pass, which can be skipped by selecting a new source.

In FMC Petri nets, delay times are specified as annotations of input places of transition nodes. The delay refers to the period of time between the transition becoming ready to fire and its actual firing. The annotation may either identify a fixed period or some range with an upper and lower bound.

A transition node referring to a process may have an annotation denoting the duration of the process. Also, this annotation may either identify a constant or

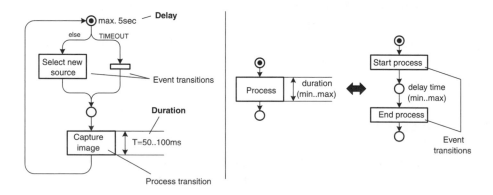

Figure 6.29: Representing timing constraints in FMC Petri nets

some range with an upper and lower bound. Figure 6.29 also illustrates how to integrate the conflicting ideas of processes having a duration, and transitions firing in zero time. Any process is defined by two events: its start and its end. So whenever, a transition node explicitly refers to some process, we may take this as a useful short notation of the refinement shown in the right of Figure 6.29. Transitions referring to start and endpoints of processes are event transitions, which consume no time when firing. The delay time between the start and end transition refers to the duration of the process.

Formally, this approach of timed Petri nets requires a safe marking of the Petri net to avoid conflicts caused by the combination of timing constraints and the firing rules of Petri nets. With this constraint, it is also possible to connect delayed input places with process transitions. In this special case, the decision for firing is confined by the delay time. The time till firing is determined by adding delay time and process duration.

6.5   Non-hierarchical transformations and semantic layers

The concept of non-hierarchical transformations (NHTs) is a special feature of FMC that is ignored – if not explicitly excluded – in most other modeling approaches. Yet, it is a very useful concept that is likely to be applied intuitively in many scenarios, sometimes without even deliberately thinking about it.

A non-hierarchical transformation is a transformation of one model into another model that cannot be explained by the strict refinement of value, behavior or compositional structures.

There are three common types of non-hierarchical transformation:

- encoding of values;

- implementation of channels and storages by active system components;

- N:M mappings of system components, e.g., multiplex (the mapping between role system and platform models, as described in Section 7.2, is a special case).

In any case, we have to consider two models – the one before and the one after the transformation. There is a break in traceability with regard to the structure that cannot be formally closed by pure comparison of the models. The break – either with regard to data, to certain operations or to system components – can only be closed by documenting the transformation that relates the two models. The following sections present examples which illustrate the idea for the first two types, in detail. The concept of multiplex is only sketched in this section. More information about multiplex and the transition from role to platform models is presented in the following chapter.

6.5.1 Encoding of values

Any information is bound to an information carrier, that is the physical form encoding the information. One task in developing an information processing system is to define this mapping, i.e., to develop a language with a terminology and notation which is appropriate to encode the information. Any information that is stored in the systems is stored with regard to that definition. To recover the information one needs to interpret the forms according to the defined semantics. Conceptually, the transition between meaning and form is arbitrary. The structure of the encoding form may not reflect the structure of the encoded information.

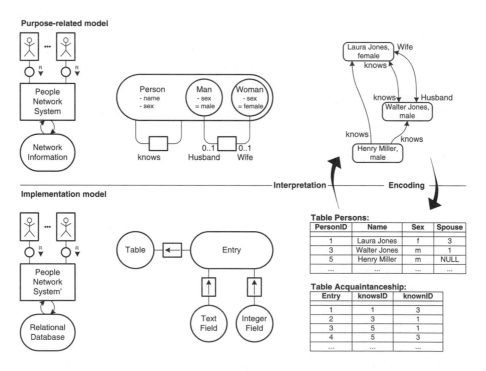

Figure 6.30: An example for the encoding of values

Figure 6.30 shows a simple example of a fictitious system for people to manage a network of contacts. People may register at the system and store references to other people they know. If two persons are married to each other, this is stored additionally. The upper part of Figure 6.30 shows a block diagram and an E/R diagram which reflect this model. The lower part of Figure 6.30 shows an implementation model of the same system. Even though the block diagram looks pretty much the same, the E/R diagram shows a completely different picture.

The data is now structured in terms of 'tables', 'entries' and 'fields' instead of 'persons', 'knows' and 'married' relationships. The change in terminology which was introduced by encoding the information, marks a change of the *semantic layer*. A mapping has to be defined between, so that the relationship between the upper and the lower model can be understood. In this case, there is one table which stores a single entry for each person and which holds its name, sex and an optional foreign key to some spouse. A second table is used to encode the knowledge about the 'knows' relationship of the upper model using a foreign key relation to the first table. Using this model, it is possible to discuss the management and access of tables.

Even though this model might possibly be useful at some level in development, it will difficult to understand the purpose of the system by mere analysis of this model. The mapping to the purpose-related model is necessary. It is typical for a non-hierarchical transformation, that this information cannot be retrieved by abstraction from implementation details. It has to be explicitly communicated.

As a way out, one might be tempted to look for a generic encoding approach. But, usually, the encoding depends on the usage of the information. For instance, an order may be stored as an XML document, if it is about to be exchanged between two ERP systems, or as a set of table entries inside a relational database for fast access to persistent data, or as a set of objects in the working memory for runtime access. So, encoding is a problem that has to be individually solved in many cases. Consequently, the discussion of different semantic layers is a task that has to be dealt with.

As a closing example, you may consider a persistency service for objects. There are many generic solutions to this problem, so one may think that defining an individual persistency encoding is no longer necessary. But there will be scenarios when a solution that provides an individual mapping to the database, outmatches any generic solution. In such a case, we have to deal with at least two different semantic layers.

6.5.2   Implementation of channels and storages

In Section 6.3.3, the concept of bipartite refinement was illustrated to simply transform abstract channel or storages into agent-based implementation. Graphically, this seems to be a simple hierarchical refinement and nobody will have a problem in understanding this transformation. Conceptually, it is slightly more complex.

Figure 6.31 shows four models of the same system which illustrates the idea. Model A shows an abstract model of two agents communicating via a channel. Model C shows that this channel is implemented using a non-transparent mediator. Non-transparent means that the sequence of values which can be observed on the channel in the upper model differs from the sequence of values which can be observed on the channels between the mediator and its users:

- Using a mediator always adheres to a characteristic bandwidth and encoding of information. There are different mediators for natural language, emails, network packages, etc.

- Additional communication with the mediator may be necessary to initiate or control the dialog between the communication partners. In communication systems with many partners, it is usually necessary to set-up a connection between the participants of a dialog. This set-up requires its own protocol as, for instance, creating a socket, binding a socket, listening to a socket and accepting an incoming call when using the Socket API.

- In any case, the transformation of one conceptual channel into several implementing location introduces a different timing model caused by transmission delays.

- Additionally, communication errors may be introduced by the use of a mediator which has to be handled appropriately.

The behavior of the communication partners of model A and C is quite different. For this reason, it is necessary to distinguish the communication partners 1 and 2 from the communication partners 1″ and 2″. It is a non-hierarchical transformation. A refinement of the mediator into two adapters – transforming model C into D – and a successive aggregation of a 1″ and 2″ with one adapter per communication partner, does not produce the original model A, but the new model B. Similar to the previous scenario, partner 1 and 2 must not be confused with partner 1′ and 2′.

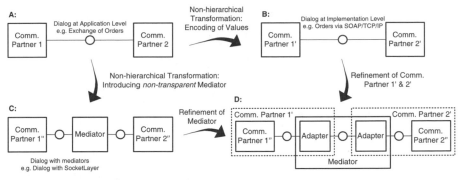

Figure 6.31:   An example of implementation of channels

6.5.3   Relevance of non-hierarchical transformations

In practice, non-hierarchical transformations are not rare exceptions. In the transition from high-level models of the application domain to the implementation model, we find them anywhere. Nevertheless, knowledge of this concept is not very prevalent – sometimes these transitions are made implicitly. For instance, in the transition from object-oriented analysis to design, changes in the identity of the represented classes are quiet common. So entity types referred to by a common name in a conceptual OO model and a corresponding design model often represent different types [Hab01]. Models that are linked by a non-hierarchical transformation may not be mapped onto each other by simple views or extensions, i.e., by abstracting from or adding model elements.

Distinctions as presented in the previous sections are rarely made explicitly, nevertheless they exist. Carefully distinguishing the different models may help to avoid severe misunderstandings and minimize complexity by the separation of different concerns.

Figure 6.32 illustrates a typical case in which the explicit distinction of several models that are partially linked by non-hierarchical transformations, helps in the understanding of the system. In many systems, a certain resource is required for different purposes. For instance, multiple web clients may use a web service to interactively define the configuration of a new car. Conceptually, we may have the idea that each client is connected to their own personal server, storing the current state of the configuration session. This is model number 1.

With a large or unknown number of clients, this is probably an equivalent model. At implementation level, a relatively small number of servers will be

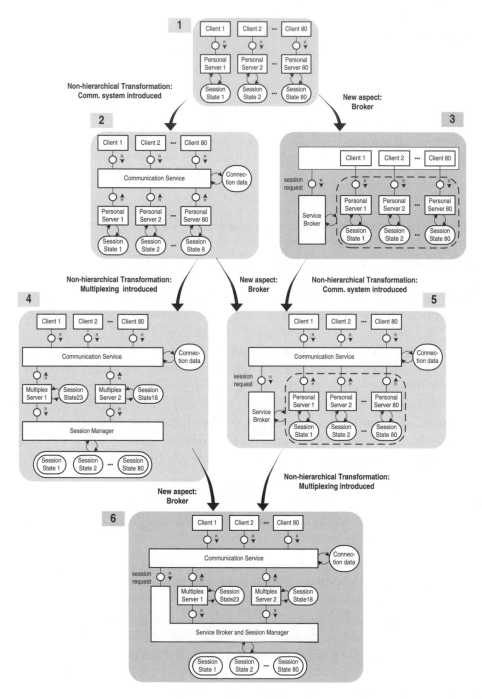

Figure 6.32: An example of a network of models containing NHTs

set-up, which handle requests from different clients in multiplex. Additionally, the clients have to find the appropriate server and the communication between the clients and the servers has to be solved. Starting with the initial model, solutions for three different problems have to be developed:

- A communication system enables the clients to dynamically connect to an arbitrary server. As presented in Section 6.5.2, this is a non-hierarchical transformation. Starting with the initial model, this transformation maps model 1 to model 2.

- Clients will need a broker to find a server that is appropriate to handle requests. For that reason, the broker needs to know about the available services. It might also be possible for a broker to activate or deactivate additional services in time, which refers to the concept of structure variance. With regard to model 1, the introduction of a broker represents a new aspect that is represented in model 3. Comparing the two models, model 1 is a view of model 3 obtained by simple abstraction from details.

- Implementing a number of personal servers with a few multiplex servers is a non-hierarchical transformation. For dialogs between a client and a server which rely on the state of previous interaction steps – typically these dialogs are called sessions – the state for different sessions with different clients has to be rolled in or out, whenever the client changes. Usually, a session manager is responsible for this task.

Integrating the different design decisions leads to model number 6 in the lower part of Figure 6.32. Conceptually, the possible sequence of design decision refers to a network of models. Usually, only a subsets of these models will be represented explicitly. For this example, model 3 and 6 should be a good choice to communicate the essential structures of the system.

This simple example demonstrates how non-hierarchical transformations may contribute to the description of systems in practice. These transformation are not formally defined. Nevertheless, this rarely constitutes a problem. Instead it helps our understanding of the transition from the application model to implementation. Patterns may be used to conserve knowledge about typical transformations. Following this idea, Chapter 11 deepens the subject of implementing client/server systems by presenting a pattern language for the design of concurrent request-processing servers.

6.6 Exercises

Exercise 6.1 Becoming familiar with the meta model

Meta models are likely to be considered as scary or annoying constructs which serve as a foundation for formal descriptions or as input for tool builders. In this context the FMC meta model may attract attention for its compact and comprehensive structure. The model captures the basic concepts that provide the framework for understanding any information processing systems.

To become more familiar with these concepts, consider Figure 6.33 and relate the entities of the meta model to the chess example.

Exercise 6.2 The concise separation of dynamic and compositional structures in FMC is reflected by two different kinds of diagrams: Petri nets and block

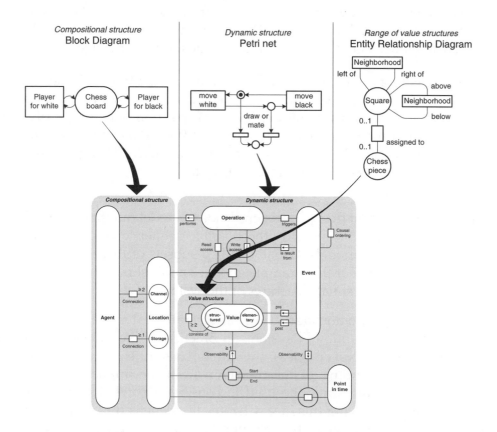

Figure 6.33: Relating an FMC model to the FMC meta model

diagrams. Give some examples which illustrate the difference between the dynamic and compositional structures.

Exercise 6.3 Dashboard device: operational versus control state

Imagine the dashboard of a car containing some interactive device which displays the measurements of different sensors such as outside temperature, inside temperature, humidity, fuel consumption, average speed, etc. The driver can select the input source by pushing a button forwards or backwards. The sequence is determined by construction and rolls back when reaching one of the ends.

Create an abstract model of that system and identify the compositional and dynamic structure. Identify the state variables and classify them as operational and/or control variables.

Carefully consider the alternatives: operational or control variables only, or a mix of both. Your model should be easy to understand and easy to adapt if the number of input sources is changed.

Exercise 6.4 Recursive Petri nets and marking of stack places

At the beginning of Section 6.4.4, a system was described which recursively computes the factorials of positive integers. Draw a Petri net describing the dynamic structure of that system. Then recursively simulate the flow of tokens for some small integer, like 3.

Chapter 7

Towards Implementation Structures

7.1 System structure versus software structure

Developing an information processing system usually starts with the acquisition of requirements. The initial structure of a system model can be identified, which meets the requirements at a very high level of abstraction. This model captures only the main requirements with regard to the purpose of the intended system. Abstracting from details of the implementation is common practice and necessary at the beginning. In this context, the *domain model* is a model of the system which abstracts from any implementation details and refers only to entities which are defined by the application domain. For instance, when considering a route planning system, there will be components like the map database, the route finder or the position finder. Components like a database buffer, a request scheduler or even the processor are probably not part of this model.

The domain model provides the input for the further development process. Implementing the system means integrating lower-level requirements and – with regard to the idea of FMC models – solving the problem to make available the agents and locations which were identified in the domain model and which do not belong to the given environment. A one-to-one mapping of these components to physical entities is rarely appropriate and is often not always possible. Conceptual channels are mapped to communication devices, different information processing components are mapped to different operating system processes on one computer system, domain specific components are mapped to objects in

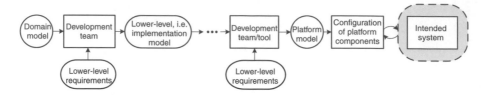

Figure 7.1:   A simple model for system development

a programmed system, etc. Figure 7.1 illustrates the purpose of this mapping process. Step by step the domain model is transformed into a *platform model*, i.e., a model that complies with all requirements and represents the system in terms of a configuration of platform components, which may be taken for granted. The platform model defines how to create the final system by programming and connecting these components.

Many design decisions are specific to a certain problem domain. However, there are a few common platform models in the context of modern software development:

- A processor is executing a program and thereby manipulating the contents of its memory and interacting with its environment.

- Many computer systems are controlled by an operating system which schedules different processes or threads, which work concurrently. Often, cooperating processes and threads may also be hosted on different computers.

- Considering the concept of object orientation, a system is described in terms of objects with attributes and methods which communicate by invoking method calls.

In this chapter, the basic patterns for mapping between these platform models and arbitrary domain models will be discussed. In that context, two types of structures must not be confused: System structure and description structure.

The structure of the system is different from the structure of the system description, i.e., the software structure.

The system structure, i.e., the structure of a system model, is defined by system components which interact with each other to implement the intended system or higher-level system components. The description structure is defined by description components which refer to each other and which describe aspects of the system structure. It is the difference between the structure of Africa and the structure of a book about Africa.

Figure 7.2 illustrates the difference with regard to programmed systems. The circles terms on the left side refer to system components on different layers of abstraction. The terms on the right side refer to descriptions: Diagram, module, DLL, class definition, program. Of course, one specific description component may describe one specific system component. There are many isomorphisms, but there are many different aspects

- Many description components specify types. Often, there is a one-to-many mapping between types and system components.

- Description components which specify abstract types do not refer to concrete system components at all.

- Description components may specify only certain aspects of one or several components as in aspect-oriented programming.

- Description components like directories, packages or tables of content support the handling of large numbers of description components. They are

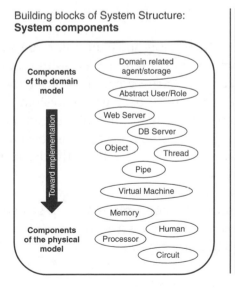
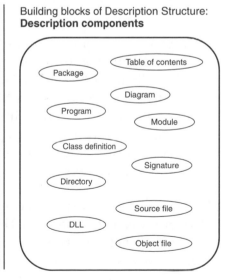

Figure 7.2: System structure differs from description structure

necessary for description management only. These description components do not describe system components.

- Description components which introduce new terms to extend the description language do not describe system components. For instance, a language that only supports integer arithmetic might be augmented by the definition of terms for floating-point arithmetic. However, this does not require the introduction of a floating point unit in the system model.

Thinking about the structure of a system description is rather different from thinking about the structure of the system itself. Both structures are very important. Software is the description of a dynamic system. The definition of the software structure is one of the most critical factors in the development of programmed systems.

In the context of this chapter, the focus is on system structures only. The reason for this is simple. Describing the system structure requires identifying the system structure first and, usually, description structures are of no primary concern when creating FMC diagrams. This seems strange, because any FMC diagram is a piece of description in itself. Even so, there is no mistake, because FMC models differ fundamentally from software with regard to their purpose:

- Software has to be complete, consistent, unambiguous, modular, re-usable, etc. The amount of software for complex information processing systems exceeds millions of lines of code. It is primarily created in order for the machines which are processing the software to become the system being described [Jac95]. Structure is important for handling this huge amount of software. Documents such as package and class diagrams, describing the description structure, are necessary in order to facilitate the division of labor during the development process.

- FMC diagrams are created to communicate conceptual system structures between human stakeholders. The amount of description is magnitudes smaller than that of software. Also for a large system, the number of FMC diagrams will not constitute a real problem. Usually, it is not necessary to provide some map for the 'architecture' of FMC-based descriptions, even for large systems.

7.2   From Processor to processes

7.2.1   Role and processor view

Often, the implementation of an information processing system or component is based on the programming of a processor system. In these cases, we have to distinguish at least two different models representing the system on different semantic layers. Figure 7.3 illustrates the fact.

The *role system model* focuses on the role of the system in its environment. This role defines the behavior and the state of the role system. For instance, a drawing system might be used to create vector diagrams. Input and output are defined by the interaction sequences necessary to create a drawing. The state of the role system is defined by the structure of the drawing, for instance, a hierarchy of composites of lines, arcs, polygons, etc.

The *processor system model* assumes a specific implementation of the role system: A generic processor system is programmed in such way that it shows the

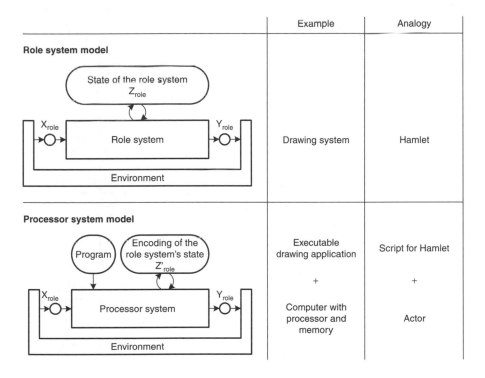

Figure 7.3:   Role and processor view

behavior which is expected from the role system. As an actor becomes Hamlet by playing the role which is described in the script, the processor system becomes the drawing system by executing the drawing program.

On this semantic level, the focus is on the structure of the processor system. The processor system might be composed of a microprocessor, random access memory and I/O devices; it could be a virtual machine or even a human strictly performing instructions. With regard to the implementation, the state of the role system would be encoded differently. A drawing system implemented by a microprocessor system would probably reveal the drawing as the operational state encoded as a structure of integers and floats. The control state would be represented by the program counter (PC) and the processor flags.

Figure 7.4 illustrates how such a model looks for a simple processor for procedural programs on a high level of abstraction [Wen91]. Program and operational data are stored in linear memory. The program counter refers to the memory cell which is collected next by the instruction reader. The separator separates instructions for the operational unit from those for the control flow unit. The operational unit performs I/O operations and computations on the operational state of the system, which is the content of the working memory. Predicates about the results may influence the control flow, so they are written to a storage that is being read by the control flow unit. By default, the control flow unit increments the program counter by one with each step it does.

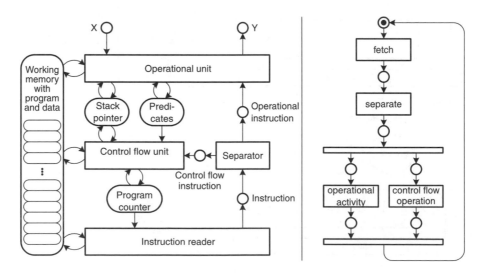

Figure 7.4:   Processor for procedural programs

Yet, predicates and control flow instructions may cause jumps in the program execution. It is a very simple processor, because it can only sequentially process a single program. However, multiple processors might be connected to constitute a network of sequential machines working concurrently.

Obviously the model for a processor for functional programs, or predicate languages like Prolog, looks very different. The presentation of those models is beyond the scope of this section. The point is that the concept of program processors is not restricted to the lowest level of system design. There are program processor on any level of abstraction. These may be processors for work flow rules, processors for XML transformation (XSLT processors), processors for layout rules (CSS), processors for picture manipulation scripts and many more. Gathering requirements for and developing those system, both role system models and processor system models are required. The conscious switch between these models is necessary to avoid confusion. There is a significant difference in talking about a specific workflow scenario using a specific configuration of ERP systems or to talk about a generic workflow engine (which may be distributed across several ERP systems).

7.2.2 Role piggyback

Developing software is about creating a complete, formal and consistent description of the future system. The repertoire of the description or programming language defines the set of elementary operations which are provided to implement the intended behavior. The language of microprocessors is at quite a low level. Software development at this level would be very cumbersome and error-prone. For this reason, most software is developed in a high-level programming or modeling language. Those language abstract from details of the processing system. The terminology of specific languages may be support of the description of systems for a specific domain. Conceptually, there are two approaches used to make these high-level descriptions accessible to the work of generic low-level hardware processors:

- translate the high-level descriptions into low-level descriptions;

- role piggyback.

Figure 7.5 illustrates the first case. The high-level description which conforms to the language L1 is translated into a low-level description which conforms to the language L2. This low-level description is written to the memory of

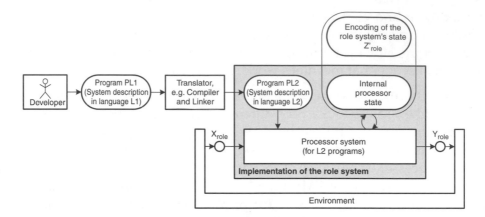

Figure 7.5:   Translation of high-level languages

a general purpose processor for L2 programs. With regard to programming languages like C or C++, the translator is the C or C++ compiler and linker. The program PL2 represents the entire software package to be installed on the destination platform, e.g., executables, DLL, etc. The model is also valid for modern development approaches like Model Driven Architecture. In this case, L1 represents another language and there is a need for a new type of translator. Yet, conceptually this does not change the idea of software development.

The diagram in Figure 7.6 shows a model of the QT development environment[1]. It is an example of a rather complex translator. The QT development environment facilitates the development of user interfaces for interactive systems. The high-level description of the intended system is composed of three different parts. These are: the description of the interface design, i.e., the form of the visual appearance; the description of the interaction model; and the description of the application core, which is independent of any interaction aspects. The translator is composed of different tools which are necessary to translate the high-level description and which have to be activated in a specific order. This model can be used to explain the different roles which can be identified when developing interactive applications using QT. It does not show the structure of the intended system.

Role piggyback is the second approach which can be used to bridge the gap between a high-level description and low-level processors. Figure 7.7 illustrates the concepts. The low-level processor is processing a program which conforms to the language L2 and which describes the behavior of a virtual

---

[1]Version 2.3.

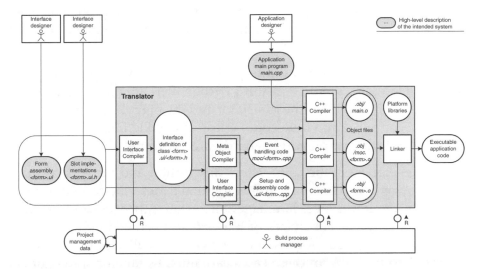

Figure 7.6: The QT development environment: a complex translator

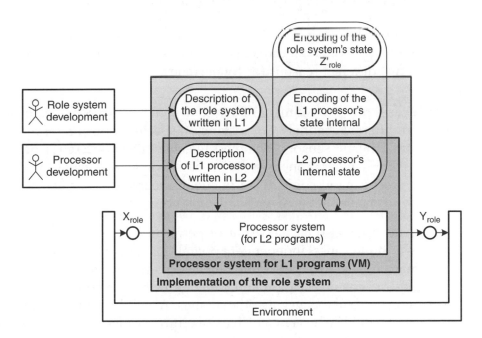

Figure 7.7: Role piggyback

high-level processor or interpreter. This virtual processor or virtual machine (VM) processes a program which conforms to the L1 language and which describes the intended role system.

The concept is very common and interpreters or VMs exist for many different programming languages. ABAP, BASIC, Python, Perl are only a few examples. JAVA development combines the translator and the piggyback approach. JAVA programs are compiled into byte-code. These byte-code files are processed by the JAVA VM which runs on various hardware platforms.

Sometimes developers of the role system description and the virtual machine work closely together. There may be a temptation to describe certain parts of the role system in the lower-level language, for instance, because of performance reasons. Certain high-level services of the virtual machine might be described using high-level language – for instance, the garbage collector of the JAVA VM can be described in JAVA. In these cases care must be taken not to confuse the role system model with the processor system model.

7.2.3 Role multiplex, interrupt handling and context switch

Usually the role system is composed of different components which have to be implemented. Often, several components can interact concurrently. Conceptually, there are two different reasons for concurrency:

- In some cases, the environment of a system can concurrently create input events on different channels. For instance, a specific control receives messages from different sensors. The messages may have different priorities. A set of event handlers concurrently process or at least register the events for later processing in some event queue. Concurrent event listeners are necessary to ensure that no events will be ignored.

- Concurrency may also be the result of performance considerations. Performing multiple, causal independent operations concurrently by different agents may be faster than performing them sequentially by one agent – yet, sometimes the communication and synchronization overhead caused by the division of labor may negate time savings. A well-known application of this concept would be servers which use a central request dispatcher which delivers an incoming request to a number of concurrently working request handlers. Also, pipeline architectures apply the concept of concurrently working agents in a processor chain.

There are different approaches used to implement concurrent systems. For example, one could provide a dedicated hardware system for each of the concurrently active agents. Figure 7.8 shows a different, but very common, approach based on programming. Each agent of the role system is implemented using a separate processor. Each of these has access to a separate storage which holds the role-specific program and the local state of the corresponding role agent or its encoding, respectively. A central communication service enables communication between the different processors and the environment as it is defined by the role system model. It also provides synchronization mechanisms to access data in the shared memory. This location implements those storages of the role system model, which can be accessed by multiple agents.

Many modern programming platforms support this model. Various programs may be processed concurrently. In a corresponding model, this can be illustrated by showing a dedicated processor for each of these programs, see the middle of Figure 7.8. The operating system provides the communication service and additional means for managing the access to common resources, like the shared memory or the environment.

Physically, many of these systems are based on a single hardware processor. This does not invalidate the multiprocessor model as long as we do not consider the actual implementation of such a system. A single processor successively plays the role of different agents including the communication service, which is usually part of the operating system. This concept is very common and may also be found on different layers of abstraction. A processor which supports this kind of *multiplex* requires specific components which enable the context switch between the execution of different programs, see the bottom of Figure 7.8. The processor core does the actual program execution of the currently chosen program. If necessary, the multiplexer can 'switch' the processor core to the next program by saving the current context (internal state of the processor core) and replacing it by another, previously saved, context.

Figure 7.9 outlines a possible implementation of such a processor. Here, the interrupt unit corresponds to the multiplexer while the other components constitute the processor core. Such a multitasking-enabled processor alternately processes different programs since, at each single moment, the processor is executing exactly one program. Therefore, the processor works very much as a processor for sequential programs. It fetches an instruction, separates control flow instructions from operational instructions and performs the corresponding operations. Specific conditions determine when to switch execution of one program to another. Such a condition may be the receipt of an asynchronous

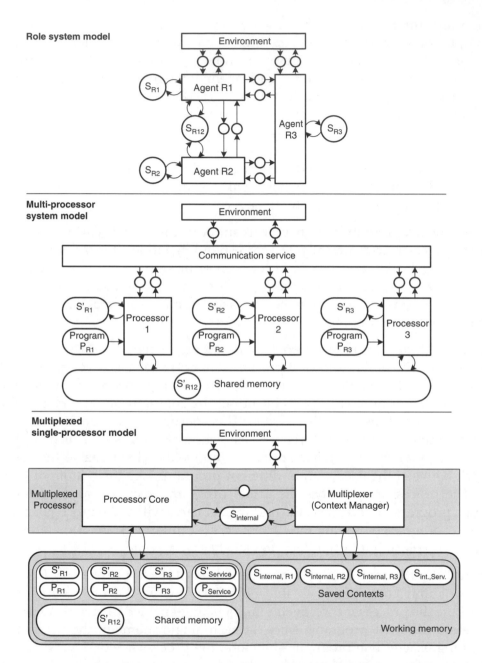

Figure 7.8:   Communicating sequential processors

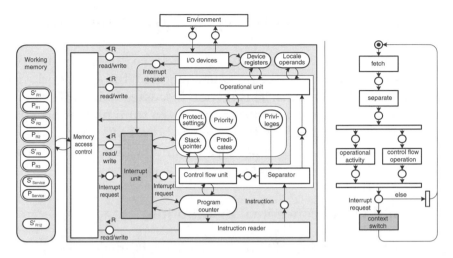

Figure 7.9: Example of a multitasking-enabled processor system

interrupt request from the environment, i.e., the I/O devices, or a synchronous interrupt request caused by the execution of a trap instruction, a processor exception, or a memory access violation.

The interrupt unit is responsible for catching interrupt events from the environment. After completion of each single instruction, it checks whether an interrupt request requires a context switch or if the execution of the current program is to be continued. Doing a context switch, the interrupt unit saves the current program counter and the predicates on the stack, which is associated with the current program. With regard to the type of interrupt, the interrupt unit selects the appropriate program for interrupt handling. The program counter is set to the start address of this program and program execution continues. The remaining registers such as the locale operands, the stack pointer, etc., are usually saved by processing the interrupt program.

Often, these interrupt programs are part of the operating system. After saving the content of the registers for the interrupted task, the operating system selects the consecutive task and restores the registers according to its previously saved context. At the end of the interrupt, the program counter is set to the position where it will continue the successor program.

This sketchy description is obviously incomplete and ignores concepts such as priority levels, privileged instructions, memory protection, etc., yet, it does provide an idea of the application of FMC in the transition from high-level agents to the very low-level structures of hardware.

7.3   Distribution, concurrency and synchronization

Today, software systems are typically distributed, i.e., their runtime platform consists of several computers being interconnected by a network, running multitasking operating systems. This section discusses how FMC can be used to describe the mapping of system components to runtime platform elements like tasks and semaphores. It will be shown how FMC models can reflect concurrency-related aspects like inter-task communication and sychronization of conflicting accesses to shared data.

7.3.1   Physical versus conceptual distribution

The term *distributed system* has different meanings for different people. It should therefore be discussed briefly. According to a typical definition [CDK94], a system is called distributed, if 'it consists of a collection of autonomous computers linked by a computer network ...' However, another definition of the term includes 'a collection of communicating processes, even when running on a single hardware installation' [Tel94]. To deal with this ambiguity, in the following, we will distinguish between two types of distribution:

- A system is *physically distributed*, if its hardware consists of several computers, which are connected by a network.

- A system is *conceptually distributed*, if it is implemented using a set of tasks.

In the first case, system components are mapped to different computers. As a consequence, some parts of the system can only communicate indirectly, using the underlying network protocol. The hardware platform itself can be described using a compositional structure diagram, see Figure 7.10.

However, in many cases we are interested in the mapping of conceptual system components to the platform. Since this is a special type of implementation, it can be shown by nesting (see Section 6.3.1), i.e., by placing conceptual components inside their corresponding hardware elements, like hard discs, RAM or computing devices – see Figure 7.11.

In case of a *conceptually distributed* system, a mapping of system components to tasks has been defined, with tasks being provided by the operating system. We use the term 'task' for both threads ('lightweight threads' sharing an address space with other threads) and processes ('heavyweight threads' with their

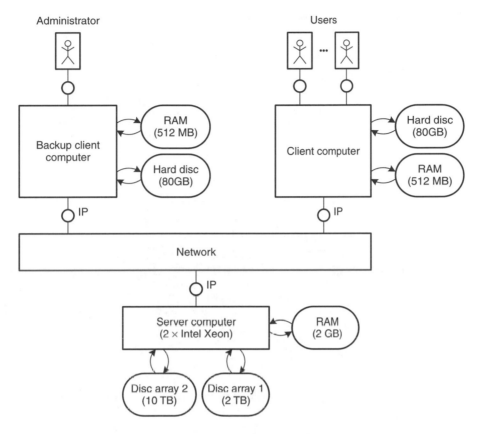

Figure 7.10: Physical distribution, platform structure

own, protected address space). A single task always constitutes a fully ordered sequence of operations.

On a single computer with only one physical processor, tasks are provided by time division multiplex of the processor, i.e., concurrency is virtually provided by interleaving different task operations. In case of a multiprocessor system, or tasks running on different computers, true concurrency can be given. As long as we ignore (abstract from) the mapping to physical processors, tasks should be viewed as working concurrently with each other, with each single task showing sequential behavior.

Concerning tasks, it is important to distinguish between compositional structure and behavior, i.e., between an agent representing a task and the sequence of operations being performed by it. When describing the compositional structure of a system, tasks can therefore be shown as agents. For example, a simple text editor being implemented as a single task can be modeled as an agent

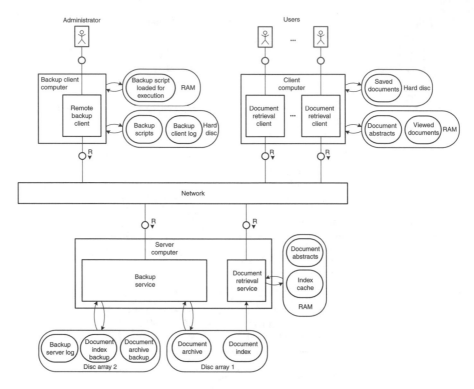

Figure 7.11:   Physical distribution of conceptual components

with its own storage for saved documents and the document currently being edited – see Figure 7.12. While this model reflects a role view (see Section 7.2.1) of the task, we can also choose to model the task as a (virtual) task processor with program and data storage (see Figure 7.12). Since this corresponds to the processor view (see Section 7.2.1), the text editor program appears as the content of the program storage. Which model we choose – task role or task processor – depends on our interest.

Describing the conceptual distribution of a system can be done by refining the abstract system model to the level of tasks and combining the two levels of abstraction within one diagram. Figure 7.13 shows such a refinement for the document retrieval clients and the retrieval service which were introduced in Figure 7.11. At this level, the usage of shared memory, private memory and files can also be revealed. Inter-task communication is simplified in this model – the channels between the tasks correspond to some communication mechanism supported by the operating system.

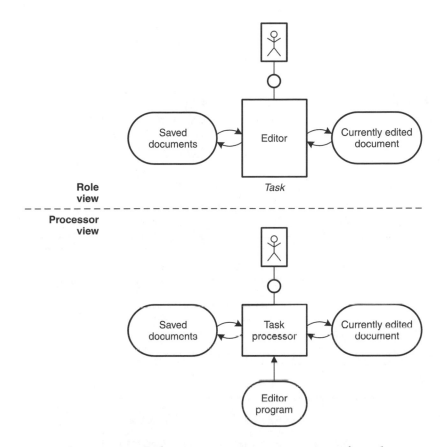

Figure 7.12: Role view versus processor view of a task

As the examples have shown, physical or conceptual distribution can be seen as a mapping of abstract system components to elements of the hardware platform or a mapping to tasks, shared memory, files etc., respectively. Since multiple tasks can be executed on a single computer, conceptual distribution can be given without physical distribution. In contrast, realizing a system on a physically distributed platform requires multiple tasks, i.e., physical distribution implies conceptual distribution, but not vice versa. Both types can be modeled by nesting nodes in FMC compositional diagrams.

7.3.2 Concurrency versus distribution

FMC clearly distinguishes between behavior and compositional structure. Following this idea, concurrency and distribution must be seen as different

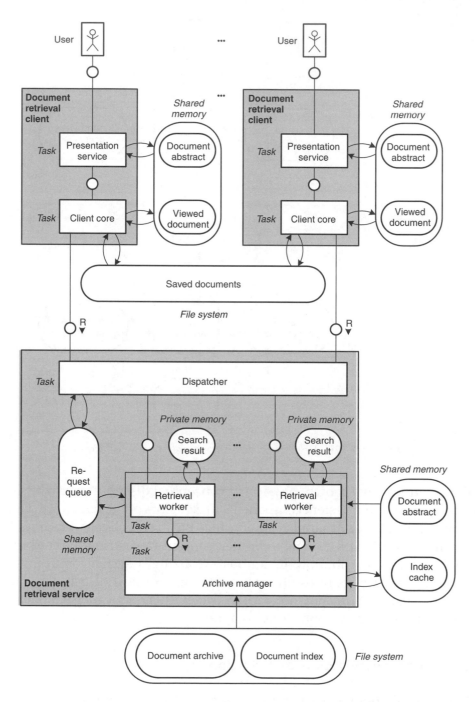

Figure 7.13: An example of conceptual distribution

things. The first refers to the behavior of the system, i.e., a concurrent system allows operations to be done concurrently (causally unrelated), while distribution refers to the compositional structure. Nevertheless, concurrency and distribution are not completely independent. In the case of today's software systems, concurrency is typically achieved by conceptual or even physical distribution. On the other hand, it is possible to have multiple tasks interacting in a purely sequential way (for example, by exchanging only synchronous messages). Therefore, concurrency implies distribution, but not vice versa.

7.3.3 Inter-task communication

Different tasks of a distributed system must communicate in order to cooperate. Different means of communication are given in a typical distributed system which can be illustrated in various ways using FMC compositional structure diagrams and Petri nets. Figure 7.14 shows block diagram patterns for typical inter-task communication scenarios.

In pattern (1) an undirected channel is used to indicate the possibility of communication, without specifying the concrete type of communication. The

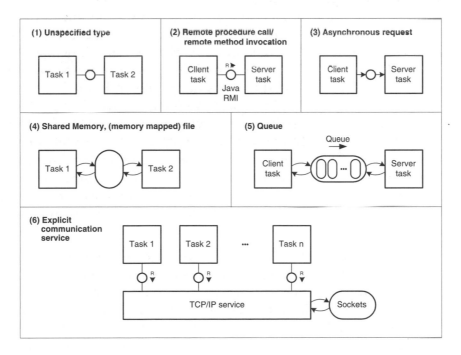

Figure 7.14: Inter-task communication: block diagram patterns

next scenario shows a remote procedure call (or remote method invocation) as a request/response channel. This channel type is chosen because typical procedure calls (method invocations) are performed synchronously. The resulting sequential control flow is shown on the left side of Figure 7.15.

Asynchronous communication can be shown as a directed channel between the communicating tasks, see pattern (3) in Figure 7.14. The upper right part of Figure 7.15 shows the related behavior. Here, the server task can receive and process requests concurrently with the client task's activities. On the other hand, the server task can (temporarily) block the client task, when it does not receive requests fast enough. In this situation, the corresponding place in the Petri net (the left input place of the 'receive request' transition) would hold a token, keeping the 'send request' transition of the client side disabled until the 'receive request' transition eventually fires. (This is an example of a Petri net with unsafe marking, see Section 6.4.2.)

Tasks can use shared memory, memory mapped files or simple files for buffered communication (see Section 2.4). A storage can be introduced in a block diagram which makes the buffering visible, see pattern (4) of Figure 7.14.

Using a queue is a special type of buffered communication which can be identified by labeling the storage ('Queue') or adding the queue entries as inner storages, see pattern (5) in Figure 7.14. Adding or removing a queue entry requires a modifying access because the changed queue depends on the queue before the operation. The direction of the queue can be indicated by an additional arrow. The corresponding behavior is shown in the lower right of Figure 7.15. In contrast to a simple asynchronous request which might block the server task (see discussion of pattern (3) above), the queue can be used to collect requests, thus avoiding the blocking of the server task. In the related Petri net, there is a multitoken place whose marking reflects the number of queue entries. This multitoken place can be given an unlimited capacity as long as the capacity of the queue is never reached. Otherwise, the upper bound of queue entries can be assigned to the multitoken place as its finite capacity (not shown in the Petri net).

Most inter-task communication is actually provided by the operating system which is not shown in the patterns discussed so far. Sometimes there is a need to model the operating system or, at least, its communication services as a dedicated agent between the tasks. This has been done in pattern (6) in Figure 7.14 where the use of TCP/IP services is shown. In this example, a storage can be introduced which contains connection-related information (namely the so-called 'socket' data structures) being managed by the operating system.

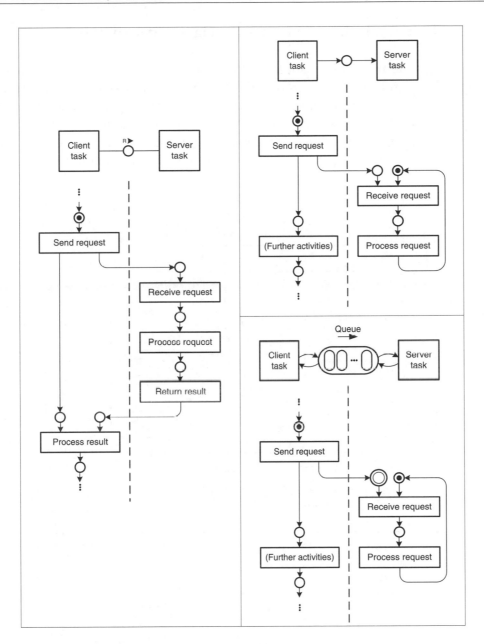

Figure 7.15: Inter-task communication: Petri net patterns

7.3.4   Modeling task and memory management activities

Starting a system is often simple in the case of non-distributed systems. A compiled program is loaded from a file and executed afterwards. In contrast, starting a distributed system often requires step-by-step creation of system components before the system is completely up and running. For example, starting the retrieval service from the example above (see Figure 7.13) may be done by first starting the dispatcher task, which subsequently creates the

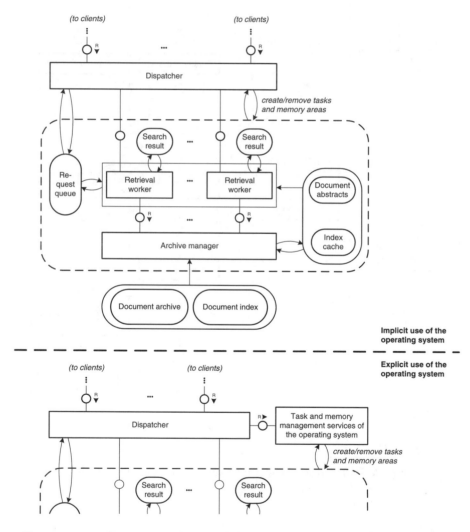

Figure 7.16:   Creating tasks and memory areas: compositional structure

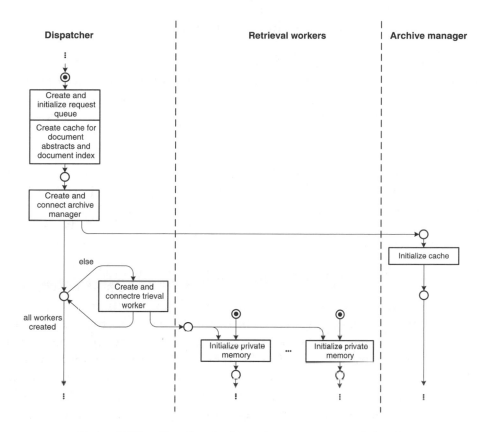

Figure 7.17:   Creating tasks and memory areas: behavior

memory areas, the archive manager and the worker tasks. The dispatcher could also be responsible for removing the other system parts when the system will eventually be stopped. This is a case of a structure variant system (see Section 6.3.4) and can be modeled as shown in the upper part of Figure 7.16. A part of the compositional structure is placed inside a structure variance storage to which the dispatcher has access, thus identifying which parts of the system are subject to the creation process and which agent is responsible for it. A possible solution for describing the corresponding behavior is shown in Figure 7.17.

In practice, tasks and memory areas are provided by the operating system, i.e., the task and memory management. If there is interest in a model to make this visible, the operating system services can be introduced in a model as an additional agent, see lower part of Figure 7.16.

7.3.5   Mapping concurrent behavior to tasks

In many cases, an abstract model of a system is given where the whole system or single agents show concurrent behavior. This behavior typically arises from the system requirements and is not related to the conceptual distribution. Instead, the mapping to tasks is yet to be found. Hence the question arises of how many tasks are needed and how to combine them in order to implement the intended system behavior. A very useful approach can be given to solve this problem. It is based on the idea that a Petri net with concurrency can be 'cut' into partial Petri nets, each describing sequential behavior, and assigning each partial net to its own task (see also [Wen79]). In order to keep the causal dependencies between different partial nets, semaphores are introduced to establish the necessary interaction between tasks.

This technique can be explained best using a simple example, see Figure 7.18, upper left. The Petri net may be seen as the behavior of a system which is to be implemented, with (a, b, c) etc., being some operation types. The concrete operation types are not important for the example, therefore they are left open. Before we divide the net into sub-nets, the minimal number of necessary sub-nets – which is also the number of tasks to be used – should be identified. This number equals the degree of concurrency of the original net, i.e., the maximal number of transitions which could fire at the same time. In this case, the number is three, because up to three transitions (b, f and g, for example) can fire simultaneously.

To avoid a subtle problem, which we have yet to discuss, we must guarantee that the net is safe. If it is not, we must transform it to a safe net, for example, by adding complementary places (see Section 6.4.2). In our example, there is place S1 which, when marked, can cause transition a to be disabled even if all input places of transition a are marked. Since this is the only marking which causes the net to be unsafe, safety can be reached by simply adding a place S1' which is complementary to S1. The resulting net is shown at the upper right of Figure 7.18.

Once the net is safe, it can be cut into sequential sub-nets. The lower left of Figure 7.18 shows the result (other solutions are possible, including those which are not minimal). These sub-nets will be mapped to tasks, with places inside each sub-net representing control states of the corresponding task. However, there are additional places (S1, S1', S2, S3) and arcs connected to them which establish causal dependencies between the three sequences. For each of them we will use a semaphore, which multitasking operating systems

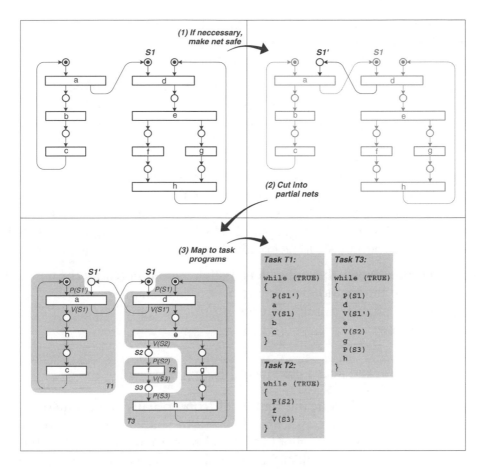

Figure 7.18:   Example of mapping Petri nets to tasks

usually provide. Each semaphore has a value which equals the number of tokens at the corresponding 'semaphore place' (see also [Pet77]). In our example, we can use binary semaphores, because all the semaphore places have capacity one (otherwise we could use multivalued semaphores). Adding a token to a semaphore place (or attempting to do so) is implemented by performing a 'V operation' (increase the semaphore value). In practice, the 'V operation' is an operating system call which blocks the calling task if the semaphore value is one (or equals the upper bound in the case of a multivalued semaphore). In order to perform the V operation and resume the task, another task has to decrease the semaphore value first. Taking a token from a semaphore place (or attempting to do so) is implemented by performing a 'P operation' (decrease the semaphore value). Again, this is an operating system call which may block the calling task, namely if the semaphore value is zero, in which case another task is needed to increase the value first. The semaphore operations needed in our example are annotated at the related arcs in the Petri net in the lower left of Figure 7.18.

Finally, the sub-nets (T1, T2, T3) and the semaphore places (S1, S1', S2, S3) can be mapped to tasks and semaphores, respectively. The lower right of Figure 7.18 shows the tasks' programs as pseudo code sequences. (For the sake of simplicity, the creation of tasks and semaphores is omitted in the code.) Studying the code examples also reveals the problem mentioned above which is the reason for making the net safe. In the original Petri net, transition a cannot fire if S1 carries a token – transition d is required to fire first, in order to free S1 from the token. But, without the additional place S1' (i.e., without the corresponding semaphore operations 'P(S1')' in the T1 program and 'V(S1')' in the T3 program), instruction a in the T1 task program could be executed even if S1 has a value of one.

It should be mentioned that other means than semaphores might be used in order to achieve the intended task interaction. For example, bounded queues (with indistinguishable 'dummy' entries representing the Petri net tokens) can serve this purpose.

7.3.6 Synchronized access to shared data

A very common problem in the context of (conceptually) distributed systems is the synchronization of conflicting accesses to shared data. Before dealing with modeling questions, we should first make clear what is meant by the term 'conflicting access'. Let us look at the example in Figure 7.19. It shows a person who can use the stock info client to request certain stock reports, for example: 'Give all stock quotes with a price between 30 $ and 40 $'. The stock report generator creates a stock report containing all quotes which meet the criteria and returns control to the client. The stock report is based on the list of stock quotes which is updated regularly by the two stock quote providers.

All transitions in Figure 7.19 represent operations, i.e., activities which are considered elementary at this level of abstraction. As already mentioned in Section 6.1, an agent makes one *access* to each affected location when performing an operation. In case of the operation 'create stock report from list of quotes', there is one *read access* to the list of stock quotes and one *write access* to the stock report, both being performed by the stock report generator. During an 'update quote' operation, a stock quote provider performs a *modifying access* to the list of stock quotes. (A modifying access is a combination of a read and a write access being performed during one operation.)

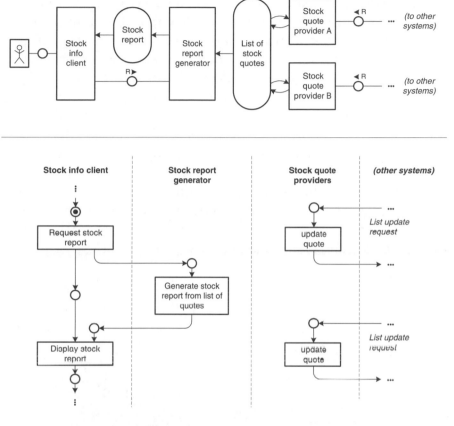

Figure 7.19:   Example of conflicting accesses

Accesses are called 'conflicting' if they affect the same location and cannot be done simultaneously.

This applies to all combinations (pairs) of accesses where at least one access is a write or modifying access, i.e., the only access types which may overlap are read accesses. As the Petri net shows, there is no explicit coordination between the stock report generator and the stock quote providers. However, these agents perform operations affecting the list of stock quotes, i.e., they perform conflicting accesses to the list. Hence the question arises of whether this model describes a properly working system. The answer is yes if we assume the following general statement:

If no explicit coordination is given, conflicting accesses are always performed in an indeterminate but defined order.

The essence of this assumption is that, if an activity is done as a single operation, each access is done atomically by definition. Of course in many cases this assumption is an idealization because access atomicity and defined order of conflicting accesses might require additional effort when implementing a system. However, these measures should be seen at a lower level of abstraction which we can cover in a more detailed model, closer to the implementation. Looking at our example again will make this clearer. Figure 7.19 shows an idealized model, i.e., it shows that we would like the agents to perform their activities as indivisible operations, performing atomic accesses to the storages. This has to be seen as a requirement which we might need to deal with at the lower level. Figure 7.20 shows our system at this level. In the refined Petri net we can see that the operations performed by the stock report generator and the stock quote providers, are actually implemented by sequences of more primitive operations, see the gray shaded sub-nets.

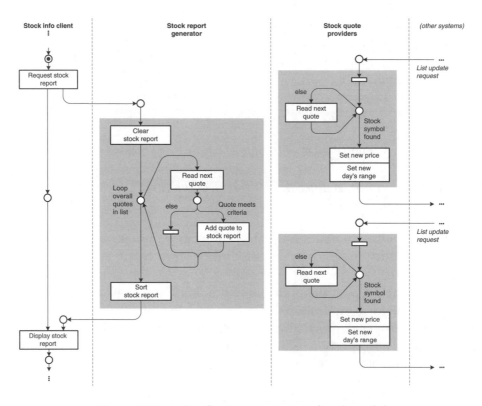

Figure 7.20:   Conflicting accesses: refined model

The consequence is that, at the level of the refined model, each of the high-level atomic accesses to the list of stock quotes is implemented as a set of accesses. Without additional coordination, these access sets could be interleaved, causing unwanted results. For example, the stock report generator could read a stock quote whose price has just been updated by a stock quote provider while the day's range is not yet set to the new values. Therefore, additional means for synchronizing the access sets must be introduced, for example, a locking mechanism. Figure 7.21 shows how the locking mechanism is reflected in both, a corrected block diagram and a corrected Petri net. Figure 7.22 shows a simpler alternative for indicating synchronization between agents. The channel allows the agents to coordinate their activities but does not show the actual synchronization mechanism.

As has been done in this example, it is recommended to keep corresponding Petri nets and block diagrams consistent with each other, i.e., either one should choose the abstract view (Figure 7.19) in which abstract operations with atomic accesses are given, or one should refine both diagram types, revealing synchronization at the lower level (Figure 7.21). The abstract view offers the advantage of being closer to the application domain, leaving out technical details of access synchronization, while the lower level view allows these details to be discussed separately.

There are several possible implementations of the locking mechanism shown in Figure 7.21. For example, locking could be done using a binary semaphore. Similar to Figure 7.18, the semaphore resembles the additional Petri net place, with the marking representing the semaphore value. The semaphore service of the operating system being used corresponds to the lock manager in the block diagram. If the list of stock quotes was implemented as a Java object (containing objects for the individual quote entries), creating the stock report and updating the list would most probably be methods of that object. In this case, these methods could be declared 'sychronized' to avoid interleaving of access sets. Albeit not being visible in the code in this case, the lock manager would still be there – it is part of the Java virtual machine: acquiring and releasing locks is implicitly done at the VM level when a synchronized method is entered or left, respectively. The modeling of shared data and synchronization issues in the context of object oriented software, is also the subject of Section 7.4.

7.3.7   Deriving transactions from FMC models

Of course, using a database is the most sophisticated solution to the problem of access synchronization. When developing a database-dependent solution,

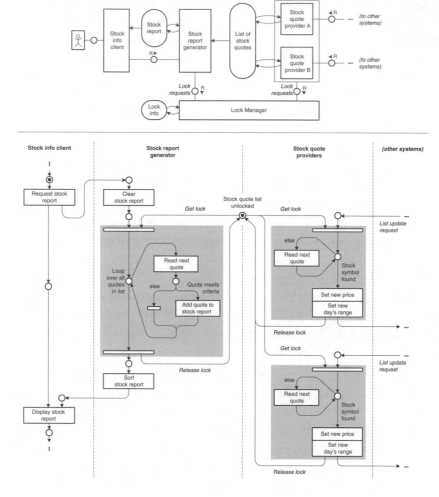

Figure 7.21: Example for coordination of accesses

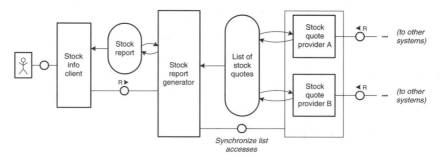

Figure 7.22: Simplified block diagram showing synchronization

identifying and introducing *transactions* [HR82] is a central design task. In fact, FMC models can be utilized to decide which operations should be organized as transactions. The approach is based on the idea of abstract operations and storages and their refinement.

In general, a lower-level model contains elements which are implementations of corresponding elements of the higher-level model, i.e., locations are implemented by locations, operations by operations, and agents by subsystems with agents and additional locations.

In most practical cases, refining model elements yields a one-to-many mapping of higher-level elements to lower-level elements. In the case of agents or locations, this is often called containment. For example, the abstract storages for the list of stock quotes and the stock report in Figure 7.19 could each be implemented by multiple storages, with a storage for each stock symbol, stock price and day's range, see left side of Figure 7.23. (The remaining parts of the stock quote system have been omitted from the diagram.)

This decomposition of the abstract storages into implementing storages, forces a developer to split abstract operations into multiple lower-level operations which access the implementing storages. For example, the 'generate stock report' operation and the 'update quote' operation could be implemented as was shown in Figure 7.20. As a direct consequence of mapping locations or operations, there is an implicit mapping of accesses.

Every time a location or operation has to be implemented by multiple locations or operations, each high-level access must generally be mapped to a set of implementing accesses. Each implementing access set is a candidate for a transaction *[Tab02, Tab04].*

Figure 7.23 shows this mapping for the stock quote example (see right side of the diagram). To be consistent with the high-level model and the assumption of undivisible accesses to storages (see Section 7.3.6), each implementing access set should ideally fulfill the so-called 'ACID properties' [HR82] which are key characteristics of transactions.

Atomicity

A set of accesses (transactions) must be performed completely or not at all, because an incomplete set of accesses cannot be interpreted as a (successful) abstract access.

Example: Writing a new stock report requires all relevant quotes to be written.

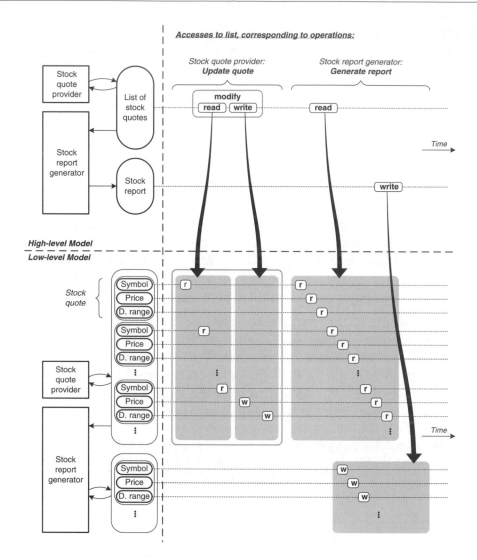

Figure 7.23:   The stock quote system, access mapping

Consistency

Intermediate values occurring between two lower-level write accesses have no meaning at the higher level (where a value change is given). Hence they must not be observable in the context of another access set. When all low-level accesses are completed, the resulting value(s) must represent (be consistent with) the abstract value after the high-level access.

Example: A partially updated quote should not be visible for the stock report generator.

Isolation (or serializability)

Conflicting abstract accesses may only occur in a defined order, i.e., they must not overlap (see Section 7.3.6). The lower-level accesses must be performed in a corresponding order (i.e., they must be 'serializable').

Example: The stock quotes are first updated, then read. The implementing accesses comply with this sequence.

Durability

The state which is reached after completion of an access set (transaction) 'survives' a system failure.

The first three properties are requirements which must be met at the lower level in order to comply with the high-level model. Durability actually becomes relevant if fail-safety is an additional requirement.

The idea of access mapping results in access sets which are *candidates* for transactions, i.e., not every access set must actually be implemented as a transaction. If durability or efficient query processing is not needed, no database is necessary. In this case, simple locking mechanisms, as discussed in Section 7.3.6, will be sufficient. If access sets do not occur asynchronously at all, even locking can be omitted. This can be given, if the system behavior precludes the simultaneous occurrence of conflicting accesses – for example, if there is no concurrency.

However, if a database-dependent implementation is required, the principle of access mapping can be utilized in delimiting transaction boundaries. As an example, we look again at the stock quote system introduced in Figure 7.19. When using a database system, the list of stock quotes and the stock report could be stored in the database. In this case, the stock quote providers, the stock report generator and the stock info client can only access the stock data indirectly via the database management system, see Figure 7.24. Beside the database contents, the database management system also stores information about existing locks and running transactions (see the block diagram). When generating the stock report, the report generator temporarily stores the required stock quotes in a

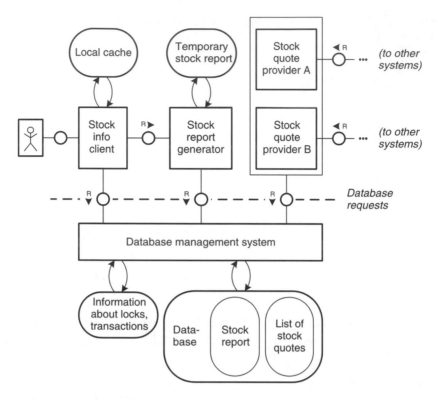

Figure 7.24:   The stock quote system, database-dependent implementation

local storage outside the database. The stock info client uses a local cache for storing a copy of the stock report before displaying it.

When implementing such a solution, certain processing steps must be grouped as transactions. At this point, abstract operations and storages from a high-level model can be used to identify transactions:

Define abstract storages and operations

In a first step, the high-level model of the application has to be defined, see Figure 7.19. At this level, the mapping of storages to the database is still left open. However, two things should be made clear.

First, it should be defined which information must be accessible as a whole when performing operations, i.e., which data should – conceptually – be readable or writeable in a single access. This results in a set of abstract storages like 'stock report' or 'list of stock quotes'.

Second, the behavior should be described in terms of abstract (i.e., as abstract as possible) operations. 'Generate stock report' and 'update quote' are examples. At this level, generating the stock report means fetching all required stock quotes in a single read access and storing the result in a single write access. Implementation details like iterative searching of stock quotes or temporary buffers are ignored.

Identify abstract accesses

Each abstract operation affects one or more abstract locations. Hence, if an operation accesses n storages, there are n abstract accesses. (A modifying access is considered one access.) For example, the 'generate stock report' operation affects two storages, namely the list of stock quotes and the stock report. Hence, there are two accesses: read list, write report. Figure 7.25 illustrates the abstract accesses in our example system.

Map conflicting access sets to transactions

When refining the system model towards a database-dependent implementation, abstract accesses are mapped to database access sets. These access sets must be grouped as transactions. As already discussed, there is no need to transform all accesses into transactions. In our example, we simply assume that all abstract accesses to the same storage can actually collide. (For example, there could be multiple stock info clients accessing the stock report concurrently with other clients and the stock report generator.) Therefore, all abstract operations

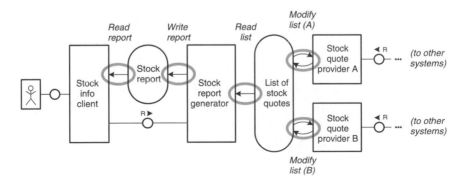

Figure 7.25: The stock quote system: abstract accesses

accessing the list or the report are realized as database transactions and we find one transaction for each abstract access, see Figure 7.26.

Each transaction is indicated by a gray shaded box, starting with a 'BEGIN' and ending with a 'COMMIT' request, see the diagram. All activities inside the gray shaded boxes are actually delegated to the database system. (For the sake of simplicity, the delegation is not shown.) Transactions have intuitive names which allow a mapping to the corresponding accesses in Figure 7.25.

The solution above is based on the assumption that the report generator first creates a temporary report from the database, sorts it and writes the result back to the database as the final stock report. Of course, other solutions and

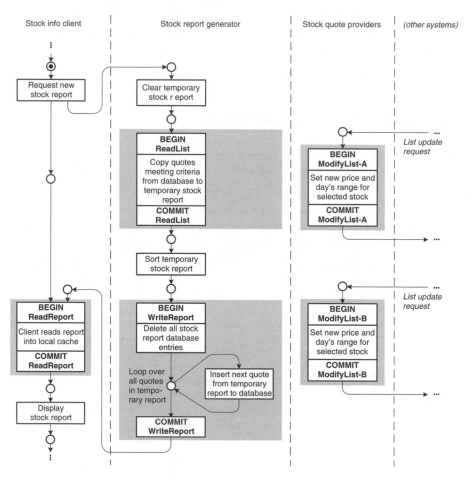

Figure 7.26:   The stock quote system, database-dependent implementation: behavior

optimizations are possible. For example, reading the list of stock quotes and writing the stock report could also be combined to one transaction. In this case, different abstract accesses are mapped to the same transaction.

7.4 From FMC to objects and classes

FMC-based models are intended to describe *system* structures, not software structures. This reflects the insight that these structures are, 'by nature', different things and that there is no simple mapping between the two. With respect to Figure 7.2, FMC covers only the left side, leaving the connection to the right side mostly open. While this focus helps in building conceptual models of the intended system, it also raises an important question:

How can we map agents, storages and channels to software artifacts?

Today, UML class diagrams and object-oriented languages like Java represent the state-of-the-practice approach to software development in many projects. In this context, object-oriented concepts like objects, classes, methods, etc., seem to be the prevalent abstractions. At first sight, there is no clear relationship with FMC modeling elements like agents or storages – we have to clarify the connection between the two worlds.

In the following sections we will show how FMC models can be related to object-oriented software structures. As we will see, there is no general 'all-purpose' transformation instead the appropriate mapping depends on the level of abstraction and the type of object. Therefore, we present several alternative mappings [TG03] and discuss which should be applied in which situation.

Actually, these mappings can be used in two 'directions'. In the context of system *construction*, they can be used to derive classes from FMC models. When *analyzing* given software, e.g., during re-engineering, they can help in building FMC models from software structures. In this context, they can be seen as possible 'interpretations' of objects and classes. Therefore, the different mappings are also called 'views' in the following sections.

7.4.1 Common views

In literature about object-oriented methods three prevalent interpretations of objects can be identified which we call the 'analysis view', the 'abstract data type view' and the 'object agent view'.

Analysis view

A typical interpretation of objects in the context of object-oriented analysis is to view an object as an abstraction of the so-called 'problem domain' where typical examples are terms and concepts such as 'customer' or 'account'. In this case, simplified class diagrams or E/R diagrams can be used to cover the terminology. In this context, objects do not (yet) correspond to elements of system models.

Object agent view

Considering an object to be an agent is a common interpretation in object-oriented design. An *object agent* is an active and abstract component of the system. Calling a method is interpreted as sending a message to a receiver object which carries out the desired operation and responds with an answer. Only an object agent has access to attributes, the data associated with an object. Methods describe which messages the object can handle, which operations on its data it can perform and which messages it sends to other objects[GR89], p. 6.

A typical example for this view in context of architecture is a dispatcher. GUI toolkits usually use a dispatcher object to react to GUI events like mouse movement to or from a defined area, or button press or release events. The dispatcher does not process the event itself but calls a method of a certain object which has been registered as handler for this event.

The block diagram in Figure 7.27 shows the example objects as agents consisting of methods and an internal storage holding object data. Only the object's methods have access to the internal storage. 'Knowing' other objects by their object ID (reference) is symbolized by a channel between them used to send messages. A direction symbol indicates which object sends and which receives a message.

This view seems natural because of its vivid association with active system components responsible for certain tasks and exchanging messages. Unfortunately, the usefulness of this view scales down in the same way as the size of the total system scales up. Given many objects of different type, this view would result in an extremely fine granular system architecture consisting of a myriad of object agents – like an ant hill. Furthermore, although this view implies that object agents can operate concurrently, there is a strict sequence resulting from the order of method procedure calls. Introducing true concurrency with threads results in severe comprehension problems: for example, no encapsulation of object data exists between two threads, and two threads can execute the same

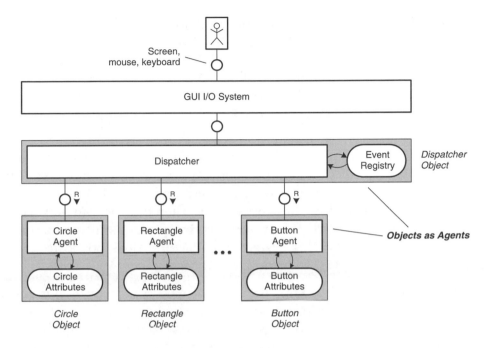

Figure 7.27:   Object agent view

method procedure with the same object. To avoid inconsistency, additional mechanisms like a lock management have to be used.

Abstract data type view

Another common interpretation can be called the 'abstract data type view'. Here, an object is seen as a storage for an abstract data type which is described by the corresponding class. Bertrand Meyer is an author who presents this interpretation of objects – he defines a class as 'an abstract data type equipped with a possibly partial implementation'[Mey97], p. 142. The class not only lists the operation types (i.e., the method signatures) of the abstract data type, it may also provide the implementation of the data storage (i.e., the attribute storages) and the implementation of the operation types (i.e., the method bodies). From this point of view, an object can be seen as a passive system component (a storage), and a method call can be interpreted as an operation which is performed on the object, rather than a message causing the object to perform an operation. The internal structure of the storages is hidden as the model does not reflect knowledge about the implementation of a data type.

Figure 7.28 shows a typical example of this type of view. The 'Vector' class defines an abstract data type 'Vector' with operation types 'scale', 'add', 'rotate', etc. The class also provides the implementation of the Vector data and the operation types. From an abstract point of view, an instance of the Vector class can be seen as a storage which holds a certain Vector value. Other system components can operate on this storage, thereby being restricted to the operation types defined for the abstract data type.

If we derived an architectural model from this view, the system would consist solely of a collection of storages (i.e., objects) for abstract data types. Since only storages with related operations have been specified, there must also be some active component doing these operations. Therefore, we can only assume a generic component, called 'the system', which performs all operations on the data – see Figure 7.28. This system 'architecture' does not foster system understanding, because it is too primitive and generic.

In the case of concurrent systems, the abstract data type view shows further limitations. The fact that an abstract operation is actually implemented by several operations on object attribute data, leads to inconsistency problems which, in turn, can only be discussed at the level of threads and their accesses to attribute data. Unfortunately, the abstract data type view hides these implementation details, which makes it impossible to understand problems of concurrent accesses or to discuss their possible solutions.

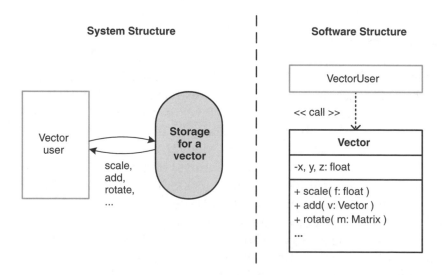

Figure 7.28:   Abstract data type view

7.4.2 Low-level mappings

The views described in Section 7.4.1 mirror the idea of encapsulation. Either the non-public attribute storages are local to the object agent or, in the case of the abstract data type view, they are not shown at all. However, there are situations where lower level models of objects are needed, which explicitly show the inner details of an object.

Data record view

Taking a closer look on how an object-oriented program is executed, you soon learn that an object is just a data record in memory. This view – which we call the 'data record view' – explicitly shows the 'inner structure' of objects, i.e., an object is described as a set of storages for attribute data. In case of the 'Vector' example (see above), the storages for the vector components x, y and z now become visible – see Figure 7.29. The implicit 'system' agent of the abstract data type view is also described in more detail: each thread is modeled as an agent operating on the (shared) objects. Each thread also has a private

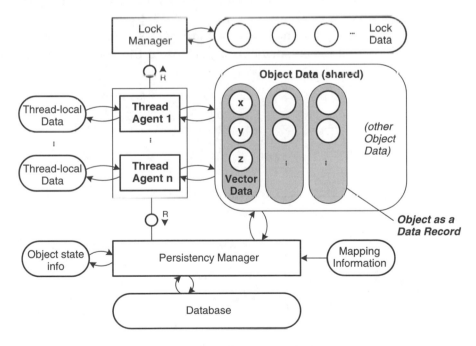

Figure 7.29:   Data record view

storage for its state, e.g., for local variables. In contrast to the abstract data type view (see above), the discussion of inconsistency problems in the context of multithreading is now possible. The architecture model makes clear that object data is shared between threads, see Figure 7.29. In a sense, multithreading breaks encapsulation because the implementation of methods and attributes causes effects (i.e., inconsistencies) beyond the scope of an object. In order to retain (or re-establish) encapsulation, the thread operations on object data must be synchronized, e.g., by using locks. Thread agents can set and release locks by sending corresponding requests to a central lock manager (e.g., an operating system's mutex service).

This view also provides an elegant way of describing object persistency. A persistency manager can access object data directly, for example, to increase performance. The persistency manager typically needs additional information for the mapping between attributes and database fields, see Figure 7.29.

Processor view

The processor view refines the thread agents of the data record view. A program thread is implemented by means of a virtual processor executing the code of the program described by the classes, see Figure 7.30. The thread-local data consists of the Program Counter (PC), the stack for parameters and local variables and other data. Each virtual processor has read access to the code in the program

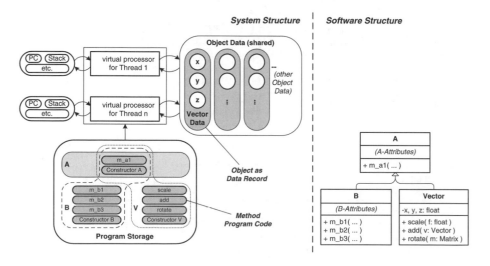

Figure 7.30: Processor view

storage. In this view we show the code which a compiler generates from an OO program and how it is executed by the machine. For example, we see that the code provides a (default) constructor procedure for every class.

The processor view can be used to discuss internal data structures and activities of runtime environments and virtual machines; for example, the Java class loading mechanism.

7.4.3 High-level mappings

The views presented above allow objects to be mapped to certain elements of architectural system models. While these mappings foster a more intuitive understanding of a single object in a certain context, they do not solve the 'granularity problem'. Reflecting each object as a dedicated element in an architectural model still yields models of (too) extreme granularity and larger systems with thousands or millions of objects cannot be modeled this way. Furthermore, such models would only present short-lived snapshots, because objects are created and destroyed very frequently. Hence, mappings are needed where a (dynamic) collection of objects can be mapped to a (static) high-level architectural element.

High-level abstract data type view

A quite obvious way to model a set of objects is to extend the idea of the abstract data type view. There are cases where the definition of a single class is not sufficient for the realization of an abstract data type. For example, a data type 'tree' might be needed, which stores arithmetic expressions as binary trees. For this purpose, one might define the classes as shown in Figure 7.31. Instances of classes derived from 'Node' would represent a tree's nodes and a 'Tree' object would be the placeholder of the whole tree. This object provides methods for accessing the whole object structure, such as calculating the value of the tree (i.e., the value of the corresponding expression).

The basic idea behind the tree-related classes is to provide the possibility of storing trees. Hence, at a higher level, the complete object set holding a certain tree can be viewed as a single storage for an abstract data type 'Tree' – see upper right corner of Figure 7.31. This 'high-level abstract data type view' yields a single storage as an abstract, compact model of an object set. This model remains valid even if the underlying object structure changes over time: at the higher level, only the current value (i.e., the tree) in the storage is changed. The

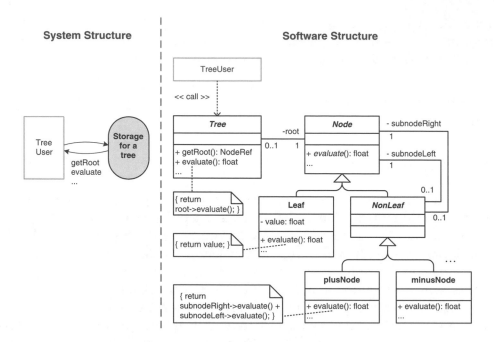

Figure 7.31:   High-level data type view

operation types defined for the abstract data type (e.g., tree evaluation) are not implemented by a single method but the combined methods of several classes (here: the 'evaluate' methods).

High-level object agent view

It is sometimes reasonable to combine many objects to one agent. Take, for example, a persistency service which consists of a singleton object of the persistency manager class and a set of class agents, one singleton object for each persistent class. Figure 7.32 shows the persistent objects, the persistency service, the transaction service and the database. The task of the persistency service is to create or load persistent objects from the database and to save altered object data whenever the transaction service requests it, in the case of a commit. The persistency manager just keeps a list of the classes, while the class agents read and write object data and create objects; they have all the information about their class and know which objects have been altered. Class agents are therefore factories for persistent objects and part of the persistency service. The persistency manager is the representative of the persistency service. The

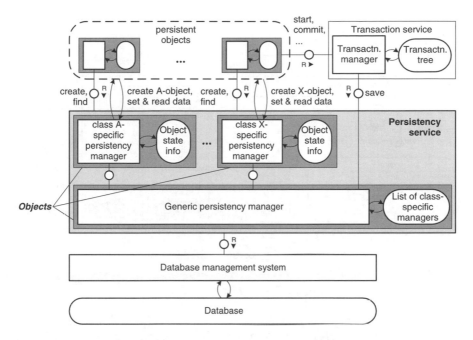

Figure 7.32: High-level object agent view

decomposition of the transaction service is not shown here; for example, the tree of the (nested) transactions can be implemented with objects of a transaction class managed by a singleton object of a transaction manager class.

It should be pointed out that, applying the high-level object agent view, would yield a model which would *not* show the *inner* structure of the 'Persistency Service' agent, thus reducing the complexity of the compositional structure.

The architecture shown in Figure 7.32 was chosen for the project 'Object Services' at SAP in 1999. The goal was a new persistency and transaction service for ABAP Objects, an OO extension of the R/3 programming language ABAP. The services had to fit as seamlessly as possible into the R/3 framework and cooperate with existing non-OO applications [Grö05].

Functional view

The high-level views presented above have in common that one architectural element (storage or agent) is mapped to many objects. However, this one-to-many mapping is not appropriate if the architectural model primarily represents a functional decomposition. Figure 7.33 shows an architectural model of a simple

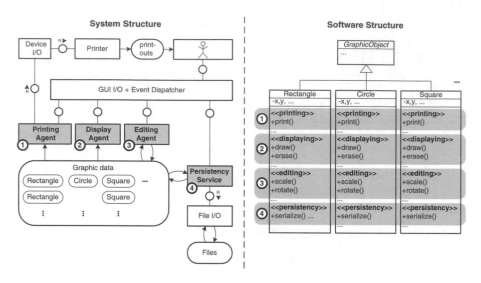

Figure 7.33:   Functional view

graphic editor where each component provides a certain functionality, namely editing, displaying, printing and persistency. The central storage holds all data describing the graphic drawing currently being modified. The agents rely on certain components of the underlying platform, e.g., the file system.

While this model is very useful in presenting a system overview, a one-to-one or one-to-many mapping of architectural elements to objects would not result in an appropriate software structure. Following object-oriented design principles, we should define a class 'GraphicObject' with subclasses for the different types of graphical elements, i.e., rectangles, circles etc.: see the right side of Figure 7.33. The implementation of displaying, editing and other operations depends on the implementation of the graphic element data. Hence, each of the classes should not only define a storage format for graphic data but should also contain methods corresponding to the various operation types. (Of course, additional classes have to be defined beside these classes.)

The example shows a many-to-many mapping of objects to architectural elements. The collective object attribute data is mapped to the 'Graphic data' storage, and all methods implementing a certain functionality (e.g., editing methods) are mapped to a corresponding agent (e.g., the 'Editing Agent'). We call this mapping the 'functional view' because the architectural model *reflects the functionality* provided by the program.

7.4.4 Additional views

Beside the mappings discussed above, additional views on objects are possible [Kle99] For example, objects can be viewed as broadcast channels or storages. This is the case if an object is used to publish data updates to dependent objects, as outlined by the 'Observer' pattern [GHJV95]. Here, the so-called 'subject' holds data which can be changed by one object (one of the 'observer' objects), causing other objects (the remaining 'observer' objects) to automatically read and process the updated value. At a higher level, the 'subject' can be seen as a simple storage which is written and observed by agents being connected to it.

Sometimes, an object is created and initialized with certain data (i.e., attributes), but is never changed during its lifetime. Instead, only references to the object or identical copies of the object are passed between other objects. An 'Order' object in an online shopping system is a typical example. If an order arrives, the object is created with product ID, quantity, customer name, etc., as read-only attributes. While the order will be processed, the corresponding 'Order' object would be transported, printed, stored in a database and be linked to an 'Invoice' object, etc., but the object attributes would remain unchanged. In this case, the object can often be simplified as a value which is passed through channels or storages between agents.

7.4.5 Guidelines for choosing a view

Each of the different views presented above is suitable, depending on the context and the type of object(s) under consideration. Hence, some criteria for choosing one of these views should be given.

The *object agent view* is suitable if an object's main purpose is controlling other parts of the system. In this case, the object can be understood best as an active system component which communicates with other components by sending requests to them. Such objects are often singletons and have a method which runs (potentially) endlessly (e.g., the request forwarding loop of the dispatcher shown in Figure 7.27). If several objects closely interact to fulfill a control function, they can be modeled as one controlling agent, according to the *high-level object agent view*.

The *abstract data type view* should be chosen if the main idea behind a class is to provide a data type which is missing from the programming language (e.g., the 'Vector' type in Figure 7.28). In this case, the methods implement operations which are typically defined with purely operational semantics, e.g., by defining pre- and post- conditions. If a set of objects is used to implement a data structure, the high-level abstract data type view is a good way of modeling this.

In general, the *data record view* is helpful if the implementation details of methods and attributes cannot be ignored and objects 'must be seen as data records'. Multithreading with shared objects (see Figure 7.29) is one example.

If aspects of code execution have to be described, the *processor view* yields a helpful model. It is also useful to explain dynamic code management like 'class loading' in Java; or object migration between processor nodes.

The *functional view* is valuable in order to keep the overview, even if the system becomes very complex. For example, the functional view helps to check if all requirements (especially functionality) have been taken into account. It shows how the components interact with each other and the environment, it also shows what kind of data is stored and which agents have access to it, etc. In contrast, a pure OO model, like a class diagram, would not offer this insight because data definitions and functionality are spread across classes, and communication links (channels) between agents are only implicitly given by certain method calls. The functional view is also useful whenever non-OO or even non-software components are involved in the system.

While we could give some criteria for the application of the views, we do not think that the mapping between object-oriented models and architecture-oriented models is always straightforward. It is a non- formal, creative task which requires experience. To support this task, patterns can be a helpful means of describing 'proven' mappings.

The mappings presented above can be used both during system analysis or re-engineering and during system construction. In the context of re-engineering, the views help in deriving high-level architectural models from an existing object-oriented code base. During system construction, conceptual architecture models can be used as a basis for object-oriented design: see [Grö05] and Section 10.2.

7.5   Conceptual patterns versus software patterns

Experience is a key factor in engineering. To benefit from other professionals' experiences, it is important to communicate them in an appropriate way, so that other people can understand them quickly. Patterns provide a common form for the transport of experiences. A pattern describes a common and proven solution to a problem that occurs in a certain context. Originally used for the architecture of buildings, they were adopted by the software engineering community in the 90s, especially for object-oriented programming.

Patterns usually come in groups. After applying one pattern, other patterns become relevant for related problems. Therefore, pattern systems describe patterns and their relationships, often supported by a guideline.

Planning large and complex software systems is the task of a system architect. This includes communication with the customer, planning the overall system structure, as well as preparing the division of labor among software engineers. An architect will also profit from former experience concerning the system's architecture.

Most architectural patterns deal with structuring the software. From the system architect's point of view, this task usually comes later, after defining the functional components of the system. Are there any patterns which are useful in the early stages when software structures are not yet an issue?

Conceptual Patterns can fill this gap. A pattern can be called conceptual, if both problem and solution belong to the conceptual view [Grö04] In this view, the functional aspects and structures of the system are relevant, while software structures or even the use of software for implementation, are not. This applies to the description of a conceptual pattern as well – common pattern descriptions focus on the structure of the software in terms of classes and their relationships. Instead, terminology and notation of the description of a conceptual pattern should be adequate for the presentation of system structures; this applies for the Fundamental Modeling Concepts (FMC).

Many existing patterns provide concepts which fit into the conceptual pattern category. Transforming such a pattern into a conceptual pattern means adapting the pattern description in order to focus on the system structures.

Conceptual patterns are useful for system architects when building a conceptual or 'mental' model of the system, in cooperation with the customer. Deriving the structure of the software from the structure of the planned system is a task which can be supported by bridging patterns, another pattern category.

Pattern systems of related conceptual patterns can transport knowledge and experience about best–practice solutions for typical problems and their alternatives.

Chapter 8

Applying FMC in Your Daily Work

FMC will benefit your work whenever there is a need to communicate information about systems, especially between people with different backgrounds and skills. This includes:

- sharing knowledge;
- presenting ideas;
- capturing decisions and experience; and
- reporting project progress.

The scenarios presented in this chapter will give you a clear idea of where the effort of modeling might be most beneficial.

8.1   Becoming comfortable with FMC

Having read the previous chapters, you may wonder how to apply FMC in your daily work. Using FMC to support communication, as stated above, requires you to find the right abstractions and draw diagrams which show the model in a comprehensible way. This can be called didactical modeling and its application requires exercise and practice.

To practice modeling, why not start with small projects first and invite frequent feedback from your colleagues or friends. Allow for iterations and compare your models. You will learn a lot about modeling.

8.1.1   Your first steps with FMC

Learn from good models and descriptions

Look for a good system description using FMC models; for example, the Apache Modeling Project [GKKS04], and then develop a feeling of how it explains the system. Familiarize yourself with the structure of the document and the layouts of the diagrams.

Model an existing system

Start modeling an existing system that is not too complex, and try to explain it to someone who is not too deeply involved into the system, but is interested in learning more about it. You may have to examine a product needed for your current project anyway. Consider Section 8.2, which deals with how to describe existing systems.

As for all modeling activities, consider the guidelines for didactical modeling, as shown in Section 8.5: namely; purpose, audience, granularity and abstraction of the models.

Model the conceptual architecture in a project

With your experience in modeling existing systems, you can start modeling the architecture in a small project. You will create a *system map*, as presented in Section 8.3.2, which will usually be subject to further refinement.

Structure the project according to your models. Although a small project might succeed without such an effort, there could be a change in the requirements and then your system map will help you to re-structure the project.

8.1.2   The next steps

After your first experiences in modeling using FMC, why not take the next step and address people other than your friends and co-workers. You will face new challenges regarding the abstraction and the effort you have to put into modeling.

It may be advisable to restrict your models to FMC block diagrams and skip 'advanced' modeling features like structure variance.

Present your models to the customer or to the management

When you have made good progress using FMC models in order to communicate with your colleagues, start applying FMC to communicate with customers or management. Use FMC block diagrams as central ingredients of your presentations, as shown in Section 8.4.2. Just use the diagrams to explain what your audience needs to know; do not emphasize the fact that you are using a specific modeling technique.

Mental prototyping

If you are involved in early project phases, use FMC block diagrams to create mental prototypes (see Section 8.3.1) and discuss them with your customer. You will create a direct feedback loop with them, and you will learn quickly whether they understand your models or not, and where they still have problems.

System map

The system map (see Section 8.3.2) plays a central role in a project because it describes the system to be built in greater detail than an introductory diagram could, and has to be understood by each and every team member. You create it during the architecture phase of the project and have to refine it with the help of the feedback given by your team.

8.1.3 Things to consider

Do I have to ... ?

FMC is not the silver bullet! If you feel that FMC will not help you to make an aspect clear, do not use it in this case. For example, some data structures like trees can be best visualized showing an example structure, whereas screenshots are usually a good way to show graphical user interfaces (GUIs).

You do not have to use all diagram types of FMC – many presentations or even reports use only FMC block diagrams as they are the most important diagram type and can also be used to explain behavior and relations, if they are not too complex.

FMC versus other modeling approaches

It may happen that you will be advised to use 'the house standard', such as UML. Even in that case, you can still use FMC diagrams, since UML and FMC can complement each other very efficiently, see also Section 10.2. The actual reason for this is that FMC is mostly useful in situations where people usually do not apply any formal notation at all. Instead, ad hoc graphics based on Power Point clip art, non-standardized boxes-and-lines diagrams, etc, can be found in practice. Since people do not expect a formal notation, FMC block diagrams are just your way of drawing these box-and-line diagrams. Of course, they will soon notice the better quality of your diagrams because you can rely on FMC's defined semantics and notation.

Purpose of a model

There is no universal model. Every model serves a purpose, and while one might be the best model to serve one particular purpose, it could fail on another. Typical purposes are:

- Communicate system structures;

- Show which problems still have to be solved;

- Show which aspects of the system are still unclear;

- Convince people to support your architecture;

- Report project progress.

So, whenever you model a system, define the purpose of your modeling.

8.2   Describing existing systems with FMC

Before you can develop a new system, you usually have to understand the existing systems such as the operating system, the development environment, the supporting systems like frameworks or middleware, and, most importantly, systems which have to be integrated into or replaced by the new system.

Often, the source code of an existing system is not available or is of limited use, due to the huge amount of it. Modeling an existing system from a functional and external view is a good starting point, especially if more than one person has to understand this system: division of labor is required for efficiency. FMC models support this process.

Imagine this situation. The project has a tight schedule, but the system can be developed in time, and some user documentation has even been written, but none of the team members is willing to maintain the software, or they are about to leave. So, you need a knowledge transfer, or even better, a way of capturing the knowledge about the product which is currently located in the code and the brains of the team members.

It is very hard to understand code written by other developers, especially if there is a large amount of it. Even worse, a lot of information cannot be found in the code; such as the requirements, a system overview, its interaction with the environment, system design decisions, alternatives which have not been used and the underlying reasons for this, and much more.

8.2.1 How to get information

Interviews The architects and developers are the most important sources of information. To lay your hands on this information, interview the architects and key developers. As they will usually be busy with other projects, you need to prepare the interviews carefully and conduct them efficiently.

FMC models can support interviews when you use them to point out what you have understood. In your models, dialog partners will usually recognize what they have told you and make sure that you have it right.

Iterative modeling Instead of one big interview, conduct a series of small interviews and at the start of each, present what you have understood so far using FMC models. Let the knowledge bearers use and correct your models.

Meeting minutes, presentation slides, white papers, documentation Any kind of written documentation, even if obsolete, can help you to grasp the big picture or understand some design decisions.

Study the system in service If available, the system itself is also an important source of information, especially in understanding details from interviews and documentation. Use the system to check whether or not your system model is already adequate. Perhaps you will have to consider different views on the system, for example, the user's view and the administrator's view.

Study the source code If available, the source code may answer detailed questions. As a prerequisite, you have to analyze the structure of the source code and how it maps to the system model. As the amount of code is usually huge, tools are required for search and navigation.

8.2.2 Documenting systems

With a good documentation, skilled readers should be able to learn all the aspects of the system which the author intends them to know. In contrast to a presentation, the author is not available to answer questions, therefore a documentation should be prepared carefully.

Do not hesitate to ask colleagues or friends to be your 'beta readers', i.e., to read your documents, jot down every arising question and give you honest feedback.

Although appreciated if it exists, writing good documentation for architects and developers is costly, therefore you should consider the hints in Section 8.6 about the costs and benefits of modeling.

Addressee of a model

Strongly related to the purpose of a model is the question of whom to address with your models. It is a question of didactics, to tailor your models to the skills and advanced knowledge of your audience, and to abstract from information which might be useless to them. A big challenge arises if you need to address a heterogeneous audience, which means that there can only be a compromise. Depending on the audience, you might have to:

- introduce the terminology;

- give a brief and concise overview of the system and its environment;

- focus on the needs of a particular role, such as the user, the administrator or the developer.

In a nutshell: What does your audience already know and which information might be useful to them?

Bridging models

Often, a report should let the readers understand the concepts behind a system and give them entry points into the implementation. To keep the gap small between the conceptual world (shown by FMC block diagrams) and the implementation world (shown by module / class diagrams), you should show some models in between: namely, bridging models.

Bridging models map structures, sometimes even single agents or storages of conceptual models to implementation–specific structures such as hardware nodes, threads or modules. For example, some transitions of a Petri net describe behavior which can be mapped to procedures.

Field report: Documentation using FMC supported the port of SAP R/3 to IBM AS/400

Between 1987 and 1992, SAP, a German software company created the technology basis of their R/3 ERP system. The basis system (without any business applications) comprised many millions of lines of code and the board became aware that too much knowledge about this new system was condensed in too few developers' brains. So in 1990 they asked Siegfried Wendt and his FMC team to model and document the concepts and architecture of the R/3 basis system.

A handful of experienced modelers interviewed the key architects and developers of the system and created models which served as a basis for discussion. Using them in the next interviews, the modelers could check that they had really understood what the developers intended to express. With this knowledge, the modelers inspected the code – they then knew where to look and which structures to expect – to create precise models of the system.

Within three years, the team published a series of technical reports inside SAP (called 'blue books', due to the color of their cover) which covered all key concepts and the architecture of the R/3 platform. As a result of the success of this modeling project, a new department was founded – Basis Modeling – which would not only document the existing platform, but would accompany further development, evaluate new technology and spread this knowledge throughout the company.

The reports were also quite useful in a project outside SAP. In 1996, IBM started to port the R/3 system to their AS/400 platform. IBM received the R/3 basis reports and the part-time support of one SAP developer, and they succeeded within the required time.

8.2.3 Preparing integration

Many projects deal with the integration of existing systems into a new one which offers new features. Most companies simply cannot afford the costs of replacing a working and reliable solution by a totally new one, which may offer all the new features but might 'hide' new bugs and problems.

The environment of existing ('legacy') systems has to be understood before it is possible to start designing a system which has to fit into this environment. This is similar to the documentation of existing systems, but for integration purposes it is necessary to focus on selected aspects of any existing systems which are needed to build the new one.

Even without 'legacy' systems, you may need to understand a complex system before you can start using it. Frameworks offer many features for application developers which may save them development time – if they can understand them.

Understanding an existing system is one aspect, but documenting it is another. The effort of modeling is justifiable whenever more than one person is involved or when it is necessary to save this knowledge for a longer period. For example, learning a framework is a time-consuming task which has to be done by a group of developers. Instead of letting each developer gather knowledge themselves, one should learn and prepare information for the others.

8.2.4   Preparing migration and re-engineering

Sometimes there is an opportunity to replace an old system by a new one which has the same features as the old one but adds some nice, 'nifty' new features. This requires a complete understanding of what the old system offers and how. Relying solely on the customer in order to understand the old system, will result in the same problems as described in the requirements engineering Section 8.3.1.

It is important to understand and document the existing system under the aspect of changing its implementation or re-implementing its functionality. FMC models can particularly help to create a functional model of the system.

8.3   Using FMC in construction

FMC can bring benefits in projects whenever communication between many people is an issue. This applies to various situations during the construction of a system.

Requirements Engineering deals with defining the project by eliciting the details of the customer's wishes. Unfortunately, the customer uses other words and may not think of every detail he or she has to decide. *Mental Prototyping* with simple FMC diagrams can be a good means of visualizing the first draft of a system which can be used and tested – mentally – by the customer to decide which requirements are still missing. This goes one step further than textual descriptions, tables or *Use-case diagrams* which visualize scenarios. The mental prototype shows a system that has been designed (on an abstract level) to comply with the requirements.

After having defined the project, you will not work on your own until the system is delivered – instead, a project manager should report, deal with customers and managers and involve different people in the development of the system. This again requires communication which can be supported by FMC models. The *System Map*, as described in Section 8.3.2, is a good tool which will give every team member a common understanding of the overall system. Furthermore, the system map gives customers and managers a good overview of the state of development.

Models evolve in time; the term *iterative modeling* emphasizes the process of changing and refining crucial system models during the requirements engineering, architecture, and design phases. In the beginning, models are subject to frequent changes. The more people that are involved in a project, due to division of labor, the more stable the central models will be.

Models reflect consensus; everyone involved in a project should know the system map which forms the result of an iteration of models and incorporates the outcome of the most important design decisions.

FMC models can also be useful in small projects with few team members, who might encounter similar problems.

8.3.1 Supporting requirements engineering with 'Mental Prototyping'

How do you get your customer involved in the development of a product? Usually, you obtain a list of requirements and a due date. Your team starts working, and whenever you need to clarify a requirement, the customer possibly adds a new one. If you present a working prototype, it seems that the customer wanted a totally different system. But the customer will not read your class diagrams. What can you do?

The solution is to involve the customer in the architecture phase. Present a *Mental Prototype* of the system. A Mental Prototype is a functional model of the intended system which already provides some design decisions without being too complex to be easily understood. The point is that there is no need to implement the system in exactly the way described in the model. You can explain what the system will do and how it may do it. Another aspect is the differentiation between the system and its environment, the interfaces and services which both provide.

The customer should be able to follow your solution and imagine how the planned product will work. In this early stage, the customer is invited to refine the requirements concerning functionality and processes.

Typical aspects of a mental prototype:

- simple model;

- shows concepts, not implementation;

- introduces a terminology;

- focuses on key aspects;

- usually incomplete: leaves open what has not yet been decided.

Field report: The project Object Services at SAP

Background SAP produces ERP software (enterprise resource planning) which runs on a platform provided by SAP as well. The development at SAP can be subdivided into basis platform technology and application development. SAP application developers have close contact with SAP customers and are themselves customers of the SAP basis developers.

One project at SAP was the introduction of object-oriented extensions to the ABAP programming language and the roll-out to the application development. To be useful in building applications, the language had to be supported by many services, starting with a persistency and transaction service which fits into the object-oriented world. This was the goal of the Object Services project.

The set-up When the Object Services project began, a small group (two architects, one developer, one manager) started with intensive communication with all groups involved. There were:

- Three groups for basis development, who had to provide service interfaces or interception points for Object Services;

- one group of application developers, who volunteered for pilot projects using the new technology;

- one group responsible for the roll-out of basis technology into the application development.

This resulted in a total of 40 basis technology developers and 30 application developers who had to be involved in the discussion of the new programming model for object-oriented applications, using the new services.

To build a working prototype, the three basis development groups had to add some extensions and hooks for the Object Services runtime and development tools, but they were only willing to do it if the application model was convincing.

The Solution The architecture team used FMC diagrams in the numerous meetings with the representatives of the groups to focus the discussion and to produce a mental prototype of the runtime system. After a month, they could present this mental prototype to all involved developers and managers (about 70 persons) and started building a working prototype.

The mental prototype and other diagrams used in the discussions were the foundation of the documentation of the object services which complemented the prototype.

The pilot projects brought new insights and requirements and finally lead to the final product. The architecture and the interfaces remained, while the implementing code was then replaced by an optimized version.

Lessons learned The project required intensive communication about the planned product and about the existing system, with a large number of stakeholders. FMC diagrams were used in every phase of the project. The requirements engineering and architecture phase at the beginning required coordination and technical discussions with many people, therefore it paid to use block diagrams from the very beginning. The documentation explained the concepts and made most of the design decisions clear, therefore it was not hard to consign the product to a successor.

8.3.2 Architecture-based design: The System Map

The System Map

Have you ever visited a team working on components of a car or a big machine? Very often, they have a large diagram pinned on the wall showing the planned machine, but the diagram seems to be ignored by the team members most of the time. But if you ask them for their current activity, they will use the large diagram to show you on which details they are working. The large diagram shows a technical drawing of the system and can be understood by non-specialists, because they can imagine the system described there.

The *Mental Prototype*, as introduced in Section 8.3.1, can serve more purposes than only for communication between the architect and customer. It may be the basis of the *System Map*, which shows an overall view of the intended system which the team is developing. The system map will include more technical decisions and refinements than a mental prototype provides. As it serves as the entry point, all team members are well acquainted with the system map. While program structures, like class hierarchies, evolve during the project, there is seldom a need to adapt the system map.

A System Map helps to structure a project and to assign tasks to all team members. They can locate their work in the system map and its relation to and dependency on, other developer's work. A project manager can identify tasks and responsibilities before one line of code has been written. Changing the project structure is easier if you can visualize the changes and their consequences in a system map.

An example of a system map is shown in Figure 8.1. In this case, colors have been used to indicate the current project status.

Writing re-usable code is about designing the software structure, which may be different from the system structure. Therefore, some tasks of the developers cannot be located in a system map. For example, the code needed to check a purchase order can be assigned to one or few agents in the system map, while database access or persistency code concerns at least a part of the system.

Project management

The project manager can use the system map to get a quick overview of the development status. This can be done by adding attributes to block diagram elements and presenting them with a tool, for example, by using a red color for critical parts. Using FMC structure diagrams for project management is a central idea of the tool ARCWAY COCKPIT (www.arcway.com).

ARCWAY COCKPIT: A specification and project planning tool using FMC
The initial stage of a project, which results in a go/no go decision, is a critical point

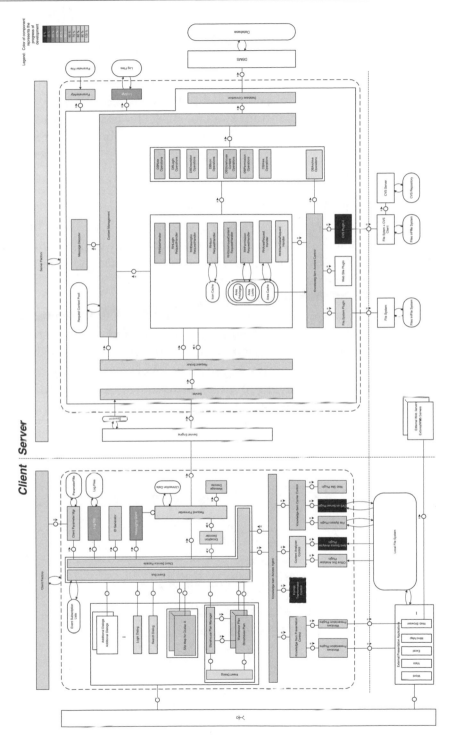

Figure 8.1: Example of a system map (original size: 600mm × 840mm)

for each project. At this stage, all the information from different stakeholders is collected and put into one common context. Thus, many different views have to be consolidated in one big picture.

ARCWAY COCKPIT is the first tool which supports the usage of FMC diagrams in the initial specification and planning stage of projects. FMC diagrams modeled in COCKPIT are stored in a central repository, together with associated secondary information like requirements, open issues, notes, related documents, project tasks and more.

The COCKPIT concept allows the provision of connected views on different levels of abstraction for different stakeholder groups. 'As is' and 'to be' business processes can be modeled as part of the analysis and requirement elicitation process. ARCWAY COCKPIT supports the mapping and validation of use-cases and requirements with the modeled processes.

Both business and technical processes can be related to the architecture of given or planned systems. The architecture and the related process steps and other information can be modeled on different interrelated levels, as shown in Figure 8.2: The executive level shows aggregated overview information. The system map on the big picture level provides an extensive overview for project management tasks. The detail and scenario level provides detailed information and process choreography issues for specialists.

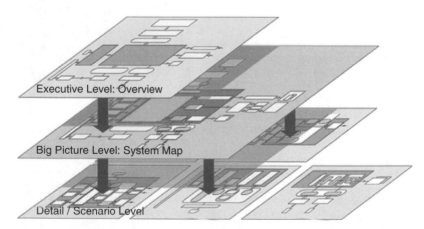

Figure 8.2:   The ARCWAY COCKPIT approach maps the process oriented business view on architectural structures on the executive level, the big picture level, and the detail / scenario level

ARCWAY COCKPIT allows different types of information arising in the early stage of the project to be linked with elements of the system model. Such information items may be:

- business or technical requirements (goals, process steps, use-cases, functions);

- requisite work items and costs as a base for an initial cost and time estimation;

- notes, hints, open points; and

- any kind of document holding relevant information.

In most cases this kind of information is spread over PowerPoint, Excel, Word or Visio files in different versions on different computers.

ARCWAY COCKPIT builds an easy to use, central integration platform for this kind of information (see Figure 8.3). The FMC block diagrams and the related process models provide a common big picture of the planned system and reflect the current status information of the project. ARCWAY COCKPIT provides the necessary foundation for the decision to start or skip the project. Also, the initial interrelated planning of the processes, architecture and the project tasks is supported by ARCWAY COCKPIT. Information such as requirements or project plans can easily be transferred to other tools already in use and established in the build stage.

8.3.3 Integrate new team members

A project may reach the point where too much work has to be done by too few developers. Often, it is not sufficient just to add new developers to the team; for example, new team members were not involved in the early phases when the initial team discussed the architecture and the requirements to be resolved. The new team members do not share the same understanding of the system as do the 'old' ones.

Usually, a new team member will have a tutor who has to show him or her the system. Perhaps the tutor will try to explain why the system is built in this way. This can be very time consuming.

The introduction to the system can be much easier if a system map already exists. The new team member will still have to examine the details of the system

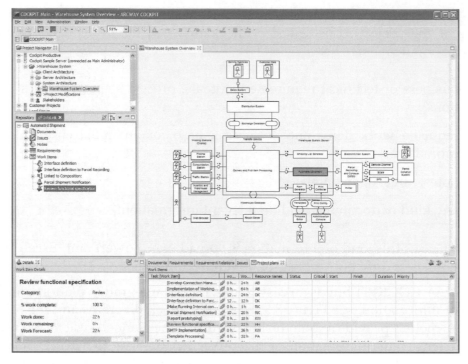

Figure 8.3: Screenshot of ARCWAY COCKPIT, a specification and project-planning tool using FMC

already built and the locations where work has to be done, but he or she can locate every artifact in the system map.

If no system map exists at this point, then this is a good occasion to create one.

8.3.4 Evolution and migration of systems

Large systems can only be developed in an evolutionary way. This requires that a team knows the architecture of the system and its environment. Before it can start to add a new feature, the team has to understand it, as described in Sections 8.2.3 and 8.2.4.

Porting a system to another platform is similar. In this case, you have to understand both the old and the new platform and which platform features the system uses. This can be a very challenging task because often no one can tell you which features of the platform the system actually uses.

Large and heterogeneous systems

The complexity of many systems is not the result of the number of lines of code of their software, but of the heterogeneity of the system components and the technology used. Typically, third-party software has to be used, starting from the operating system and database management systems. Larger systems have been developed over many years, adding new technology without discarding the old. This results in a mixture of technology like programming languages, hard–and software platforms, libraries, frameworks, and so on.

Especially in embedded systems, there is a high degree in hard–and software codesign. Parts of a system are simply not implemented using software but have to be integrated into the system as well. They cannot be modeled like software.

As FMC models use a higher level of abstraction, they can serve the purpose of coping with the heterogeneity. For example, an agent can be a thread executing some code or an integrated circuit, a channel can be a network allowing remote procedure calls or a bus. You can describe the system, being precise about the information processing, without having to decide which technology to use.

Another feature of FMC is the possibility of being precise at one place and keeping things open at another. You will not be forced to specify a system part if you do not want to in this project phase – because no implementation will be generated from the model.

8.4   Using FMC diagrams to support communication

FMC can bring a benefit for your work whenever there is a need to communicate information about systems, especially between people with different backgrounds and skills. The scenarios presented in this chapter will give you an idea of where the effort of modeling is beneficial.

During *meetings and discussions*, having a simple notation for ad hoc diagrams at hand can greatly improve efficiency. Using diagrams minimize the danger of talking at cross purposes although using the same words. This can happen all too quickly when people with different backgrounds are involved, and when crucial terms have different meanings for them.

In *presentations*, you may have to deal with a mixed audience as well. As time matters, you have to use graphics to be more efficient; therefore you need a simple but precise notation which can be understood quickly. Such a presentation should be prepared carefully considering its purpose and the audience.

Finally, *reports* about technical systems or concepts are read by different people who have not been involved in the matter as deeply as the author, or may even lack the background to understand the problem at all. In this case, a quick but precise introduction is required which gives the reader a comprehensive overview of the system, its environment and which problems have been solved.

Training or teaching classes do not have to be as compact as presentations. Nevertheless, didactical issues are to be considered, i.e., comprehensive diagrams offering an overview can be used to let the audience locate and classify details and remember their inter-relations more easily.

8.4.1 Using FMC in interviews, meetings and discussions

How much time have you wasted in meetings where people seemed to talk about different things although they appeared to use the same words? And do you remember what happened after someone drew a simple sketch on a blackboard or a flipchart? When using a diagram, there was immediately something 'to point at', something which focused our thoughts and allowed everybody to be more precise than words would normally allow us to be.

It would seem to be a good idea to be as precise as possible in meetings, and particularly with the notation used for diagrams. At the same time, it should be easily possible to draw such diagrams by hand and use a notation that can be learned and understood quickly.

According to our experience, few people have had difficulty in understanding the system structures depicted by FMC block diagrams, whatever their background. The reason is that it is simple and close to the real-life experience of information processing. The advantage of an FMC diagram is its precision on one hand, and the possibility of leaving things open on the other.

Ad hoc modeling

If the situation cries out for making things clearer in order to avoid confusion, use ad hoc modeling. A large sheet of paper, a flipchart or a whiteboard are sufficient to quickly draw a sketch and give items their proper names. Often, these sketches form the basis of more precise diagrams to be prepared for the following meetings. Figure 8.4 shows an example.

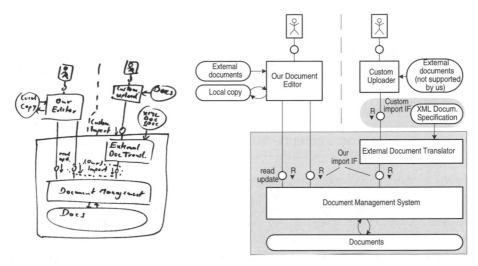

Figure 8.4: Example of an ad hoc sketch of a model and a reworked version for the meeting minutes

Prepared models

Ad hoc models are often the basis of system models and architecture. Meetings become more efficient if carefully prepared, for example, if the participants receive a model in advance which they can discuss in the meeting. Furthermore, they can use a prepared model as the basis for further refinement.

This is the typical form of a prepared model:

- a document of a few pages containing the diagram and some supporting text;

- a slide or an enlarged version of the diagram to be shown in the meeting.

Prepared models are often a good starting point for going into greater detail, thus forming a basis for modeling. The same applies to locating a problem and finding unclear descriptions and, in this way, serving as a basis for remodeling.

Meeting minutes / protocols

It is important to keep track of both the discussion and the decisions taken by jotting down the minutes of the meeting which include the models created, presented and changed. Even if the final project report contains only a fraction of the information, these minutes may come in handy at some future time.

8.4.2 Presentations

Presentations are usually required to be brief. If you want to communicate technical information, e.g., to make the audience understand your proposal and vote for it, what you then need is an alternative to marketing clip-art diagrams and highly technical specifications. On the one hand, you need precision, while on the other hand your time is too limited to explain a complex notation. If you are going to address an audience with different skills and backgrounds, you need a way to be understandable without sacrificing precision. In a nut shell, you need to transport knowledge in a short time.

Before you start preparing the presentation, carefully consider the purpose and the audience, i.e., the addressees of your talk. The notation of diagrams should be quick to grasp and may be introduced quickly during the presentation. FMC block diagrams offer a good solution. If they have been prepared with care, regarding granularity, level of abstraction, labeling, and layout, then the audience will have no problem reading them without further instruction. Therefore, FMC block diagrams focusing on the aspects which are important to you should play a central role in your presentation.

A typical presentation using FMC models may follow a structure like this:

1. The introduction: A system model giving an overview over the system with its environment, including a simple legend.

2. One or more detailed models showing aspects of the system to be discussed or deepened, supported by some catchwords.

3. The conclusion.

The presentation focuses on explaining the system and the chosen aspects using the diagrams. The slides containing the catchwords are included for summary purposes and for people who are not able to attend the presentation and will read the slides later. During the presentation, you lead your audience through the models and explain what you regard as important.

FMC block diagrams play a central role because they show structures with agents processing information and communicating with other agents. As this view is close to the way information is processed by human beings, the audience will not have a problem in understanding them. You can also show what happens in your system by explaining the sequence of actions and pointing to the agents involved. Therefore, you normally do not show Petri nets to explain behavior, except for more complicated cases.

Figure 8.5 shows some example slides taken from a presentation on the Apache HTTP server. The diagrams are the central part of this presentation.

Diagrams should not be too complex. All labels must be readable by everyone in the audience, but sometimes you need to explain a bigger diagram step by step. In this case, you can show the overall diagram and then zoom in on the parts, or you can enlarge the diagram so that everyone can see it while you present further slides, or else hand out a copy of the diagram to your audience, but be aware that they will look at their copy instead of looking at you.

8.4.3 Using FMC in documentation and reports

There are many purposes of a report, for example:

- it allows usage or modification of an existing system by a team;

- it reports the status or progress of a development project;

- it describes the system and the design decisions to allow handing over system responsibility to another team.

According to our experience, a reader needs to visualize the system structures to get an overview of the system, and to be able to locate further details in this 'big picture'. FMC block diagrams form a graphical representation of system structures and should be the cornerstones of the introductory part of a documentation.

A typical report using FMC models follows this structure:

1. An introduction and a system overview depicted by an FMC block diagram, including a simple notation legend.

2. One or more detailed models showing aspects of the system to be discussed or deepened, and explanatory text.

3. Conclusion.

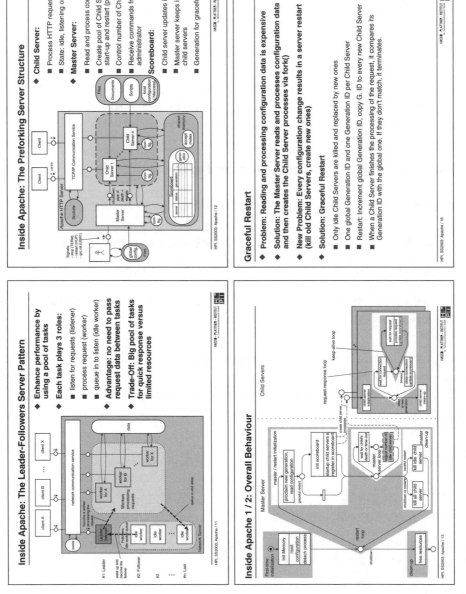

Figure 8.5:   Excerpt from a presentation using FMC diagrams: Inside Apache

The accompanying text should guide the reader through the models. It is a good idea to explain a diagram to someone and keep in mind how you explained it, and which questions your listener asked you for clarification. Keeping this method of explanation in the supporting text will, in most cases, work for other readers, too.

Which FMC diagram types should be used?

Depending on the nature and subject of the report, you will not be able to show everything you want by using block diagrams alone. Some behavior which could be explained in a presentation by pointing to the agents and storages on a block diagram, must now be made explicit using Petri nets. Furthermore, you may want to give a more detailed description than you are able to in a presentation. On the other hand, do not think you are doing something wrong if your report does not contain either an E/R diagram or a Petri net – not all three diagram types are required every time! On the other hand, be open to use other visualization means such as screenshots or exemplary data structures whenever you feel that they will improve the readers' comprehension of the subject.

Example documentation: The Apache Modeling Project

Figure 8.6 shows two pages from the Apache Modeling Project [GKKS04], a documentation of the Apache HTTP server. After a short introduction into the subject (here: a common pattern for a multitasking architecture), a FMC block diagram is shown and then explained in the following text.

8.4.4 Technical training and teaching

The issues of a presentation also apply to technical training and teaching classes. One difference is the amount of technical details and 'know how' to be transferred.

FMC models can help you to explain concepts and serve as an introduction to a topic. They will not help you to teach how to use a tool or which source code to type in, in order to produce a specific behavior.

The task pool must be created at server start. The number of tasks in the pool should be big enough to ensure quick server response, but a machine has resource restriction. The solution is to control the number of tasks in the pool by another agent: the master server.

Preforking Architecture

The Preforking architecture was the first multitasking architecture of Apache. In Apache 2.0 it is still the default MPM for Unix The Netware MPM very closely resembles the Preforking functionality with the exception that it uses Netware threads instead of unix processes. Summarizingly the Preforking architecture of Apache takes a conventional Approach as each child server is a process by itself. That makes Preforking a stable architecture but also reduces performance.

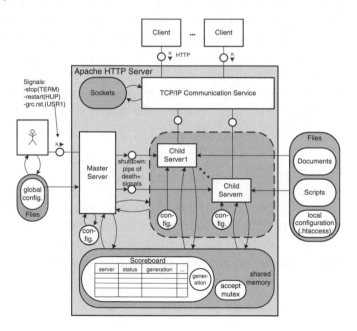

Figure 4.6: The Apache 2.0 Preforking MPM

The structure diagram in figure 4.6 shows the structure of the Preforking architecture of Apache 2.0 and is important for the description of the behavior of Apache. You can see which component is able to communicate with which other component and which storage a component can read or modify. The block diagram for the Apache 2.0 MPM version of the Preforking architecture very much resembles the version that was used on Apache 1.3, however there is one difference: The Master Server uses a "pipe of death" instead of signals to shut down the child servers for a (graceful) restart.

Figure 8.6: Excerpt from The Apache Modeling Project, a typical report using FMC diagrams

The Preforking architecture shown in figure 4.6 seems to be very similar to the inetd archi-tecture in figure 4.3 at first sight. There is one master server and multiple child servers. One big difference is the fact that the child server processes exist before a request comes in. As the master server uses the fork () system call to create processes and does this before the first request comes in, it is called a *preforking* server. The master server doesn't wait for incoming requests at all — the existing child servers wait and then handle the request directly.

The master server creates a set of idle child server processes, which register with the TCP/IP communication service to get the next request. The first child server getting a connection handles the request, sends the response and waits for the next request. The master server adjusts the number of idle child server processes within given bounds.

General Behavior

Figure 4.7 shows the overall behavior of the server, including the master server and the child servers.

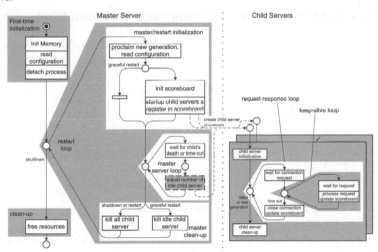

Figure 4.7: Overview: The behavior of Apache

Independently from the underlying multitasking architecture, Apache's behaviour consists of a sequence of the following parts which will be discussed individually for each of the architectures:

- First–time initialization:
  Allocate resources, read and check conguration, become a daemon.

- The restart loop:
  (Re–)read conguration, create task pool by starting child server processes and enter the master server loop.

Figure 8.6: *continued*

Some suggestions:

- Most people can remember simple graphics better than text.

- Do not let your audience get lost in a complex diagram appearing out of the blue, it is better to construct it step by step.

- Repetition helps to keep things in mind; you can repeatedly use an overview FMC model to show which topic you are discussing next.

- Diagrams are a contrast to text, so variety keeps the attention of your audience.

8.5   Guidelines for didactical modeling

FMC models serve the purpose of supporting technical communication between humans. Therefore, the following didactical issues have to be considered before you start:

- the purpose of the models,

- the audience or readers resp.,

- the aspects,

- adequate granularity and abstraction.

8.5.1   What is the purpose of the models?

Every model serves a purpose. The general purpose of FMC models is communicating system information. This is one aspect, other purposes of the models may be:

- a base for discussion

- to show problems which still have to be solved

- to show aspects which are still unclear

- to convince people to support your architecture

- to share knowledge about details

- to document project progress

8.5.2 Who is my audience?

It is important to know the skills and interests of your audience. If you choose the wrong aspects or level of abstraction or granularity, there might be a big danger of irritating or even frustrating your audience. For example, the ERP system SAP R/3 provides business applications running on a complex application server platform. A group of people, such as system users, administrators, application developers or integrators, are interested in information about the system, but they all have different expectations regarding relevant aspects and level of detail.

Communicating with a heterogeneous audience is always a challenge. The proposed structure of presentations and reports can help to some extent. By giving a compact introduction and overview of the system using a system map, you can involve people who have no deep technical knowledge, they will at least recognise the environment and some elements by location. People who already know a lot about the system may be more interested in the more detailed models.

The same applies to the terminology. You have to choose between more general terms (without falling into marketing slang) or specific terms which are only known to a smaller group. Be careful with abbreviations and product names.

8.5.3 Which aspects do I want to show?

Do not try to show everything in one diagram. A good didactical model shows only one or few aspects of the system. Your audience then does not have to look for the aspect you want to show, it should be evident.

Typical aspects can be:

- functional model of information processing
- location of information
- mapping to machines and threads
- communication infrastructure
- pooling, multiplex of resources
- configuration, loading and changing the program code.

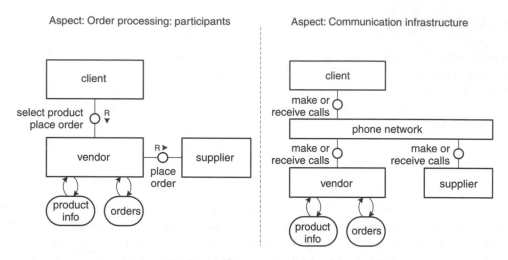

Figure 8.7:   Aspects and levels of abstraction. Either show the communication between
participants or the communication infrastructure

Showing different aspects of the system in different models results in a set of
diagrams. The reader must be able to combine these views to form his or her own
model. To link the diagrams, choose plausible names for agents and storages
and keep them consistent in different models. Furthermore, use a similar layout
throughout the diagrams. These issues are described in sections 9.3 and 9.4.

8.5.4   Which granularity and level of abstraction should I choose?

The level of abstraction and granularity strongly depends on the audience and
the purpose of a model. Do not put too many aspects in one diagram; on the
other hand, do not bore or annoy your audience with trivial diagrams.

Some information which can be clearly seen on a higher level of abstraction can
hardly be seen on a lower level. For example, if you want to show which agents
are sending requests to other agents, you can show it very clearly and precisely
in a high-level model. If you show how they communicate, that is for example
using a communication infrastructure, you may not see the kind of requests
they send to each other as the communication infrastructure just connects every
agent to all other agents. Figure 8.7 shows the difference.

Of course, the granularity and size of diagrams depends on the audience
and purpose. FMC models for presentations are small and can be understood
quickly, while a system map can contain more detailed levels in one diagram

and will be bigger. For example, the system map in Figure 8.1 is supposed to be printed on a large sheet of paper and should be discussed by architects.

8.6   Cost and benefit of modeling

Modeling with FMC requires time and effort. In contrast to models which are close to the implementation, like UML class diagrams, FMC models are usually not used to generate code or other software structures – the purpose of FMC models is to support knowledge transfer between humans.

While code can be quantified by software metrics, the efficiency of knowledge transport is hard to measure or to be expressed in dollars or euros. Nevertheless, if you are the one who has the knowledge, with some exercise and experience you can create FMC models quite quickly.

Creating abstract but nevertheless informative models, is a hard task which requires a broad knowledge of the system. Writing a report as described in Section 8.4.3 is time-consuming and should be considered only if many people are to be addressed or if the knowledge needs to remain in the company for a couple of years. Examples are documentation for end-users, developers or administrators.

FMC models can support the process of obtaining knowledge from another's brain, as described in Section 8.4.1, which may reduce costs.

A rule of thumb: Modeling with FMC brings a benefit whenever:

- more than one receiver is addressed in the knowledge transfer

- knowledge transfer is required at different times and locations

- the technical background and skills of the receivers differ and therefore require a more abstract description

- the unavailability of key developers / knowledge bearers due to fluctuation is likely

- the modeled structures do not change too frequently (which is a typical property of architecture)

- the models do not just show obvious or well-known structures

- it is important to show the environment of the system

- the system uses heterogeneous implementation techniques (for example, hard–and software codesign). As a result, there are isolated descriptions while the big picture is missing.

- there is a need to structure the development which gives some benefit for maintenance (locate problems / responsible persons quickly)

- new developers must be integrated in a project quickly, which requires a low effort to understand the system.

The effort and quality of FMC documentation strongly depends on the audience (their skills, their number): In case of a small project, use a mental prototype, a system map and the meeting minutes to add new team members and as basis for a small project report. In bigger projects, you need to keep the system map up to date, document each design decision, put effort and time into presentation and documentation, as you have to convince customers, consider a project handover and finally handle and maintain a complex system.

An Example

Project handover   Michael and George have finished their project and have to hand it over to a team of four people. Two of them start immediately while the other two will join the team a few weeks later, so Michael and George have to explain the system twice.

Whether they have used FMC models throughout the project or need to prepare new models now, in both cases they can use those models now for a quicker and more thorough knowledge transfer.

Explaining the system without the help of models can be tiresome and take more time, depending on the system. On the other hand, preparing models for knowledge transfer consumes time as well. In our example, the overall effort with or without FMC models is probably similar.

Delays and an additional presentation   Imagine this change in the set-up. Instead of starting in two groups, the team members start one by one and, out of the blue, their boss wants Michael to make a presentation for the board. Michael and George would have to do knowledge transfer four times and additionally create a presentation about the same topic, but on another level of abstraction.

In this scenario, the initial modeling effort pays off: the shortened and more effective knowledge transfer consumes less time and the FMC models can be used to prepare a successful presentation.

Fluctuation After handing over the project, Michael and George leave the company. Three months later, all four members of the new team are hired by a head hunter and leave the company as well. The company now fully depends on written documents describing the system. The worst case would be that knowledge transfer has been carried out without any written documents or diagrams.

In this scenario, any document aside from the code helps. Good FMC models, either used for development or prepared for knowledge transfer will help anyone unconnected with the subject to understand the system, as they provide the overview and some links to dive into the code.

As you can see, even in small projects knowledge transfer can easily take more time and effort than expected.

Chapter 9

Modeling and Visualization Guidelines

9.1 Introduction

If you have read this book from the beginning, you have seen many FMC diagrams by now. Perhaps you have recognized that most diagrams in this book have a similar style which is not only the result of the FMC specific notation. Certain guidelines exists that help you to create valuable and comprehensible models.

Of course, guidelines are not rules. There is no algorithm for the creation of the perfect model and its representation. The problem starts with the purpose of diagrams. Diagrams are means of communication. Before creating a diagram you should know your communication partners, their language, their previous knowledge, their expectations and your own intention. Effective and efficient communication always seeks a balance between referring to familiar issues and relating them to new ones.

There are two different tasks in the creation of a useful diagram:

1. Develop a model which represents your understanding of the system and which fulfils the purpose of this endeavor, for instance, the promotion of an overall system comprehension or of a specific design decision.

2. Find an appropriate representation of that model which is likely to be accepted and understood by your communication partner.

In practice, you may find it hard to clearly separate these activities as modeling is usually an iterative process. Once a diagram is created, it provides input for reconsideration. Questions may arise and the model may be changed. Often, there is some kind of interaction between the author of a diagram and the diagram itself. A diagram may influence its author's understanding of the system and it drives the modeling or design process. That is why the representation of a model is very important in communication scenarios and also in personal use.

Independent of any specific application domain, the quality of a diagram depends on:

- the ability to perceive the diagrams' nodes and arcs as well as their labeling,

- the plausibility of the diagram with regard to its structure and labeling

- the ease of recognition of familiar structures

Appraising these aspects for a given diagram is rarely a choice between right or wrong. There is a smooth transition and fixed criteria are hard to define. Therefore, this chapter illustrates these aspects basically by discussing many examples, by contrasting good and bad examples, and by presenting patterns that evolved over time and that worked in practice. With this chapter, we hope to foster the awareness of diagram quality, which is more useful than any checklist can ever be.

9.2   Increasing the reader's perception

This section refers to a small set of design principles which help the identification of the nodes and arcs of a diagram, as well as their labeling. This includes the recognition of hierarchies or containment relationships as well as affiliations and alignments.

Basically, this chapter is about form, layout, fonts and colors. Yet, most of these principles are more about reducing the mental effort in reading a diagram than considering the mere physical limitations of our senses. This effort may even include a psychological component. For instance, my personal willingness to deal with a diagram is much higher if the layout is neat and the labeling was done carefully. Wasting time in order to obtain a sufficient understanding due to bad layout can be very annoying. Universal validity of a diagram may not be increased by choosing a layout just by chance.

Strive for a layout that is likely to attain an overview of the model quickly and which is easy to memorize and to remember.

I remember two developers discussing in front of a blank wall. Both were talking about the structure of a content management system. They were pointing left and right, up and down at this absolutely empty wall and discussing the interaction of some obviously invisible components. This rather strange behavior was easily explained. Both developers were remembering the structure of a block diagram they knew and they were projecting – in their mind's eye – against that wall.

Often the impression of a diagram is the only thing that lives on in people's memory. Effort is wasted if people cannot even remember the basic structure of a diagram.

9.2.1 Linestyles

Lines are the basic means of representing arcs and the outline of nodes. The weight, color, pattern and corner roundings of lines, all influence the perception of arcs and nodes.

Usually lines in FMC diagrams are continuous and black. Colored or dashed lines are reserved for special purposes. But lineweight and corner roundings are a simple means that may easily be used to increase the perception of a diagram, significantly. The lines used to delimit the outline of nodes should be thicker than those representing arcs between nodes.

Figure 9.1 shows three different representation (a, b, c) of three different graphs (1, 2, 3) to illustrate the idea. Confined to simple graphics, Figure 1a, 2a and 3a may be considered to represent a pile of three rectangles. With rectangles representing nodes, each of these figures would represent a graph of three isolated nodes. Yet only graph 3 has this structure. As the labeling suggests, graph 1 is composed of one node (N) and two relating arcs (R1 and R2), and graph 2 is composed of two nodes (N1 and N2) and also two relating arcs (R1 and R2).

The layout of the variants b and c is less ambiguous. The different lineweight eases the distinction of arcs and nodes. Corner roundings and shadings emphasize the effect.

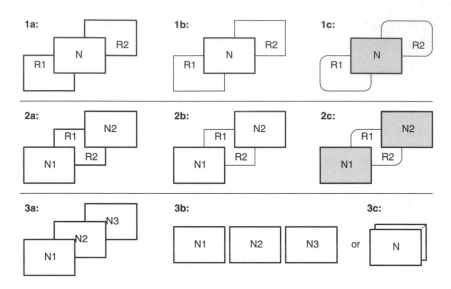

Figure 9.1: Distinction of edges and nodes

What looks rather academic in this context has a real background. I remember a diagram similar to Figure 2a causing some colleagues several minutes of guessing until the correct interpretation was found. It was a UML class diagram with all labels being single nouns and without much difference in the meaning of the class and role identifiers.

9.2.2 Arcs and arc trees

The arrangement of arcs contributes much to the readability of diagrams. A higher perception is achieved by avoiding the cluttering of arcs and by harmonizing the layout. The following guidelines outline the basic principles:

- avoid unnecessary crossing of arcs; arcs should never cross nodes

- avoid unnecessary detours of arcs, the connections between nodes should be perceptible without effort

- minimize the number of line directions (most lines run vertically or horizontally) to harmonize layout

- use corner roundings for edges to direct the reader's eye.

The avoidance of crossing and detours has much to do with the arrangement, i.e., the alignment and shape of the nodes. A little effort may pay off and layout patterns can support the task of placing nodes. Sometimes we have to find a trade-off between crossings and detours. Yet, creating a diagram is also a trade-off between usability and cost (mostly time), so striving for the perfect diagram is the exception.

A reduction in the visual complexity can also be achieved by applying the concept of *arc trees*. Different arcs being connected to the same node can be converged, so that they share a common path from this node up to a junction. For this common path a single line represents multiple arcs.

As Figure 9.2 suggests, this example is especially useful for the representation of alternatives in Petri nets. Apart from the reduction of lines, the concept of arc trees may reduce the complexity of the labeling and contributes to the harmonization of the layout by supporting the minimization of line directions.

Arc predicates, such as for instance arc weight or branch conditions, may be placed once beside the common part of the tree if they are valid for all converged arcs of that section. Predicates which are not valid for all arcs have to be placed beside the separated paths. In the example, one place is connected to five transitions. Each arc is labeled with predicates. The root of the arc tree is not labeled because there is no predicate that is valid for all arcs. The predicate a = 2 is written next to that branch which combines the arcs with this predicate. The horizontal or vertical alignment of arcs also facilitates the placements of labels. Even though both Petri nets in Figure 9.2 represent the same graph structure, the right diagram seems to be more comprehensive and compact.

Our experience shows that arcs with corner roundings are easier to follow than arcs with straight edges. The rounding smoothly directs the readers eye into the new direction. While this seems to be a very subtle aspect, corner rounding can be necessary to resolve ambiguous scenarios. The top of Figure 9.3 shows a simple structure of three connected nodes. Without providing additional information different interpretations are possible. Corner roundings provide this information.

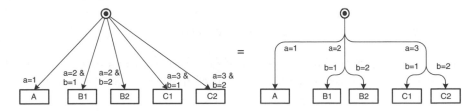

Figure 9.2:   Facilitating layout with arc trees

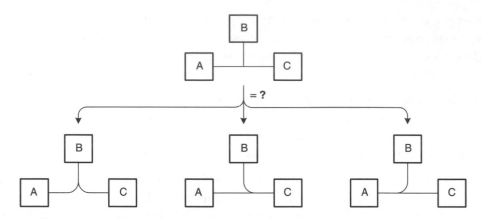

Figure 9.3:   The purpose of rounded arcs

9.2.3   Shape and arrangement of nodes

There are only two types of node within any FMC diagram – those with corner roundings and those with straight edges. Their outline is usually based on rectangular or circular shapes, even though every form which is composed of horizontal and vertical lines is allowed. There is much freedom for design. The shape and arrangement of nodes can help perception and highlight implicit relationships between nodes, but can also confuse the reader. The leading principle is to keep it simple! Some more specific guidelines are presented below:

- Avoid unnecessary variations in size or shape – use simple forms.

- Avoid unnecessary parallel offsets between nodes by emphasizing for instance itemizations, data flow or sequential orders. Alignment contributes to the harmonization of layout and helps perception.

- Alignment can also be used to highlight implicit relationships between nodes which are not connected by arcs as, for instance, similar transition nodes in two concurrent branches of a Petri net.

- Nodes with a short distance with regard to semantics or graph structure should be placed near to each other thus creating clusters of related nodes.

- Structural containment should be represented by visual containment (nested nodes).

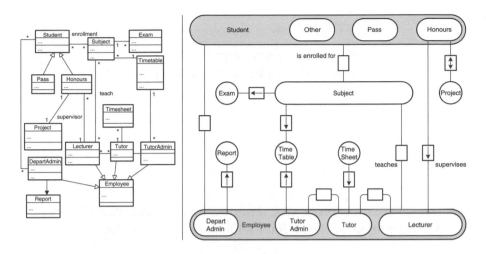

Figure 9.4:   Arrangement of nodes: an example based on [PAC01]

Figure 9.4 illustrates these points. The figure shows the entities and relations of an educational institution. The left diagram shows an UML representation with a typical layout that already conforms to many layout principles, but still leaves room for improvement. The right diagram represents the same structure using an E/R diagram. Visual containment is used to represent the containment of sets. In doing so, the main entity sets of the institution, i.e, students and employees, are represented by the dominant nodes in the diagram. The nodes inside and between these two nodes are aligned with each to other. The nodes 'exam', 'subject' and 'project' are aligned because they represent entities which are directly related to student activities. The nodes 'report', 'timetable' and 'timesheet' represent organizational information. They also are aligned.

This additional graphical structure is likely to increase perception and memorability. Of course, memorability does not imply that anybody needs to remember the entire diagram. At least, when working with the diagram, you should be able to relocate the major components without delay.

Considering the size of nodes, only the entity nodes are different. The main nodes, student and employee, will probably attract the eye first. Most other entity nodes have a rather unobtrusive and almost identical layout. The subject and lecturer are an exception, in some parts for layout reasons (to avoid arc bendings), in some parts for semantic reasons (because lecturers teaching different subjects represent the purpose of an educational institution).

9.2.4   Colors and shading

Readability and acceptance of diagrams can also be influenced by the color and shading of nodes. Generally, the colors or shadings can be used to:

- ease perception,

- encode additional information and

- influence the emotional effect on the reader.

In particular, the distinction of nested nodes can be easier when colors are used. Figure 9.5 illustrates a few guidelines which are discussed below.

- Nodes on the same level should have the same color. Specific nodes may be highlighted to encode additional information or to emphasize their importance, which provides an exception to this point.

- Generally, use one hue and either alternate or increase or decrease the brightness. The use of different colors should be constrained to encode additional information as is discussed later.

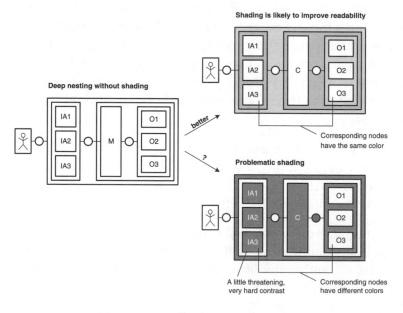

Figure 9.5:   Shadings and nesting

- Certain colors may have a specific meaning in a certain context. For instance, red signals mean attention or danger. Avoid conflicts with those conventions. Usually, pale colors or a simple gray, work best.

Colors and shadings are often used to separate different aspects visually.

- Colors and shadings may be used to encode additional information which might alternatively be added in textual form. Figure 9.6 shows a diagram as it could be used in the development of a system which is to be built of in-house components, third party components and legacy components. Colors are used to distinguish the different types.

- Colors and shadings which encode additional information should be confined to a small number (maximum of 4 colors). If many aspects are to be visualized create multiple diagrams or use a tool to turn aspects on and off interactively. Add a legend to explain the meaning of colors and shadings.

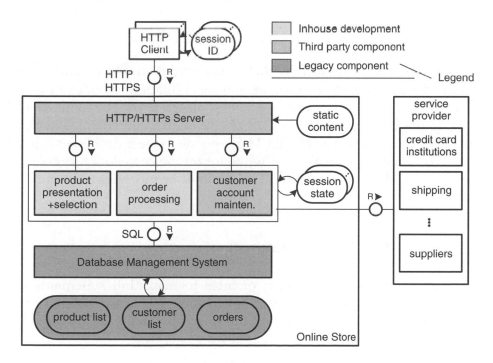

Figure 9.6: Encoding additional information

- Colors that encode additional information have to be easily perceptible. Different colors should also have a different brightness. This facilitates access for people who are colour blind and also prevents problems with black and white copies.

Often colors are used for the simple accentuation of important structures. In this case, bright colors are likely to achieve the focus, while it is also possible to tone down less important parts of a diagram. As arc colors are likely to be overlooked in certain conditions, a stronger lineweight may be chosen to emphasize an interesting case, or dashed lines to tone down less important connections.

Colors also have an emotional effect on the reader. I still remember a former colleague of mine saying "your diagrams always look sad, why don't you use colors". In my next presentation, I had used very bright colors in my diagrams, so my colleague was happy, but some others were a little confused. Generally, it is acceptable to polish up your diagrams slightly, but always consider the addressee. Be careful not to 'jazz up' your diagrams, because people may have different tastes. When considering the presentation of system structures, engineering effort may be wasted if the design detracts from the content.

9.2.5   Fonts

Any labeling employs fonts that define the layout of the character string. Generally, the text should be readable and the affiliation to nodes or arcs has to be unambiguous. Usually, a node's label is placed inside the node. The label of an arc is placed close to the arc. The choice of size and colors is as much a question of design as of readability. Many people have a problem with small fonts and low contrast. Use black or white for text since yellow text on a white background and blue text on a red background, or vice versa, do not please the eye.

9.3   Increasing comprehension

FMC diagrams are more than neat pictures to relax dull statements about information processing systems. They represent models of an existent or future systems. A good model is concise and binding. The quality of the model may be appraised by working through the following checklist:

- Is the labeling complete and comprehensive?

- Does the model pass a plausibility check?

- Does the model represent a comprehensive system regarding the addresses and the purpose of the model?

9.3.1 Labeling

Most nodes in FMC diagrams require a label to understand their meaning. What happens when a certain transition fires, what kind of information is communicated via a certain channel, what class is represented by a certain entity node? There are a few exceptions though, since most places in Petri nets require no label and sometimes relation nodes in E/R diagrams or channels in block diagrams may remain unlabeled. A good label precisely and concisely characterizes the node in the context of the diagram type. Again, there are no hard and fast rules, so the following examples contrast the good and bad solutions.

Figure 9.7 shows two block diagrams representing the compositional structure of an address management system. Both block diagrams have the same graphical structure, but a different labeling. While the labeling of the diagram on the left clearly shows the purpose of the system components, the one on the right creates more questions than answers.

Abbreviations like 'MTerm' and 'QTerm' may have a meaning for insiders, but they are not appropriate for communicating with non-experts or with experts from different domains who need to learn about the system. Abbreviations may be unknown or have a different meaning in a different context. Of course, there

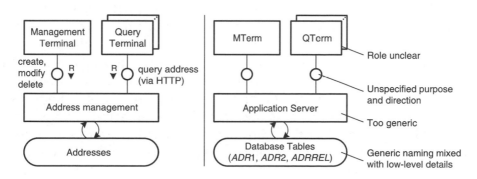

Figure 9.7: Block diagram example of good versus bad labeling

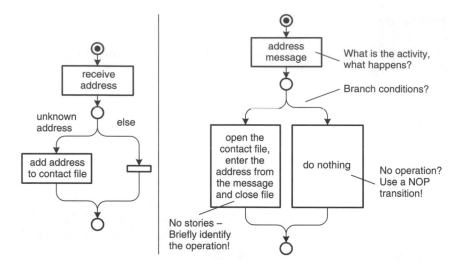

Figure 9.8:   Petri net example of good versus bad labeling

are a lot of abbreviations which are commonly used and often so-called TLAs[1] may be very useful. Nevertheless, abbreviations should not be used without an introduction. Often they may be avoided.

Referring to the diagram on the right, the labels 'Application Server' and 'Database Tables' do not provide any useful insights into the address management system. What is the purpose of these system components? What do they do? What information does the database store or what kind of database is used in the system? Only from the table names may one *guess* about the type of information being stored in the database. On its own, the diagram on the right is completely useless. Its creation would be a waste of time.

Figure 9.8 shows a similar comparison between two Petri nets describing the behavior of some address-collecting component. While the diagram on the left has compact, complete and comprehensive labeling, the other diagram is quite the opposite. The labeling of its transitions illustrates two typical mistakes. In an attempt to create a brief label characterizing the transition in note form, the verb was omitted. Even though the author of this diagram probably knows what this transition stands for, the label does not identify an activity. So we cannot be sure what happens when this transition fires. The left transition, following the conflict point shows the opposite extreme. The activity is described in unnecessary detail and too much prose for one transition. It will be hard to

---
[1]TLA = three letter abbreviation.

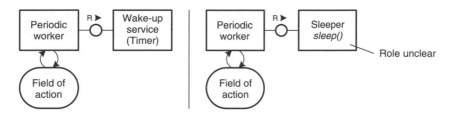

Figure 9.9:   Good versus bad labeling: check the suggested names

remember and difficult to relocate when scanning a complex diagram for the second time.

Names of software packages, product names, development names and marketing names are another source of confusing labels. Apache, Beans, Chicago, Java, Mandrake, San Francisco, Struts and Windows may appear to a non-expert like the memories of a globetrotter and craftsman. So, when adopting a name from one of these sources, make sure that it really identifies a system component. Sometimes these names represent a generic technology, an entire platform, or a conceptual framework. In the upper example only Apache identifies a cohesive system component (an HTTP server). If a system component is identified by a very fancy name, it may be appropriate to look for a name that is more likely to describe the character of the component. Of course, introducing a new name may be a trade-off between three aspects: the publicity of the established name, the perspicuity of the alternative and sometimes political issues. As a compromise, both names might be given.

When re-engineering software products, procedure and method names may inspire the naming of system components. Also in this context, a simple adoption of names may provide irritating results. Figure 9.9 shows a little example of this category: A worker which is performing a periodic task is calling a procedure *sleep()* to communicate its wake-up time to a wake-up service before entering its sleep state. A sleeper would not reliably provide this service.

9.3.2   Checking plausibility

Even though layout contributes much to the readability of a diagram, the value of the diagram mainly depends on the quality of the represented model. Does a block diagram identify the relevant system components and their connections? Does a Petri net identify the relevant activity types and the causal dependencies for a certain type of process? Does an E/R diagram identify the relevant data structures of the system?

Of course, relevance depends much on the personal interest and often domain-specific knowledge is required to answer these questions. However there is a difference between weaknesses in presentation and errors in the model. While rarely an issue to insiders, those errors may create severe problems for people who need to learn about the system. The following checklist provides a set of clues which may help to challenge a given FMC model and may discover possible weaknesses, especially with regard to the compositional structure of the system.

1. Scrutinize the purpose of any system component:

   - What is the purpose of a component according to its name? Be aware of fuzzy components that do everything or nothing (see also the previous section).

   - Identify isolated system components or clusters of system components. System components with no connection (direct or indirect) to the environment do not affect the behavior of the system. They may be removed, otherwise connections are missing.

2. Scrutinize the responsibility for any system activity:

   - For any type of activity that is identified in the model, one or more responsible system components have to be identified. These assignments are mandatory. Activities which cannot be assigned indicate a vacancy in the compositional structure.

   - Strive for a closed system: components in the environment which provide input to or receive output from the system should be visible.

   - Complex systems perform a huge variety of different tasks. However, there is no need to explain systems with only one model, but do strive for a comprehensive picture in detecting and dissolving incompatible statements in the different models.

3. Scrutinize the purpose and availability for any information in the system:

   - Which information is necessary to fulfill a certain task and which information is generated?

   - How is the information obtained and where is it sent to or stored?

   - Are sender and receiver compatible with each other?

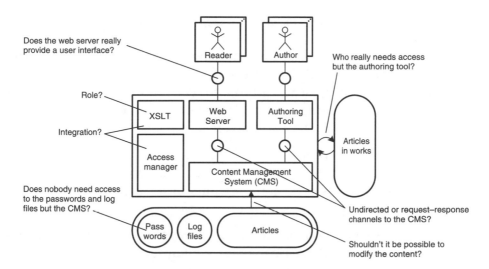

Figure 9.10: An example of identifiable weaknesses

The example in Figure 9.10 shows the model of an authoring and publications system which illustrates a few of these points. Authors may write and edit articles. Readers may request articles via a web server. A content management system is used to store articles which are to be published. The system also contains an access manager and an XSLT converter. However, there are a lot of questions and obvious weaknesses. The access manager and XSLT converter are isolated and therefore without any meaning to the users, so how do they interact with the rest of the system or are they part of some other system component? Also, the represented connections between storages and agents are likely to miss the actual needs namely, who really needs access to the articles in work, the log files or the passwords? Why isn't it possible to store information in the database of the content management system? For a real system, these questions would have to be answered and the diagram should be changed accordingly.

A critical attitude when reading diagrams is necessary in order to improve the models. This also helps to increase their acceptance. In this way, the previous checklist is not only useful for authors of FMC diagrams, it may also help people to work with a model, identify its weaknesses and give feedback about it. This is especially important when diagrams are interactively developed in the early stages of system development.

9.3.3   Component hierarchies versus semantic layers

Layering is a common approach for enforcing the separation of concerns. It is based on the idea that each layer provides a foundation for the next layer directly above it. But the character of those foundations varies very much with regard to the type of layering. Layers of system components are completely different from terminological layers or layers of models.

Figure 9.11 illustrates the problem which occurs particularly in the context of a block diagram. The figure shows four block diagrams which refer to the same system. Nevertheless, only the diagrams in the upper part represent a meaningful model.

Diagram 1a represents a domain model. A user is interacting with different applications which have a database management system.

Diagram 1b shows an implementation model with a focus on the operating system. Each application, as well as the DBMS, which is identified in diagram 1a is transformed into a domain-specific application core which uses the platform services of the operating system. The operating system provides a means for the different application cores to communicate with each other and with the environment. So the interface to user as well as the access to the mass storage for the database is encapsulated by the operating system.

Finally, diagram 1c shows a very low-level model (see also Section 7.2) which illustrates the implementation of the system by programmable hardware components. This model may be used to discuss the processor and the way the multiprocessing is managed by a scheduler.

Each of these models belongs to a different semantic layer, i.e., the mapping between these models involves non-hierarchical transformations (see Section 6.5). Of course, components identified in a model belonging to a lower semantic layer provide the foundation for components identified in a model belonging to a higher semantic layer. Nevertheless, any attempt to map this layering of models to a hierarchy of interacting system components must fail.

The lower part of Figure 9.11 shows the typical outcome of such an equivocal attempt. Block diagram 2 does not represent a meaningful compositional structure. The idea of the operating system communicating on one side with the application and on the other with the processor, is a paradox. Of course, a model may contain high-level and low-level components interacting with each other. But a component never communicates with its own implementation. *It does not make sense to share the responsibility for a certain functionality between a conceptual*

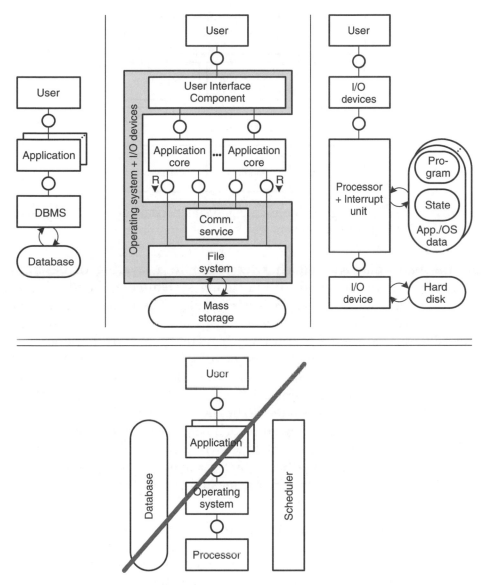

Figure 9.11: Component hierarchies versus semantic layers: four diagrams referring to the same system

system component and its implementation. Also the role of system components, like the database which becomes visible on all semantic layers, is obscured in that model – who accesses the database: the application, the operating system, the processor or all of them concurrently?

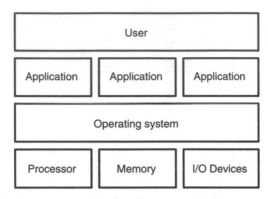

Figure 9.12:   'Brick-art' diagram representing the relationship between components of different semantic layers.

There are many diagrams which refer rather to a layering of descriptions and models than to a network of interacting system components. Typically, confusion between these two aspects arises quite often in scenarios dominated by components and pseudo-components with fancy names. In these cases, it is impossible to deduce the purpose or character of such a component, either from its name or from its structural embedding, even though its role may be vital to the understanding of the system. In these cases, informal (not to say fuzzy) notations as shown in Figure 9.12 may be the right choice, for the strict semantics of block diagrams is likely to be misleading. For instance, marketing diagrams referring to the architecture of IT systems often rely on a simple layering of colorful and labeled rectangles which may not reflect a meaningful compositional structure. Nevertheless, any system designer or analyst should stop at this point and ask for the precise meaning of the representations.

9.3.4   From naive models to abstractions

Each model represents a selection of facts which characterize the subject being modeled. The selection of these facts determines the particular aspect represented by the model. An electrical model may describe the frequency response of an amplifier. A geometrical model may describe the dimensions and the shape of the connectors of the same amplifier. Creating an FMC model involves identifying the relevant system components, the relevant activities and the relevant values structures on a certain layer of abstraction.

Naive approaches are based on a very simple mapping from the subject to the model. For instance, when modeling the organizational structure of a company, people, technical devices, files and folders may be identically mapped to agents and storages. Or when modeling a programmed system, packages, classes or procedures may be mapped directly to a compositional structure. Generally, these naive approaches produce very limited results. More sophisticated abstractions are necessary. For instance, Section 7.4 introduces common abstractions for object-oriented system implementations. Yet, many abstractions are domain-specific and awkward to specify formally. One reason for this is that each model should serve a dedicated purpose which is not easy to formalize. So, instead of searching for the global mapping instruction, check whether a model is appropriate for its purpose – if not search for appropriate alternatives.

To illustrate this statement, Figure 9.13 shows two models of a very simple filter system, which is described by a short procedural program. The layer diagram of this program is shown on the left. It represents the call hierarchy of the involved procedures. A naive mapping of procedures and variables to agents and storages, would produce the lower block diagram. A 'main control agent' instructs the memory allocator to provide two buffers, one for input and one for output. The filter triggers a reader which in turn triggers the file system to fill the input buffer. The filter reads this information to create the data for the output buffer, which is written to the output file.

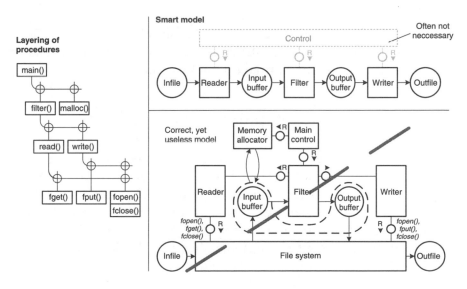

Figure 9.13: Naive mapping to code

The model is correct, but glutted with details related to the trivial functionality of the system. The purpose of this system is hard to discover. A better model may be found when considering the following guidelines:

- Basic operations (with regard to the purpose) do not need to be represented as discrete system components; they may be considered to be part of the caller. Related activities and operations may be assigned to a single component.

- The causal relationship between activities of different system components may involve a complex network of event channels. In particular, when trying to map a call hierarchy to a network of channels, it can easily become confusing. The approach of the 'discrete control loop' (Section 6.2.4) provides an elegant solution for minimizing this complexity. The network of direct event channels between the different components is replaced by a structure with each component being connected to a central controller unit. The connections between the different components are now restricted to the exchange of operational data, i.e., the data flow. The controller unit may even be omitted if the data flow structure is likely to be understood on its own. (Figure 9.13, upper block diagram).

- To carve out the relations between storages and accessing agents, we may abstract from storage managers like a file system, a database management system, etc.

- Structure variance does not need to be shown explicitly in all cases, particularly when the system structure does not change after start-up and the model focuses on the normal operating mode.

9.4   Secondary notation, patterns and pitfalls

Representing similar system structures by a similar layout will help with the recognition of familiar structures. In this context, layout patterns are typical arrangements of node structures in a diagram which has evolved over time by re-using previously used and reasonable arrangements. Their use increases the ease of perception and the memorability of the diagrams. Over time, these layout conventions create some language above the basic diagram semantics, which is called secondary notation. The character of an entire sub-net of nodes may be recognized by a reader as a whole, if he or she is familiar with the layout pattern.

Sometimes, the human ability to recognize patterns can also create a risk. If the layout of a graph structure coincidentally resembles a layout pattern which is used to represent a different type of structure, readers may be misguided[Pet95]. This is no reason to avoid layout patterns. Deliberately obfuscating layout is no alternative. But knowledge about patterns is also useful in order to avoid a few typical pitfalls which may cause misunderstanding.

For block diagrams and Petri nets in particular, some basic guidelines may contribute to an increase in the quality of diagrams and may reduce the layout effort. Most of the points are rather intuitive, so the intention of the following section is to create an awareness and idea of the topic rather than to provide a complete pattern catalogue.

9.4.1 Block diagrams

Taking advantage of similarities

Often multiple diagrams are necessary in order to represent different aspects of the compositional structure of a system. It may even be necessary to represent the same model in different contexts, for instance, in different documents or presentations. However, if the same structure is to be represented, there is no reason to change the layout. If refinements or similar structures are represented, a similar layout should be used.

Figure 9.14 shows four block diagrams to illustrate this basic idea of layout patterns. The block diagrams 1a and 2a represent the same compositional structure. A refinement of that structure is shown in diagram 1b and 2b. Again, both diagrams represent the same structure. Even though all diagrams are closely related to each other, only the relationship between 1a and 1b on the one side and between 2a and 2b on the other side, is evident. So any other combination of diagrams should be avoided when discussing the structure of this system.

Incompatible layouts are rarely the result of intentional decisions. Usually, they emerge when diagrams are created independently of each other. For instance, if several people or different modeling tools supporting automatic rendering are involved. A central (and managed) repository of the available diagrams may provide a utility for dealing with these problems and may avoid or eliminate severe incompatibilities. Of course, modeling tools should support this aspect of handling layout information.

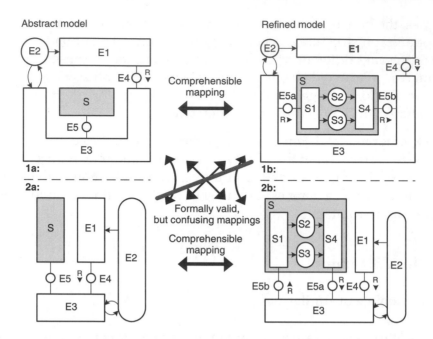

Figure 9.14: Traceability of diagrams

Compositional patterns

The structure of a system depends on its purpose. But, there are generic system patterns which can be applied in the design of different systems of different domains (see chapter []). Consequently there are layout patterns representing these structural patterns. Figure 9.15 illustrates a few very simple, but widely applicable patterns of this category. Basically, layout patterns are based on the idea of working out the control flow and align nodes of a similar semantic level.

Visualizing the bridge to code structures

Much of the effort in developing information-processing systems goes into the development of the software that is required to implement these systems on the basis of programmable platforms. For this reason, it is often useful to visualize the relationship between the conceptual system components of lower-level models and the code packages describing these components.

Quite often, software packages are mapped easily to a single component or a group of system components, which are closely related or which are of a certain

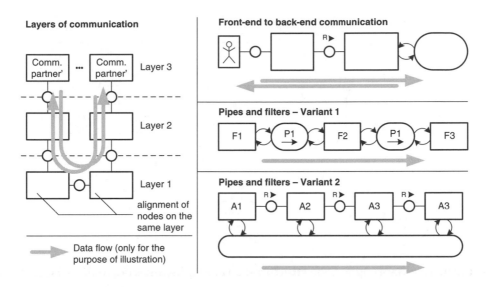

Figure 9.15:   Common patterns in block diagrams

type. Of course, a one-to-one mapping is not always reasonable or possible (as Section 7.4 illustrates). But this section is not about discussing the quality of software structures, but about visualizing the relationship between existing software structures and system structures.

In the case of a simple one-to-one mapping, a comment which refers to the package name can be added to the label of the corresponding node. It is good style to use a font which is different from the one used to label the system components. Shading a group of components with the same color or surrounding them with a connective background can be used to represent a package that refers to multiple components. Figure 9.16 shows a simple example of mapping agents to a package of procedures. Additionally, the labeling of certain channels may refer to API calls which are associated with a specific component. For instance, the queue manager understands messages of the type 'Get' and 'Peek'.

9.4.2   Petri nets

Most of the layout patterns for Petri nets have already been introduced. For instance, the representation of sequences, loops, alternatives and concurrency (see Figure 3.5).

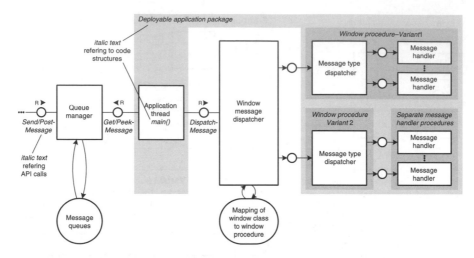

Figure 9.16:   Mapping to code structures: an example (referring to the MFC library)

Compact representation of sequences

Default sequences of actions are arranged from the header towards the bottom of a page. Because long sequences consume much space, a short notation has been introduced. For a simple sequence, successive transitions may be placed immediately below each other – the place and arcs in-between are omitted in that case. As Figure 9.17 illustrates, this pattern may be used to group related actions. In the example, the first block represents actions for order acquisition, while the second block represents actions for order processing.

Different styles of representing alternatives

The representation of alternatives depends on the focus of the diagram and the semantic of the different alternatives. Conceptually, there are two different scenarios as Figure 9.18 illustrates. If the alternatives are considered to be of the same value, with regard to context and semantics, they should be represented equally as shown in the diagram on the left. If an alternative represents the choice between an exception and the standard flow of control, then the standard case should be emphasized as shown in the diagram on the right.

Standard flow of control and exception handling

The representation of multiple exceptional cases may confuse a diagram very easily. Often many of these cases may be ignored in the diagram, but this is

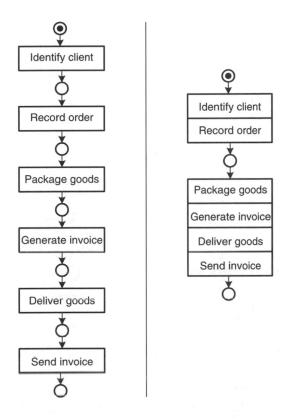

Figure 9.17: Compact representation of sequences

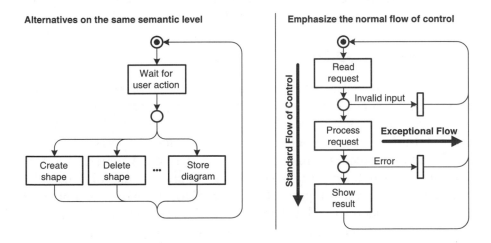

Figure 9.18: Representation of alternatives

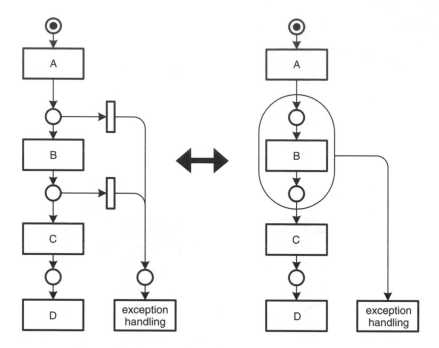

Figure 9.19: Short notation to simplify the representation of exception handling

not always possible. A short notation as shown in Figure 9.19 can be used to reduce the visual complexity. A similar notation might be used to simplify the representation of interrupt scenarios. Conceptually, this short notation complies with the idea of bi-partite refinement, i.e., the surrounding circle in the left diagram includes a place–bordered subnet.

From code structures to Petri nets

As noted in Section 9.3.4, a one-to-one mapping of program statements to transitions of a Petri net is not always advisable. In particular, representing the entire hierarchy of procedure calls is rarely appropriate. Whether a statement or a group of statements is represented by a transition depends on the level of detail and the functional aspect represented by the Petri net. A general limitation of levels in the representation of call-hierarchies will not be useful. Particularly in OO frameworks, when striving for a high level of software re-use, some methods may only offer hooks for further extension, without providing functionality by themselves. When describing the behavior, those simple delegations may be skipped: Simply focus on the operations which really work on the data and which have some meaning for the purpose of the activity being described.

In the case when describing an operation with many agents involved, especially in the case of a simple mapping of procedures to agents, the swimlane layout very quickly becomes confusing. A stack of horizontal arcs is bouncing back and forth, obscuring the essential structure of behavior. In this case, it is a good solution to abstain from the swimlane layout of sequence charts and focus on the primitives of the Petri net patterns: sequences, loops, alternatives and concurrency. Having achieved a clear arrangement of the arcs and nodes, additional background shadings can be used to visualize the mapping to agents or software components.

Figure 9.20 shows an example representing the control flow of a Smalltalk system being based on the Model–View–Controller framework. Such a system is usually composed of a large hierarchy of views, controllers and models interacting with each other. Inheritance and a deep nesting of methods, make it difficult for the beginner to understand the system. The Petri net abstracts from all these details and focuses on the essential operations. At any point in time, only one controller is processing input from the user. It is called the active controller. The active controller is determined with regard to the view that is identified by the pointing device. Control may be passed to the a superior controller when the pointer has left the associated view area, and control may be passed to a subordinate controller when the pointer has entered a lower-level view area. In the case when the controller keeps control, it performs a controller and application specific I/O step.

The mapping of these operation to methods of Smalltalk classes is represented by the background shading. The hierarchy of method calls is mapped to a hierarchy of nested background shading. For instance, the generic controller method *startup* calls the generic controller method *controlLoop*, which calls the method *controlActivity* of some specific controller class. The latter calls the method *controlActivity* of the generic controller superclass and triggers the specific I/O step of the controller. Even though the shading represents a six-level hierarchy (of twelve levels in the actual framework implementation of Squeak Smalltalk V1.20), the Petri net remains clear.

Common mistakes

Probably, the most common mistake is to forget the initial marking of the Petri net. While this is no problem for simple nets with one obvious place initially marked, a faulty marking may cause substantial confusion for more complex nets. So take a little time to check the tokens.

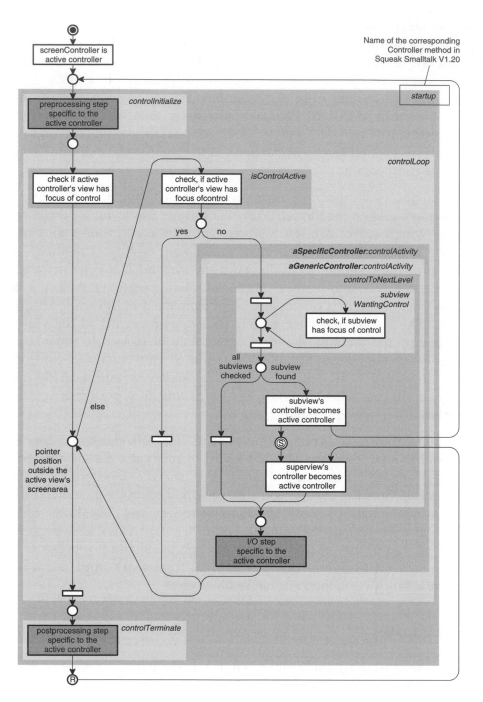

Figure 9.20:   Control flow of an MVC based system [Knö04]

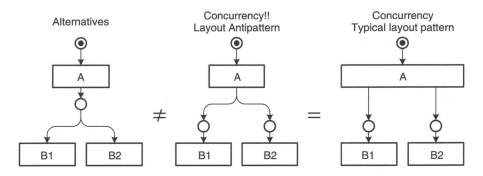

Figure 9.21:   Confusing alternatives and concurrency

Figure 9.21 illustrates a common pitfall in the creation of Petri nets. We found that people who are not familiar with Petri nets sometimes create diagrams as shown in the middle of Figure 9.21 to express alternatives. While experts easily recognize that this pattern represents potential concurrency, caution might be advisable in the context of modeling 'novices'. For this reason, we suggest generally avoiding this layout antipattern.

9.4.3   E/R diagrams

There are no real patterns in the layout of an E/R diagram. But, there is a common pitfall in reading E/R diagrams with regard to the meaning of visual containment. As mentioned before, a node which is surrounded by another node represents a part of the surrounding node. In the case of an E/R diagram, a surrounded node represents a set of entities which is part of an even larger set of entities of a supertype. This is different from block diagrams, where components can be composed of inner components. Referring to the example in Figure 9.22, the node 'employee' denotes the set of all employees. This set contains managers, engineers and others. While the HTTP server is composed of a master server and several workers, an employee is obviously not composed of a manager, an engineer and some other employee.

9.4.4   Annotations

Textual or graphical annotations to FMC diagrams may be used to increase understanding. Conceptually, this can be any kind of additional information characterizing a certain aspect of the system, system structure, design decision or

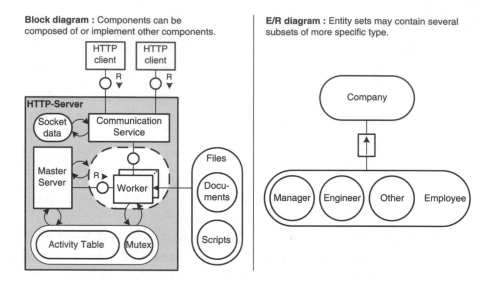

Figure 9.22:   Compound components versus containment of sets

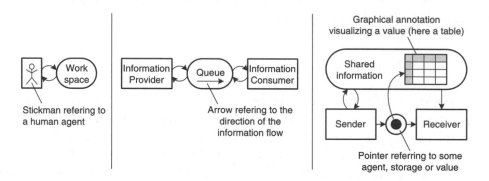

Figure 9.23:   Common stereotypes of annotation

even references to the development process, in more detail. A stickman inside an agent node referring to a human agent; a specific color visualizing the progress of implementation; or background shadings referring to the corresponding source code packages, are examples of those annotations. However, annotations should be used with care as they may supercede the actual diagram.

Since conceptually there is no fixed notation for annotations, any form which seems appropriate may be used. But of course, there are a few common stereotypes which provide a certain *de facto* standard as their are used quite often. Figure 9.23 illustrates these annotations.

While the stickman symbol is included in so many FMC diagrams that it seems to be already part of the notation, the following annotations are less popular.

A queue is a first-in–first-out storage. Very often, a queue enables buffered communication between one or more information providers and one or more information consumers. Conceptually, the provider as well as the consumer are modifying the information stored in the queue – the provider by adding elements from the queue, the consumer by removing elements from the queue. Even though on a higher level of abstraction, such a queue implements a directed channel from the provider to the consumer side, the pure FMC representation of the queue does not show the direction of information flow. By annotating the queue node with a uni-directed arrow, the direction becomes graphically visible.

The example on the right of Figure 9.23 demonstrates the illustration of values. For instance, a location storing a table may be represented by a storage node containing a little table drawing, or a storage containing images may be represented by a storage node containing a miniature of some example image. Pointers are a special case of values. As the example illustrates, pointers are represented by a bound arrow starting with a small, filled circle and ending on the referenced objects. This object can be an agent, a storage or even some value inside the storage. The arrow is bound to better distinguish it from the read and write arcs of the FMC notation. In the example, the sender communicates a pointer identifying a specific table entry to the receiver. However, this type of annotation should be used in a very limited fashion since diagrams can become obscured very quickly.

Finally, Figure 9.23 shows four instances of simple textual annotations. They are used to explain the graphical annotations in this example.

Chapter 10

Relationship with Other Modeling Approaches

10.1 Comparing FMC with Structured Analysis

Those taking only a short glimpse at FMC may be reminded of Structured Analysis (SA) and might wonder if FMC is an attempt to re-establish SA, which many consider outdated. The following is a comparison between SA, as described by DeMarco [DeM78], and FMC. It carves out similarities and differences in the purpose, the modeling approaches and the relationship with the process of the software development of both approaches.

10.1.1 Background of Structured Analysis

In the seventies, Structured Design was developed to achieve a higher quality of computer programs in terms of efficiency, reliability, maintainability, modifiability, etc., [YC79]. It conveys the idea of a development process, where different people act in different roles. Typically starting with the idea of the user; systems analysts, systems designers, programmers and coders incrementally refine and formalize a description of the system to be built, resulting in the software package to be delivered.

With that background, Structured Analysis (SA) emerged as an approach, how the system analyst should transform the initial ideas of the system, the requirements of the user, into a specification, which is appropriate to methodologically design an information processing system. The well-known book by DeMarco *Structured Analysis and System Specification* [DeM78] describes this approach. SA consists of three integral parts:

- modeling and description concepts

- management of the description units

- guidelines for the development process.

10.1.2   Modeling and description concepts

Data Flow Diagrams

According to SA, modeling an application domain reveals a structure of interconnected processes. During each process, information may be retrieved, transformed, transported or stored. A network of processes is identified, with the processes being coupled by input and output of a certain type. Information which is passed from one process to another may be transmitted immediately or may be buffered in a file or some kind of information storage. Those networks may be visually described by Data Flow Diagrams. Figure 10.1 shows an example of a system supporting enrollment for seminars (from [DeM78]).

As we can see, an incoming request ('transaction') triggers the edit and route process, visualized by a circular node. During this process, the request is being analyzed and finally an appropriate subsequent process is triggered, which relays on some data being produced during the edit and route process. This flow of data is visualized by the arcs connecting the process nodes.

Processes are found by analyzing systems built of physical components, which exchange information between each other. Examples of these components are employees, customers, computers or some enterprise. Each of these components performs specific actions, which can be assigned to one or more processes serving a specific purpose or function. The network of processes is what remains, when abstracting from the physical components. Obviously, Figure 10.2 illustrates the same model adopting the FMC notation for block diagrams.

Without doubt, to understand a complex system, it is essential to abstract from concrete implementation details. Nevertheless, the SA terminology has some problems. A process is a temporal structure, which is defined by at least two events: its beginning and its end. Processes should be carefully distinguished from the building blocks of a system, the physical or virtual components

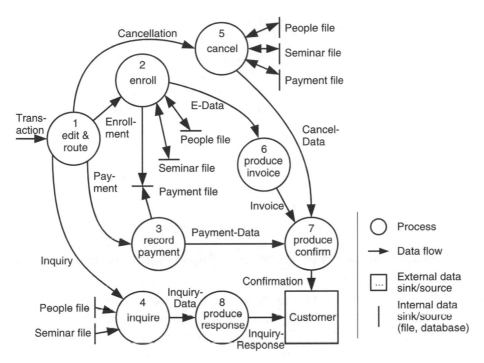

Figure 10.1: Example of a Data Flow Diagram, [DeM78]. Published with permission of Pearson

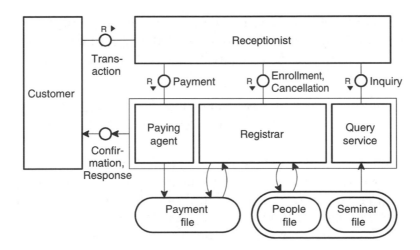

Figure 10.2: FMC counterpart to the previous DFD

which are driving these processes sequentially or concurrently. For example, a journalist may be writing a newspaper story. The process of writing is defined by the journalist beginning to write and finally finishing his story. There is no meaning in saying that the process did the writing. Now try to reduce your imagination to the abstraction of a DFD, that there is a set of processes P_i during which input data Din_i is required, and output $Dout_i$ is provided. To be honest, this is a little difficult to imagine and that is why it may be appropriate to think of a DFD as a compositional structure of – at least virtually – physical components, though SA is not specific about this.

Processes and behavior

Each system description based on structured analysis contains one DFD providing an overview of the system. For complex systems, this diagram cannot and should not reflect all the details in which we might be interested. When analyzing a system, DFDs being created in the early phase will reflect the physical structure of the system. In this case the nodes represent physical components of the system. This might be users or some part of the infrastructure being used. Abstracting from the concrete physical implementation, a logical model is found. Each physical node is replaced by one or more process nodes, reflecting the process or processes which the physical component is driving. Such a transition from a *physical* to a *logical* model, as they are called in SA, combines two conceptual steps.

1. The semantics of our model changes – we are no longer interested in the physical properties or the identity of the system components, whose behavior is observed. With regard to the system's realization, the model becomes more abstract.

2. The resolution of the processes and data flows being identified may be increased. With regard to the system's functionality, the model is refined.

For complex systems, it is usually not appropriate to show the whole functional structure in one single DFD. Refining complex processes in multiple DFDs which are separated from each other and only logically connected by their ingoing and outgoing data flow, is one solution to that problem. The result is a set of DFDs which are hierarchically ordered. Lower-level DFDs describe only a part of the system, but with a higher level of detail. The procedure of refining processes and data flow is based on the idea that processes serving a specific,

```
=======================================================
                POLICY FOR INCOICE PROCESSING

If the amount of the invoice exceeds $500,
        If the account has any invoice more than 60 days overdue,
                hold the confirmation pending resolution of the debt.
        Else (account is in good standing),
                issue confirmation and invoice.
Else (invoice $500 or less),
        If the account has any invoice more than 60 days overdue,
                issue confirmation, invoice and write message on the
                credit action report.
        Else (account is in good standing),
                issue confirmation and invoice.


=======================================================
```

Figure 10.3: Example of structured english, [DeM78]

but complex, function may be decomposed into smaller functions, which rely on each other, but which still are conceptually closed. This approach is usually called *functional decomposition*.

DFDs describe no causal dependencies in terms of the conditions that trigger the different processes, so at some point you need to stop breaking things down into finer and finer pieces, and actually document the makeup of the pieces.

Structured english, *decision tables* and *decision trees* are used to describe the structure of the elementary processes in a procedural, mainly textual, semi-formal way. Flowcharts were considered to be unacceptable to most users and a waste of time. The idea of structured english is to describe procedures using natural language (enriched by mathematical expressions) in an unambiguous way. Therefore a set of rules was defined to restrict the grammar and the set of verbs, objects, qualifiers, conjunctions and attributes to be used. That is why procedural descriptions based on structured english are already slightly reminiscent of programs. An example is shown in Figure 10.3.

Description of data structures

In DFDs each data flow or file is associated with a unique name. The structure of data flows or files can be described either by a textual or graphical representation. As depicted in Figure 10.4, the textual representation follows a simple grammar-like notation, which allows one to express EQUIVALENCE, AND, EITHER-OR,

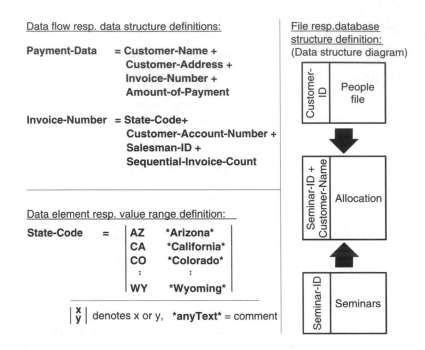

Figure 10.4:   Examples of data structure definitions in SA

ITERATIONS and OPTIONAL substitution rules. Complex data structures representing multiple entities and their relation between each other may be described graphically using *data structure diagrams*. A reader who is familiar with UML might be reminded of simple class diagrams. But data structures do not necessarily describe implementation structures. Data structure diagrams may be used to describe the 'logical', i.e., the conceptual, relationship between the pieces of information held in the systems, as well as the 'physical', i.e., the implementation structures, for instance, on the database level. According to the original proposal by [DeM78] and different from other ERD−like notations, there is no way of classifying different types of relationship. Everything is just a refers to relationship.

10.1.3   Document management and data dictionary

Data dictionary denotes the infrastructure; the tool enabling the management and maintenance of any piece of description, which is created during Structured Analysis. The purpose of this database is to keep track of any DFD, data structure definition, procedural process description or supporting document and to provide access to these documents for the people involved in the development process.

A data dictionary can be anything from a collection of ink-written papers and index cards to some IT-based solution. To ensure the quality of the dictionary's entries, one or more librarians scan these entries for inconsistencies, missing entries, redundancies, misfiled entries, etc. Workflows may define how dictionary entries are created, modified and checked in and out.

10.1.4 Development process

Originally, Structured Analysis was used to analyze the business processes of organizations, which were planning to automate certain areas of their paper-work. Structured Analysis aims to gather and present knowledge about existing processes in order to prepare the design of the intended automation system. The approach clearly focuses on the early phases of a development project.

Basically, Structured Analysis is not bound to a certain implementation methodology. At the time DeMarco wrote his famous book about SA, the implementation of many programmed systems was based on the ideas of Structured Design [YC79]. So it does not surprise us that two of the three design approaches in [DeM78] are about Structured Analysis. A third alternative is roughly sketched, and this is called data-driven design, which shows the characteristics of object-oriented design. A good description of how to 'Integrate Object Orientation with Structured Analysis and Design', for embedded systems, is found in [War89]. However, Structured Design does not end with design. It also influences testing. Structured Analysis defines how to derive test cases from the entries stored in the data dictionary.

10.1.5 Comparing FMC and SA

The focus of this comparison is on the modeling and description concepts. The reason is simple: As shown in Figure 10.5, the process of software design and the management and maintenance of system descriptions are not an integral part of FMC. Of course, guidelines describe how FMC might be applied in practice, but FMC does not promote a distinct process model or methodology. The concepts of FMC may be used in any situation where people need to understand a dynamic and discrete system.

	Fundamental modelling concepts (FMC)	Structured analysis (SA)

Modeling and description concepts	• Purpose: Enhance communication about discrete/information systems
	
	• Multiple system models:
	  Integral units of a compositional, behavior and value structure
	
	• Principles of abstraction:
	  + Free choice of resolution
	  + Free choice of semantic layer
	  + Explicit distinction of
	    * System structure and
	      structure of system description
	    * Active and passive components
	    * Control and operational state
	
	• Relevance of layout & didactics
		• Purpose: Enhance communication about discrete/information systems during analysis to prepare design
		
		• One hierachical system model:
		  Hierarchy of processes coupled by in-/outcoming flow of data with a low-level behavior structure
		
		• Principles of abstraction:
		  + Free choice of resolution
		  + Abstraction from physical layer

Management and maintenance of descriptions	• Not integral part of FMC	• Data Dictionary is the mandatory, central database for managing and maintaining all description units • Guidelines for process integration
Relationship to the development process	• Not integral part of FMC, yet guidelines for a transition to design	• A process model for analysis • Guidelines for a transition to design • Guidelines to derive test cases

Figure 10.5:   Comparing FMC and SA

Modeling concepts

Usually, FMC models are created to capture the system at architectural level [WK03], which abstracts from the implementation details. But FMC is not restricted to that level. FMC models may be used to describe a dynamic system on any semantic layer and resolution that is confined to discrete values and behavior. As Figure 10.6 illustrates, each of these models is composed of a compositional structure, a behavior structure and a range of value structures. For each type of structure, there is a dedicated notation. Obviously, in practice there is no need to create a triad of diagrams for each model. If it is appropriate, diagrams may be omitted and substituted by a verbal description or an illustrative example. However FMC defines no alternative representations from which to choose.

Applying SA, results in a strict hierarchy of models. Analysis starts with a model, which captures the physical entities of the application domain, such as people, organization units or IT installations, and the data flows between them.

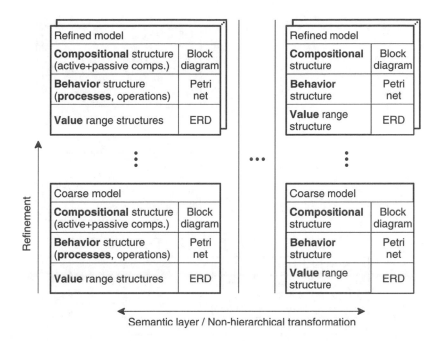

Figure 10.6: FMC showing choice of semantic layers and refinement

Because many of these entities act in several, conceptually independent roles, it is necessary to change the semantic layer so that the logical structure of the system becomes visible and so that the purpose of the system may be described (see Figure 10.7). Subsequent modeling activities are refinements on the same logical layer; so SA results in statements covering two semantic layers as a maximum. Applying FMC, semantic layers may freely be chosen with regard to the purpose of the models. For instance, apart from the physical and logical structure of an application system implemented with the JAVA programming language, one might also be interested in the structure of the JAVA virtual machine used to process the application program.

Logical higher-level SA models represent the system in term of processes which are coupled by data flows. Data flow diagrams, which are used to describe these models as well the physical model, do not reflect when and why things are happening. DFDs describe static structures and, at first glance, they may be associated with the compositional structures of FMC. In consequence, we might be tempted to put structured english on a par with Petri nets and the data-type definitions with ERDs. But there are differences:

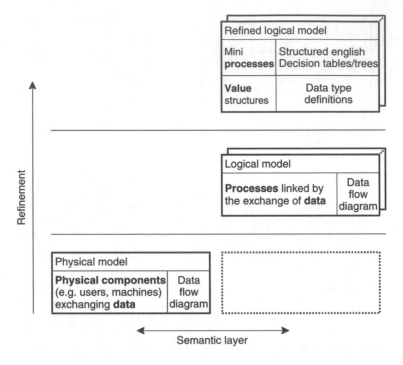

Figure 10.7:   SA with choice of semantic layers and refinement

- If we are serious about terminology, then agents are something different from processes. In that case DFDs and block diagrams express different things. Even if there is a one-to-one relationship between processes and responsible agents, flying is something different from an aircraft.

- Discussing an FMC block diagram, one might ask for the behavior of each single agent. Talking about DFDs, behavior becomes visible only at the ultimate level of refinement.

- DFDs only show data flow (a data flow may be associated with a channel in a block diagram). In contrast to block diagrams, where there are channels to control or trigger other agents, feedback and control flow should not be shown in DFDs [DeM78]. Following this rule, It is not possible and there is no meaning to the representation of components which act exclusively as controllers. (In fact, there are real-time extensions for SA, which ease this restriction and make it possible to represent the flow of events in DFDs [War89].)

- There are system components, which concurrently perform different operations. With Petri nets, as used in FMC, concurrency can be described easily. Structured english, as defined in [DeM78], defines only sequence, decision and repetition, in order to specify the behavior of a process.

- Initialization, termination and exchange of system components are crucial activities for the operation of complex systems [Gal98]. FMC block diagrams may be used to model these aspect based on the concept of structure variance. There is no way of expressing these aspects using SA.

Both FMC and SA aim to enhance the communication about IT systems. SA clearly aims to develop a system and to define a software structure. FMC is open on that point. It may be applied to the development of systems as well as to gain and communicate an understanding of existing systems.

Description concepts

Both FMC and SA define a graphical notation, which is used to describe the corresponding models. The quality of the descriptions primarily depends on the elements, which are identified in the model and the names which these elements were given. This is valid for FMC, SA and almost any other modeling approach. Differences in presentation are:

- FMC comes with exactly one graphical notation for each of the three complementary system aspect: block diagrams, Petri net and ERDs. The decision to develop and visualize an FMC model is a trade-off decision based on the estimation of potential benefits and cost. Textual descriptions may be added, where they are considered to increase understanding. SA offers DFDs to visualize static structures and fosters a textual way of describing value structures and behavior. In contrast to FMC, SA defines additional alternatives as there are decision trees used as a graphical means to express alternatives and data structure diagrams to visualize data structures. Other extensions to SA make use of the ERD notation introduced by Chen. While FMC defines a graphical notation to describe behavior, DeMarco Portrays flowcharts for SA as unacceptable to most users and a waste of time.

- The layout of DFDs is mainly composed of equally sized process and data nodes, which are distributed in such a way that the connecting arcs have as few crossings as possible. In general, the result is a network of very similar-looking elements and a graphical structure that is hard to remember. The layout of SA diagrams rarely has any special meaning. For FMC diagrams, comprehensive visualization guidelines have been defined to ease the pure perception of graphics as well as to identify, recognize and memorize system structures. The use of layout patterns is expected to facilitate the recognition of patterns in the system structure. In order to enhance the didactic value of a diagram, its nodes may be transformed, adjusted and/or grouped with regard to their semantic relationship.

In summary: Structured Analysis focuses on the process of software development. SA models may be mapped to FMC models. SA directs the identification of models toward implementation by refining DFDs until the level of elementary behavior is reached. In contrast, FMC models may describe the compositional structure, behavior and values on any resolution and semantic layer. Basically, the concise conceptual foundation of FMC is independent of any purpose. FMC abstains from different alternatives for notation, but promotes an emphasis on layout and secondary notation.

10.2   FMC and the Unified Modeling Language

At first sight, FMC and the Unified Modeling Language (UML) might be seen as direct competitors. Against the background of UML's alleged or actual dominant position among other modeling approaches, FMC seems to be in a David-against-Goliath situation. However, the fact is that FMC is not meant to replace UML nor can it be replaced by UML. Behind the obvious dissimilarities of the diagram types, UML and FMC show significant differences with respect to both concepts and purpose. This section not only discusses these differences but also shows how UML and FMC can effectively complement each other, integrating model-based communication and development.

10.2.1   Differences in focus

Before choosing a notation, you should first ask for its purpose. This is also true for UML and FMC, which have different backgrounds and focus.

In the late 90s, UML was initially created to integrate different object-oriented modeling and design methods [Boo94, RBP+91, JCJ92]. At this time, this convergence was important to foster object-oriented technology and to strengthen the commercial viability of the emerging tools. While UML has its roots in object-oriented modeling, it has increasingly been influenced by the needs of the vendors of development tools. These companies are the driving force behind the Object Management Group (OMG), UML's standardization body. As a result, UML has continuously been extended to better support tool-based model creation, verification, transformation, code generation, etc. The OMG's Model Driven Architecture (MDA) [Fra03] represents the latest and probably the most far-reaching effort in that direction, see also Section 10.2.5.

This trend fits well to the way UML is used in practice today. A recent survey among software companies [Kel03] revealed that UML is primarily used for code-near documentation, during later software design and development. In this context, UML can be considered the *de facto* standard' it is often claimed to be. The many tools supporting UML appear to be a crucial factor here.

However, when it comes to early development phases and architectural modeling of systems, the situation turns out to be different. According to the survey [Kel03] and our own experience, UML is almost irrelevant in this context. Instead, ad hoc graphics (e.g., PowerPoint, Visio) and FMC diagrams are preferred. This is not surprising since such models are used to grasp ideas, to sketch and refine architectural structures, to discuss them with different stakeholders, etc. Tool-based model processing or code generation is simply not an issue here. Simplicity and readability of diagrams is much more important. [KTA+02].

To put it briefly, UML is primarily suited for *the description of software structures and machine-based model processing*. In contrast, FMC has a strong focus on the *communication of conceptual system structures*. So the question is not which is the better notation, but which fits your needs better.

10.2.2 Differences in notation

The manifold purposes and the 'historical' background of UML has significantly influenced the notation. In its early days, it was quite compact and had a strong focus on object-oriented development. In the meantime, UML picked up many ideas to meet the needs of more users and new markets. To accomplish this, new diagram types and syntactical elements were introduced. Since further specialization is always possible, sophisticated extension and metamodeling mechanisms have also been added. The latter is also needed for MDA [Fra03] model transformation and repository tools.

Inevitably, this development increased the complexity of UML. A few years ago when UML 2.0 [COR03] was still on the horizon, *Communications of the ACM* published a collection of articles where several experts presented their ideas about the future direction of UML. All of them, except one, called for a fundamental redesign, primarily to reduce diagram complexity and redundancy.

However, this did not happen. While there have been efforts to clarify the inter-relationship between diagrams, UML 2.0 has added gratuitous complexity as a result of the standardization process. Instead of dropping or actually unifying diagram types, further diagrams have been added to the collection.

It seems unavoidable that an all-embracing solution like UML tends to be full of compromises, trade-offs and potentially unnecessary options. Consequently, it is not the best solution if you are aiming at one particular problem. In this case a simple solution, tailored for the problem in hand, is preferred. If you intend to cut down a tree you will favor a saw over a Swiss army knife.

FMC has a strong focus on one problem, namely the communication about conceptual system structures. Hence it offers a concise set of concepts and notations, strictly optimized for this purpose. In contrast, UML contains many elements needed for generating code from models or vice versa, to support automated checking against formal specifications, etc. For example, the 'visibility' types of attributes and operations (method declarations) in UML class diagrams resemble the corresponding concepts of popular programming languages. (This influence of programming languages has also been a point of criticism in [Mil02].) Such elements have deliberately been omitted from FMC because they are negligible for system comprehension and would make things unnecessarily complicated.

Another principle behind the simplicity of FMC is the avoidance of notational redundancy. For each of the three fundamental aspects, i.e., compositional structure, behavior and value structure, there is only one diagram type. UML obviously favors diversity over simplicity and offers thirteen different, partially interchangeable variations of diagram. For example, there are four different diagram types for behavioral modeling (activity diagram, sequence diagram, state machine diagram, communication diagram) which can even be mixed (in the so-called interaction overview diagram).

Due to its focus on communication, the notation of FMC is optimized for readability and ad hoc usage. Its few graphic elements can easily be used without extensive notation guidelines and pervasive tool support. If necessary, the basic reading of FMC diagrams can be learned 'as you go'. This is particularly important during architectural design where people often do not have a deep knowledge of modeling notation, e.g., the customer, the non-technical management or engineers from other disciplines. Our impression is that UML's steep learning curve and dependency on tools are the major reasons for its lack of acceptance in this field.

10.2.3 Differences in concept

A comparison of FMC and UML must go beyond the number of diagram types and the shape of graphical nodes. Probably more important than asking how things are depicted, is the question about the concepts behind the graphics. A major difference is that UML, due to its history, has its roots in object-oriented methods, while FMC does not. Describing object-oriented design models is still a typical application of UML. In contrast, FMC does not even offer objects and classes as basic concepts.

When object orientation became popular in the late 80s and early 90s, it helped in the realization of complex, larger systems. But software systems became even larger, so objects and classes turned out to be too fine-grained for building high-level, architectural models. Therefore, people started looking for more suitable abstractions which were typically based on 'components' and 'connectors' [MT00, Cle96, SDK+95].

FMC follows a similar idea with its block diagrams. These show the 'long-lived' compositional structures of the system and help to localize fundamental functionalities, namely processing (agents), storing (storages) and communication (channels). In contrast, object structures present short-lived, complex snapshots because thousands or millions of objects are typically created and destroyed during runtime. Though class diagrams describe static structures, they do *not* describe the *system architecture* but outline the *modularization of the code*. This is a quite different thing since, following object-oriented principles, functionality is often scattered over multiple methods of different classes (see, for example, Figure 7.33). There are very good reasons for this, but it makes it difficult to localize these functionalities or track the control flow.

UML 2.0 introduced additional diagrams and elements which actually improved the notation's capability of modeling above the level of objects and classes. But the related concepts – components, ports and interfaces – are obviously tailored for component-based software development, using popular platforms like Microsoft's .NET Framework, CORBA Components or Enterprise Java Beans. A direct mapping to FMC compositional structures is not possible since UML does not distinguish between active (agents) and passive components (storages, channels) or enforce a bipartite structure. (UML offers the concepts of 'active' classes and objects but these are semantically different from FMC agents.)

Further differences in concept become visible when comparing the meta models of the two notations. For example, the inter-relationship between the concepts of operation, access and location is very specific for FMC and cannot be found in the UML meta model. However, these terms are important elements of FMC because they constitute the conceptual basis for dealing with synchronization issues and transactions, see Section 7.3.6.

10.2.4   Complementary usage of FMC and UML

After the discussion of the differences between FMC and UML you might have the impression that these notations are simply incompatible approaches. But the differences stem from different focuses, i.e., they are solutions to different problems. This means that you can choose from and combine the two languages in a complementary way, depending on the context.

Is FMC compatible with object-oriented concepts?

It has been emphasized that UML is strongly connected to object oriented methods, while FMC is not. This raises the question of how FMC, with its different concepts, fits with object-oriented methods.

Following a purely object-oriented approach, classes would initially be derived from terms or concepts of the so-called 'application domain', as a result of the 'analysis' (OOA) phase. In the subsequent 'design' (OOD) phase, this model is enhanced by refining the class hierarchy, adding cardinalities and visibilities or introducing additional methods and attributes, see Figure 10.8.

This sounds alluring, because it describes a (seemingly) straightforward mapping from things in the application domain to classes in the program code, without a need for any system model. In the case of simple systems, it does even work – the transition from the OOA model to the OOD model appears to be seamless because it requires only few refinements to the classes. However, the seamlessness of this transition is an illusion because 'OOA and OOD objects are inherently different things' [Kai99]. A 'customer' object, in the context of OOA, represents a person, while in the context of OOD it merely represents a data record in your system, including a set of related procedures (methods) to access it. In the first case, removing a customer object leads to imprisonment, while in the second case it gives you some extra bytes of free memory. A method named 'makePersistent' does not make sense in the first context, while it does in the second, etc.

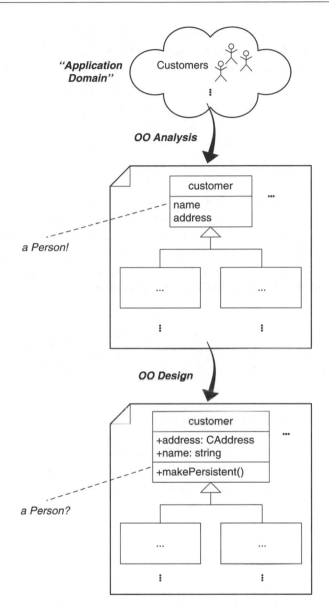

Figure 10.8:   A simplified pure object-oriented approach

This example reveals that the transition from application domain objects to OO software artifacts is far from being as natural as is often described [Gla02]. The problem is that the object-oriented approach tries to circumvent an explicit system model. However, in the case of complex systems, such a system model is needed in order to establish a shared understanding of what is to be developed. So instead of avoiding such system models we should utilize them by making them explicit and integrating them in the development process (see Figure 10.9):

The 'application domain' is replaced by an explicit system model which resembles a high-level, application-related view of the required system. This mental prototype (see also Section 8.3.1) integrates information which would otherwise be scattered over many requirement descriptions and use-cases. Here, a 'customer' object represents *an abstract description* of a customer being kept in an (abstract) storage. A corresponding class 'customer' can be defined, including application-level attributes like 'name' or 'address'. During architectural refinement, additional system models can be created to reflect further, mostly non-functional requirements. For example, a database management system might be introduced to meet the requirement of persistency. In the resulting refined system model, data from a customer object must occasionally be copied to the database storage. With this system model at hand it is no longer strange to add 'makePersistent' as a method to the 'customer' class, see Figure 10.9.

Combining FMC with object-oriented methods allows us to describe what is otherwise only given implicitly, namely a model of the system and its refinements. By doing so, we do not actually avoid object-oriented methodology, but enhance it.

Usage in different development phases

Since FMC is optimized for communication and modeling at the architectural level, it is primarily useful in the early phases of development. Here, details can still be unclear and a mapping to software artifacts is postponed because it is not yet possible, or of no interest at this time. The development, presentation and discussion of the system model is needed first.

UML shows its strength in later phases when a strict mapping to code artifacts is needed. In this context, there are typically many models which may change rather frequently. In order to keep code and models consistent, tool support for code generation or even round-trip generation of models is definitely desirable. In contrast, FMC is typically used to describe high-level, architectural system models. Even for complex systems, the number of such models is rather small, and, due to their focus at the architectural level, they remain mostly stable over time. Therefore, manual maintenance is no problem. (If it becomes a problem, you should check your system's architecture!) In the following, we discuss which notation is more useful in each context of the development process. However, we do not assume a certain development process model.

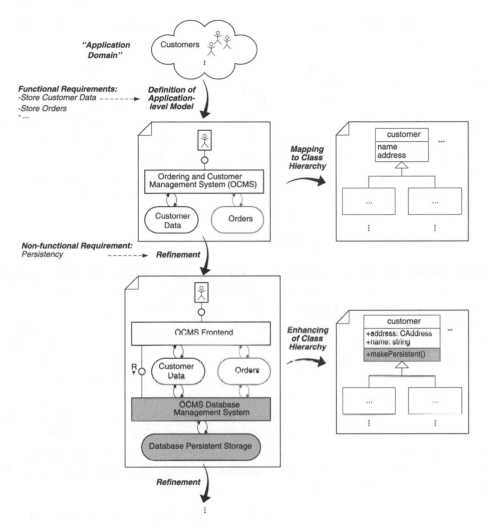

Figure 10.9: Integrating FMC and object orientation

Architecture elicitation/re-engineering

Let us assume that a large system has been developed over a long time and several major releases. Due to missing documentation and/or time pressure, architectural erosion can be given. In this context, the main problem is to redefine the architectural model of the given system and to discuss whether it is still a sustainable basis for future development. Often it is impossible to extract this knowledge from code because third-party binary components are integrated, or code-analysis tools do not support legacy languages. Here, UML is of limited use because the models neither have a direct mapping to code nor can they be generated.

In this case, third-party documentation, manual code inspection or interviews with developers form the sources of information. Based on this, an integrative architectural model must be built. This can be achieved by developing a first version of the model, asking the relevant developers (and other stakeholders, if necessary) for their feedback and updating the model if required. This can be done incrementally until there is consensus about the model's adequacy. Due to the high degree of communication and human interaction, FMC is a good candidate to describe the evolving model and its iterations [TG05].

Requirements analysis / mental prototyping

Requirements are often collected as textual descriptions or UML use-case diagrams are used to show inter-relationships between use-cases and involved users. Though this is necessary to fully understand the purpose of a system, it does not create an idea of the system itself. We have found that FMC can help a great deal in creating a first, application-oriented sketch of the system and in making this mental prototype (see also Section 8.3.1) explicit, see Figure 10.10. In particular, a block diagram can be used to represent the various required functionalities (agents), to show which application related data is kept in the system (storages), as well as the interactions (channels) within the system or between the system and its environment. In addition, high-level Petri nets can be used to summarize use-cases or important business processes, showing which agents and storages are affected. If necessary, E/R diagrams can be used to describe abstract data structures.

The mental prototype helps to verify a common understanding of the intended system between customer and development team. With respect to communication and simplicity, FMC diagrams have a clear advantage here.

System architecture refinement

In order to address non-functional requirements like robustness, scalability, performance or security, the mental prototype must be refined and augmented with mechanisms which meet these requirements. Examples are the introduction of caching, replication or the adding of infrastructure components like a request broker, a key server or a dispatcher. Utilizing architectural patterns, like the server patterns described in Chapter 11, is the preferred way to achieve this,

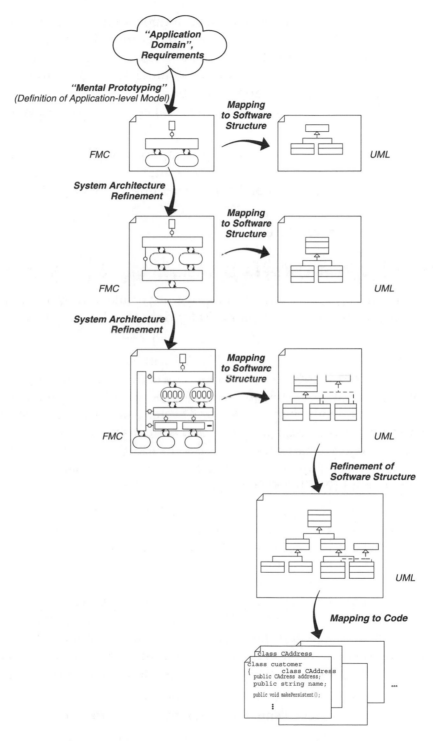

Figure 10.10: Combined usage of FMC and UML

because the resulting models remain valid, independent of the chosen implementation in the code. The purpose of the architecture refinement is to develop a system model which, after all, 'fits' to the chosen runtime platform, i.e., it builds upon the underlying middleware, operating system, libraries, database system, etc. For example, the mapping to tasks, (shared) memory, files, tables and the introduction of synchronization mechanisms can be described here (see also Section 7.3).

Using FMC diagrams (block diagrams and, optionally, Petri nets) allows the architect to incrementally refine and describe these system models and, at the same time, to stay independent of the implementing software structures.

Mapping to software structure

As soon as the mental prototype has been defined and subsequent refinements made during architectural refinement have taken place, the mapping to structures in the program code can be done in parallel. Since object-oriented languages are widely used, this is typically done by defining a hierarchy of classes and interfaces.

The first choice for describing the result is UML, in particular its class diagrams. These are optimized to cover the corresponding code artifacts in object-oriented programming languages. This structure shows a higher granularity and is changed more frequently than architectural system models. Therefore, an automatic mapping between class diagrams and code, as provided by many UML tools, is desirable. UML packages can be used in addition, for example, to group parts of the class hierarchy which realize a common functionality, i.e., a certain agent in the related FMC block diagram.

In the case of large systems, a direct and complete transformation of a high-level FMC model to object-oriented software artifacts is usually not possible. The reason is that classes do not only reflect things from the application domain, but also many technical aspects and decisions. While some classes like 'order item' or 'customer' may be derived from an application-related model, other classes like 'transactionManager' cover architectural refinements such as the introduction of a database system interface. The 'translation' from architectural system models to objects and classes is therefore done incrementally, based on the various refinements of the system model. The mapping itself can be achieved in a defined manner by applying the mappings described in Section 7.4.

It should be pointed out that FMC should not be refined to a degree where each object or class is represented as an own agent, storage or channel. FMC block diagrams should primarily define major building blocks which might be realized each by a set of several related classes. (The high-level agent view and the high-level data type view, in section 7.4.3 describe such scenarios.)

Refinement of software structure

Since FMC models describe primarily architectural system structures, they are mostly independent of the chosen realization in terms of interfaces, classes, methods, etc. Therefore, many refinements of the class hierarchy require additional UML models (mostly class diagrams) or changes to existing UML models, while the related FMC models remain valid. This is particularly true for modifications which improve the comprehensibility or changeability of the software, but do not affect the functionality. Refactoring, the introduction of interfaces (or pure abstract classes) and the application of certain design patterns, are typical examples.

Mapping to code

Finally, code has to be written according to the models or it can be generated from them using tools. This can begin as soon as the first software structures are defined. Herein lies the strength of UML, since many UML tools can generate code from models and even *vice versa*.

The above paragraphs outline typical situations during a software project and describe which notation is useful in which context. However, it should *not be seen as a proposed development process*. Depending on the chosen process model, the phases may overlap, be combined, be passed through iteratively, etc. It is even possible that 'reverse feedback' effects occur. For example, writing and testing parts of the program can reveal deficiencies in the class hierarchy or even in architectural modeling.

10.2.5   Model Driven Architecture

Many software systems are built on runtime environments, middleware products or application servers provided by third-party software vendors. Sun's J2EE (Java 2 Platform, Enterprise Edition), platforms based on the Object Management Group's CORBA (Common Object Request Broker Architecture) or Microsoft's .NET framework, are typical examples. Using such a platform often requires significant adaptation of the software, e.g., by using vendor-specific

APIs (application programming interfaces), tools, languages or pre-built components. The result is that platform-specific details are often spread over the code, mixed up with other aspects. Thus changes to the underlying platform or even switching the platform imposes pervasive, tedious changes to the software.

In order to reduce this platform dependency and the related costs, the Object Management Group (OMG) announced Model Driven Architecture (MDA) as its strategic direction in 2002. This initiative aims at providing tool support for the automatic adaptation of software systems to different platforms, based on UML models.

MDA model transformation

The basic idea behind MDA is outlined in Figure 10.11. The developer describes the desired system as a UML model which is still independent of the target platform. For example, a class 'account' would include the application related attributes (account ID, bank ID, etc.) but not methods for writing account data to a database. This Platform Independent Model (PIM) can be mapped (translated) by a model transformer to the Platform Specific Model (PSM) which contains the extensions necessary for a specific target platform. For example, the transformer could add a method to the 'account' class for writing account data to the database. The mapping to the chosen target platform can be controlled by 'marking' the PIM, i.e., by adding information to customize the transformation process. The resulting PSM can be enhanced manually, if necessary.

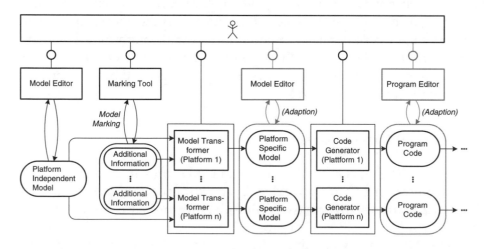

Figure 10.11: Simplified MDA process

In the next step, the PSM can be transformed into program code by a platform-specific generator. This tool can add platform-specific parts to the code which have to be written by hand otherwise, e.g., the implementation of the method for writing account data to the database. Since generating the complete code will not be possible in all cases, manual additions or changes to the software might be necessary.

MDA and FMC-based models

MDA is sometimes touted as a solution which will eventually replace programming completely. Following this vision, software could be fully generated. Instead of writing code, developers (modelers?) would define Platform Independent Models, choose their target platforms, perform the necessary model marking and let tools generate the code. In this scenario, there seems to be little need for models which serve solely as a means of communication, such as FMC models.

However, it seems unrealistic that this scenario could become a general reality, particularly for complex systems. The basic question is: *Can model transformation and code generation fully replace high-level conceptual models and their architectural refinement (as outlined in Figure 10.10)?* There are several reasons why the answer is no and these are given below.

Abstraction is more than platform independency

It is a valuable advantage that MDA removes the burden of adapting code to third-party programming interfaces or mapping objects to a database. However, there are many other technical details which are not platform related but which nonetheless have to be hidden in higher-level models. In the case of complex software systems, there is a significant difference between a system model which is suitable for discussion with the customer and an MDA Platform Independent Model.

Creativity and experience cannot be formalized

Architectural refinement of a system is a challenging task which requires the broad knowledge and creativity of an experienced system architect or chief developer. It comprises not only simple decompositions, but also sophisticated design techniques such as non-hierarchical transformations (see Chapter 6.5) or the application of conceptual system patterns (see Section 11). This repertoire of solutions can hardly be replaced by a predefined set of automatic model mappings, even if transformation tools allow some customization.

Means for communication versus transformer input

As an input to a transformation tool, a model must be formal, complete and free from inconsistency or ambiguity. However, these are secondary issues if a model is used for communication between humans. In this context other criteria like simplicity or layout become more important, see also Section 10.2.2. A model can simply not be optimized for both man and machine.

Complexity at the next level

To put it briefly, MDA uses UML as a high-level programming language to abstract from the underlying platform – just as conventional programming languages abstract from the underlying hardware. Following this analogy, MDA raises the level of abstraction again. But it would be shortsighted to expect reduced complexity in the long term. Whenever complexity is decreased by better abstractions, new complexity is added by increased functionality which now becomes possible – the same thing happened when object-oriented languages became widely used. In order to create a purely MDA-based application, the new functionality must be fully described using the modeling notation, sometimes including algorithms. These descriptions take over the role of conventional program code and also its complexity. As soon as a certain level of complexity is given, efficient means of communication are needed again.

MDA will surely bring more efficiency to software development, particularly in phases where the transition from models to code is carried out. But, for the reasons discussed above, we do not expect it to replace modeling approaches like FMC. These are still needed in contexts where efficient communication between humans is most important and complex architecture refinements need to be documented.

Chapter 11

A System of Server Patterns

This chapter introduces a system of conceptual patterns (see Section 7.5) which describes various solutions for request-processing servers using multitasking. The system was created after studying several server products and has been presented at the Viking PLoP pattern workshop in 2003 [GT03]. Section 11.3 shows some examples of server products where the patterns can be found.

11.1 Application domain

11.1.1 The system

The patterns focus on request-processing servers which offer services to an open number of clients simultaneously.

Figure 11.1 presents an abstract conceptual model of the server type under consideration. For each client, it shows a dedicated session server inside the server. Each session server represents an abstract agent which exclusively handles the requests of a corresponding client, holding the session-related state in a local storage. This abstract view leaves open whether or not a session server is implemented by a task (process or thread). Ideally, a client–server pair are isolated from each other so that clients will only learn from other clients if a conflict concerning access to a common resource occurs.

Before clients get their individual session server, they must first send a session request to the Listener. The Listener sets up a connection between the client and session server and is not involved in further communication between them.

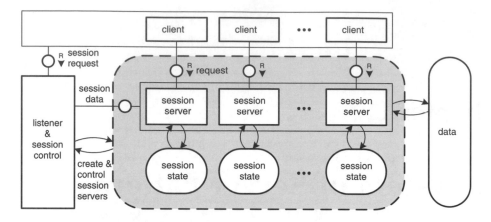

Figure 11.1:   Clients and its corresponding servers

11.1.2   Requests and sessions

A *session* starts with the first request of the client and represents the context of all further requests of the client until either the client or the server decides to finish it, which usually depends on the service and its protocol. Because each session server is only needed for the duration of the session which it handles, session servers can be created and removed by the session controller on demand.

During a session, a client can send one or many requests to the server. For each request the server returns a response. In the following, we will exclusively focus on protocols where each client sends a sequence of requests and the server reacts with a response per request.

In this context, we have to distinguish between one-request sessions and multiple-request sessions. In case of one-request sessions, the session is limited to the processing of only one single request, see Figure 11.2(a). This is a typical feature of stateless protocols like HTTP. In contrast, a multiple-request session like an FTP or an SMB session spans several requests, see Figure 11.2(b). In this case, a session server repeatedly enters an idle state, keeping the session state for subsequent request processing until it is finally removed. If the client manages the session state, it sends the context to the server with every request, therefore the server can be simpler as it only has to manage single request sessions (The KEEP SESSION DATA IN THE CLIENT pattern in [Sø02]), but this solution has many drawbacks. In this paper, we will focus on the server's point of view of multiple request sessions which results in the KEEP SESSION DATA IN THE SERVER pattern [Sø02].

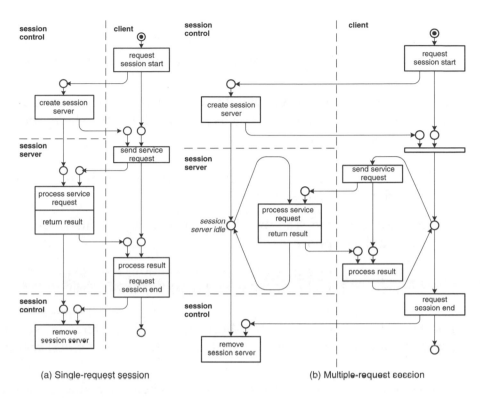

Figure 11.2: Behavior of client, session server and session control

Setting up connections

If a dedicated connection between a client and server (e.g., a TCP/IP connection) is used for communication during a session, the first request is a *connection request* sent by the client to the session controller. This request sets up the connection which can then be used to send service requests and return results. To set-up the connection, the server has to accept the connection request. After establishing the connection, the TCP/IP service creates a new handle (socket) to access the new connection. The LISTENER / WORKER pattern shows this behavior in detail.

Multitasking

To serve multiple clients simultaneously, a server is usually implemented using processes or threads (tasks) of a given operating system. While the maximum number of concurrent clients is in principle open, it is actually constrained by the resource limitations of the server platform.

11.1.3   Forces

There are some forces which are common to all patterns in the pattern system.

Response time   A network server should accept connection requests almost immediately and process requests as fast as possible. From the client's point of view, these time intervals matter:

t_{conn} Connect time. The time from sending a connection request until the connection has been established.

t_{res1} First response time. The time between sending the first request and receiving the response.

t_{res2+} Next response times. The time between sending a subsequent request using an established connection and receiving a response.

The connect time t_{conn} should usually be short, especially for interactive systems. Minimizing the first response time t_{res1} is important for single-request sessions.

Limited resources   Processes or threads, even when suspended, consume resources such as memory, task-control blocks, database or network connections. Hence, it might be necessary to minimize the number of processes or threads.

Controlling the server   The administrator wants to shut-down or restart the server without having to take care of all processes or threads belonging to the server. Usually one of them is responsible for all other processes or threads of the server. This one receives the administrator's commands and may need some book-keeping for the processes or threads belonging to the server.

11.1.4   Conceptual focus of the pattern language

The patterns presented in this paper are not design patterns [GHJV95] in the narrow sense, i.e., they do not suggest a certain program structure such as a set of interfaces or classes. Instead, each pattern's solution is described as (part of) a *conceptual architecture*, i.e., as a dynamic system consisting of active and passive components without implying the actual implementation in terms of code elements, written in some programming language. The resulting models mostly focus on the conceptual view or execution view according to [HNS00], but not the module view or code view. While this approach leaves some (design) burden for a developer, it allows the presentation of the patterns in their wide applicability – they are not limited to a certain programming paradigm, but in practice can be found in a variety of implementations, including non–object–oriented systems.

Because the patterns are related to a common application domain, they form a system with strong dependencies between the patterns: a pattern language. In this paper, three basic dependency types are relevant.

Independent patterns share a common application domain but address different problems. Both can be applied within the same project.

Alternative patterns present different solutions for the *same* problem. Only one of the patterns can be applied, depending on which of the force(s) turns out to be the dominant one(s). In the case of such patterns, the dominant force(s) is/are identified as such and the alternative patterns are put in contrast.

Consecutive patterns. In this case, pattern B (the consecutive pattern) can only be applied if pattern A has already been applied/chosen, i.e., the resulting context of A is the (given) context of B. Such patterns are described in order of applicability (A first, then B) with B explicitly referencing to A as a pre-requisite. This aids sorting out 'secondary' patterns which become relevant at later stages or will not be applicable at all.

11.2   A pattern language for request processing servers

11.2.1   Overview

In the following, a system of seven patterns for request processing servers is presented. Figure 11.3 and the following table give an overview. The LISTENER / WORKER describes the separation of connection request and service request processing. Then there are two alternative task usage patterns, namely FORKING SERVER and WORKER POOL. For the latter, two alternative job transfer patterns are presented which are consecutive to the WORKER POOL pattern – JOB QUEUE and LEADER / FOLLOWERS. As an additional, independent pattern, the SESSION CONTEXT MANAGER is discussed.

Pattern Name	Problem	Solution
LISTENER / WORKER	How do you use processes or threads to implement a server offering services for an open number of clients concurrently?	Provide different tasks for listening to and processing requests: one listener for connection requests and many workers for the service requests
FORKING SERVER	You need a simple implementation of the LISTENER / WORKER server. How can this server respond to an open number of concurrent requests in a simple way without using many resources?	Provide a master server listening to connection requests. After accepting and establishing a connection, the master server creates (forks) a child server which reads the request from this connection, processes the request, sends the response and terminates. In the meantime, the master server listens for connection requests again.
WORKER POOL	How can you implement a LISTENER / WORKER server providing a short response time?	Provide a pool of idle worker processes or threads ready to process a request. Use a mutex or another means to resume the next idle worker when the listener receives a request. A worker processes a request and becomes idle again, which means that his task is suspended.
WORKER POOL MANAGER	How do you manage and monitor the workers in a WORKER POOL?	Provide a WORKER POOL MANAGER who creates and terminates the workers and controls their status using shared worker pool management data. To save resources, the Worker Pool Manager can adapt the number of workers to the server load.
JOB QUEUE	How do you handover connection data from listener to worker in a WORKER POOL server and keep the listener latency time low?	Provide a JOB QUEUE between the listener and the idle worker. The listener pushes a new job, the connection data, into the queue. The idle worker next in line fetches a job from the queue, reads the service request using the connection, processes it and sends a response back to the client.

Pattern Name	Problem	Solution
LEADER / FOLLOWERS	How do you handover connection data from listener to worker in a WORKER POOL server using operating system processes? How do you keep the handover time low?	Let the listener process the request himself by changing his role to 'worker' after receiving a connection request. The idle worker next in line becomes the new listener while the old listener reads the request, processes it and sends a response back to the client.
SESSION CONTEXT MANAGER	How does a worker get the session context data for his current request if there are multiple-request-sessions and he has just processed the request of another client?	Introduce a SESSION CONTEXT MANAGER. Identify the session by the connection or by a session ID sent with the request. The session identifier is used by the session context manager to store and retrieve the session context as needed.

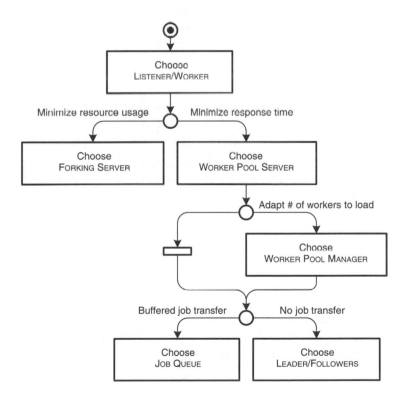

Figure 11.3: Overview of the pattern language

11.2.2   Guideline for choosing an architecture

In the following, a simple guideline for selecting patterns from the pattern system is presented. It helps in deriving a server architecture by choosing a pattern combination appropriate to the intended server usage. The guideline presents the patterns according to their dependencies and fosters pattern selection by questions aiming at dominant forces, see also Figure 11.3.

1. Clarify the basic context for LISTENER / WORKER.

   - Is the server's type a request processing server or a different one, e.g., a streaming server? Should threads or processes provided by the operating system be used, including IPC mechanisms? If not, the pattern system might not be appropriate.

   - Does a session span multiple requests? Then consider 4.

2. Select the task usage pattern.
   Is saving resources more important than minimizing the response time? If yes, choose a FORKING SERVER. If not, apply the WORKER POOL pattern instead.

3. When using a WORKER POOL:

   - Choose a Job Transfer pattern. Is transferring job data between tasks easier than changing their role? If yes, introduce a JOB QUEUE. If not, apply the LEADER / FOLLOWERS pattern.

   - Does the number of concurrent requests vary over a wide range? Then use a dynamic pool instead of a static pool. In this case the WORKER POOL MANAGER dynamically adapts the number of workers to the server load.

   - Choose a strategy to select the next worker task from the idle worker set: FIFO, LIFO, priority–based, undetermined.

4. If a session spans multiple requests:

   - Does the number of concurrent sessions or their duration allow one to keep a worker task exclusively for the session? If not, introduce a SESSION CONTEXT MANAGER.

   - Can the listener retrieve the session ID of a client's request? Then choose central context management, or else local.

11.2.3 Patterns for request processing servers in the literature

For this domain, several patterns of this system have already been published in different forms. A good source is [SSRB00] – in fact, most patterns described in this paper can be found in this book in some form. Some, like the LEADER / FOLLOWERS pattern, can be found directly, others only appear as variant (HALF-SYNC / HALF-REACTIVE) or are mentioned as part of one pattern although they could be considered as patterns of their own (like the THREAD POOL in LEADER / FOLLOWERS).

Apart from books, some pattern papers published for PLoP workshops cover aspects of request processing servers: The REQUEST HANDLER pattern [VKZ02] describes what the client and server have to do to post and reply to requests in general. The POOLING [KJ02b], LAZY ACQUISITION and EAGER ACQUISITION patterns [KJ02a] describe aspects of the WORKER POOL mechanisms. The KEEP SESSION DATA IN SERVER and SESSION SCOPE Patterns [Sø02] are related to the SESSION CONTEXT MANAGER.

11.2.4 The LISTENER / WORKER pattern

Context You want to offer services to an open number of clients using connection–oriented networking (for example TCP/IP). You use a multitasking operating system.

Problem How do you use tasks (processes or threads) to implement a server offering services for an open number of clients concurrently?

Forces

- It is important to keep the time between the connection request and establishing the connection small (connect time t_{conn}). No connection request should be refused as long as there is any computing capacity left on the server machine.

- For each server port there is only one network resource, a socket, available to all processes or threads. You have to make sure that only one task has access to a server port.

Solution   Provide different tasks for listening to connection requests and processing service requests (see Figure 11.4):

- One *listener* listens to a server port and establishes a connection to the client after receiving a connection request.

- A *worker* uses the connection to the client to receive its service requests and process them. Many workers can work in parallel, each can process a request from a client.

Consequences

Benefits   As the listener's only task is to accept connection requests, the server is able to respond to connection requests quickly. Therefore it does not matter much that there is only one listener task per server port, or even for all ports. A client sends its connection request and finds that the connection will be established quickly and that he is connected to a worker exclusively listening to his request.

Liabilities   Although it is obvious that the listener has to exist at the start of the server, you can still decide when to create the workers. You can either choose the FORKING SERVER pattern, where the listener creates the worker on demand, that is for every connection request; or choose the WORKER POOL pattern and

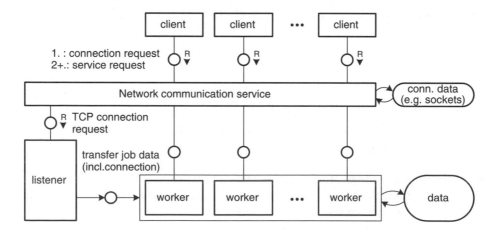

Figure 11.4:   The LISTENER / WORKER pattern

create the workers in advance. Transferring the job data (in this case, just the connection to the client) from listener to worker must also be implemented. For this, the patterns FORKING SERVER, JOB QUEUE and LEADER / FOLLOWERS offer three different solutions.

Response time   There are four time intervals to be considered for a LISTENER / WORKER Server:

t_{listen} Listener response time. The time the listener needs after receiving a connection request until he establishes the connection.

$t_{latency}$ Listener latency. The time the listener needs after establishing a connection until he is again ready to listen.

$t_{handover}$ Connection handover time. The time between when the listener establishes the connection and the worker is ready to receive the service request using this connection.

t_{worker} Worker response time. How long it takes for the worker from receiving a request to sending the response.

Assuming that a worker processes a request exclusively, the Worker Response Time, t_{worker}, will be the same for all patterns in the system. The same is true for the Listener Response Time, t_{listen}, if the Listener sets up the connection after receiving a connection request.

From a client point of view, the response times described in Section 11.1.3 relate to the intervals as follows:

t_{conn} Connect Time. The interval between sending a TCP connection request and when the connection has been established, fully depends on the listener. If the listener is idle, then $t_{conn} = t_{listen}$ is true. Maximum throughput of the listener is $\frac{1}{t_{listen}+t_{latency}}$.

t_{res1} First Response Time. It takes $t_{res1} = t_{handover} + t_{worker}$ to answer the first request after the connection has been established. The Connection Handover Time varies from pattern to pattern.

t_{res2+} Next Response Time. The time needed to answer subsequent requests over an existing connection equals t_{worker} and is not dependent on a specific server pattern.

Known uses   Most request processing servers on multitasking operating system platforms use the LISTENER / WORKER pattern. Some examples are: the inetd, HTTP/FTP/SMB servers, the R/3 application server, database servers, etc.

Related patterns   FORKING SERVER (11.2.5) and WORKER POOL (11.2.6) are two alternative consecutive patterns which address the creation of the workers. SESSION CONTEXT MANAGER (11.2.10) deals with the session data if workers should be able to alternately process requests of different sessions.

The ACCEPTOR–CONNECTOR pattern in [SSRB00, p. 285] describes the separation of a server into acceptors and service handlers. The REACTOR pattern [SSRB00, p. 179] is useful if one listener has to guard more than one port.

11.2.5   The FORKING SERVER pattern

This is also known as THREAD PER REQUEST [Sch98, p. 56]

Context   You implement a LISTENER / WORKER server (11.2.4) using tasks of the operating system.

Problem   You need a simple implementation of the LISTENER / WORKER server. How can this server respond to an open number of concurrent requests in a simple way without using many resources?

Forces

- Each operating system task (process or thread) consumes resources like memory and CPU cycles. Each unused and suspended task is a waste of resources.

- Transferring connection data (the newly established connection to the client) from listener to worker can be a problem if they are implemented by operating system processes.

Solution

Provide a *master server* task listening to connection requests. After having accepted and established a connection, the master server creates (*forks*) a *child server* which then reads the service request from this connection, processes the request, sends the response and terminates. In the meantime, the master server listens for connection requests again. The forking server provides a worker task for each client's connection.

Figure 11.5(a) shows the runtime system structure of the FORKING SERVER. The structure variance area (inside the dashed line) indicates that the number of Child Servers varies and that the Master Server creates new Child Servers.

The master server task is the Listener who receives connection requests from clients. He accepts a connection request, establishes a connection and then, in the case of a UNIX environment, executes a `fork()` system call which creates another task which then becomes a child server that also has access to the connection socket. While the listener returns to wait for the next connection request, the new child server uses the connection to receive service requests from the client. Figure 11.5(b) shows this behavior.

Consequences

Benefits   The usage of server resources corresponds to the number of connected clients. The implementation of a Forking Server is simple:

- Connection handover: As `fork()` copies all the process data from the parent to child process, this also includes the new connection to the client. If tasks are implemented with threads, it is even simpler because all threads of a process share connection handles.

- An idle Forking Server needs very little system resources as it creates tasks on demand only.

- The Master Server only needs to know which workers are not yet terminated as this helps to limit the total number of sessions (and therefore active workers) and makes shutting down the server quite simple.

- Handling multiple request sessions is easy because a worker can keep the session context and handle all service requests of a client exclusively until the session terminates.

Liabilities   A severe drawback of this kind of server is its response time. Creating a new task takes some time, depending on the current server load. This will increase both $t_{latency}$ and $t_{handover}$, which results in a bad connection response time and (first) request response time. If you need a more predictable response time, use the WORKER POOL. This also applies if you want to limit resource

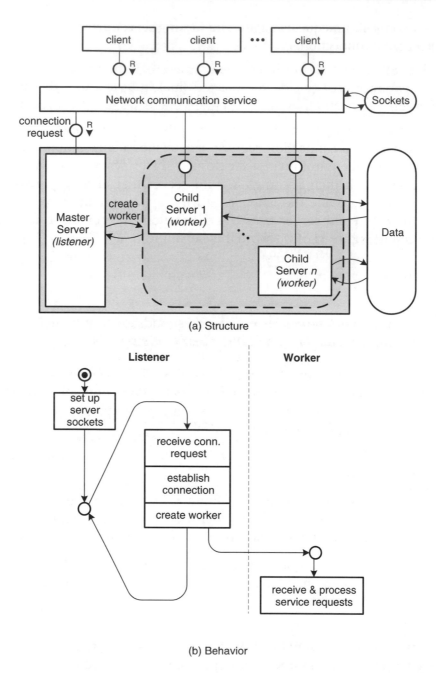

(a) Structure

(b) Behavior

Figure 11.5: The FORKING SERVER pattern

allocation and provide less workers than client connections. In this case you need a scheduler for the workers and a context management, for example, the SESSION CONTEXT MANAGER.

Known uses

Internet Daemon   The Internet Daemon (inetd) is the prototype for the forking server which starts handlers for many different protocol types like FTP, Telnet, CVS – see Section 11.3.1.

Samba smbd   Using the smbd, a Unix server provides Windows networking (file and printer shares) to clients. The Samba server forks a server process for every client.

Common Gateway Interface (CGI)   An HTTP server which receives a request for a CGI program forks a new process, executing the CGI program for every request.

Related patterns   The WORKER POOL (11.2.6) pattern offers an alternative solution, if a short response time is a critical issue. The SESSION CONTEXT MANAGER (11.2.10) is an independent pattern which can be combined with FORKING SERVER, if a session spans multiple requests and it is not desirable to keep the according worker task for the complete session (for example, because the session lasts several hours or days).

The THREAD-PER-REQUEST pattern [PS97] is very similar to the FORKING SERVER. The THREAD-PER-SESSION pattern [PS97] describes the solution where session data is kept in the worker task instead of using a SESSION CONTEXT MANAGER.

Example code

```
while (TRUE) {
  /* Wait for a connection request */
  newSocket = accept(ServerSocket,...);
  pid = fork();
```

```
if ( pid == 0 ) {
  /* Child Process: worker */
  process_request(NewSocket);
  exit(0);
  }
[...]
}
```

11.2.6   The WORKER POOL pattern

This is also known as the THREAD POOL ACTIVE OBJECT [SSRB00]

Context   You implement a LISTENER / WORKER server (11.2.4) using tasks of the operating system.

Problem   How can you implement a LISTENER / WORKER server providing a short response time?

Forces

- To minimize $t_{latency}$, you have to make sure that the listener is quickly ready to receive new connection requests after having established a connection. Any actions that could block the listener in this phase increase the listener latency time.

- Creating a new worker task after establishing the connection increases $t_{handover}$.

- Every task, active or idle, consumes system resources.

Solution   Provide a *pool* of idle worker tasks ready to process a request. Use a mutex or another means to resume the next idle worker when the listener receives a request. A worker processes a request and becomes idle again, which means that his task is suspended.

In addition, the strategy for choosing the next worker can be customized to gain a better performance. The straightforward way is using a mutex. This usually results in a FIFO order or a random order, depending on the operating system

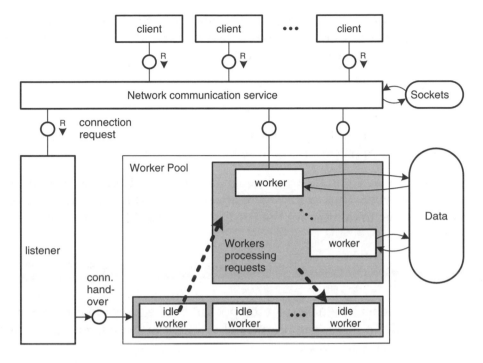

Figure 11.6: The WORKER POOL pattern

resource used for the mutex. Another strategy could implement a LIFO order to avoid paging of task contexts.

The WORKER POOL pattern is a good solution if the server's *response time* should be minimized and if it can be afforded to keep idle processes or threads in a pool between requests. In contrast to the FORKING SERVER, this pattern avoids creating a process or thread for every session or request, which therefore increases the response time (see Figure 11.6).

Consequences

Benefits

- As the worker tasks are created in advance, the time taken to create a task no longer affects the response time so $t_{latency}$ is therefore very short.

- You can limit the usage of server resources in the case of a high server load. It is even possible to provide less workers than clients, which then requires a SESSION CONTEXT MANAGER.

Liabilities

- The worker tasks in the pool have to be created when the server starts and have to be terminated when the server is shut-down.

- You need a way to handover the connection data from the listener to an existing worker. This strategy will affect $t_{latency}$ and $t_{handover}$. The two alternatives ways to do this are the JOB QUEUE and the LEADER / FOLLOWERS patterns.

- Usually, more worker tasks exist than are really necessary, consuming extra resources.

- A static number of workers in the pool might be a problem for a varying server load. To adapt the number of workers to the current server load, use a WORKER POOL MANAGER.

Known uses

Apache web server   All variants of the Apache HTTP server use a WORKER POOL. Most of them use a WORKER POOL MANAGER to adapt the number of workers to the server load. See Section 11.3.2 for further details.

SAP R/3   The application server architecture of SAP R/3 contains several so-called 'work processes' which are created the start-up of a server and stay alive afterwards to process requests. Usually there are less work processes in the pool than clients. As R/3 sessions usually span multiple requests, the work processes use a SESSION CONTEXT MANAGER. See Section 11.3.3 for a more detailed description.

Related patterns   The FORKING SERVER pattern (11.2.5) is an alternative pattern which minimizes resource consumption, but increases response time. The WORKER POOL MANAGER (11.2.7) is a consecutive pattern which provides a manager to control the workers. The SESSION CONTEXT MANAGER (11.2.10) is an independent pattern which can be combined with WORKER POOL if a session spans multiple requests. JOB QUEUE (11.2.8) and LEADER / FOLLOWERS (11.2.9) are consecutive patterns which deal with the transfer of job–related data from listener to worker.

A detailed description of a thread pool can be found in [SV96a, SV96b, SV96c] and in the LEADER / FOLLOWERS pattern in [SSRB00, p. 450ff]. It is also mentioned in a variant of the ACTIVE OBJECT pattern[SSRB00, p. 393].

The POOLING Pattern [KJ02b] describes in a more general way, how to manage resources in a pool. The creation of idle worker tasks at start-up is an example of EAGER ACQUISITION [KJ02a].

11.2.7   The WORKER POOL MANAGER pattern

Context   You have applied the WORKER POOL pattern.

Problem   How do you manage and monitor the workers in a WORKER POOL?

Forces

- At the server start, a certain number of worker tasks (processes or threads) have to be created before the first request is received.

- To shut-down the server, only one task should receive the shut-down signal which will then tell the others to shut-down too.

- If a worker dies, he must be replaced by a new one.

- To avoid the case that a request arrives while there is no idle worker in the pool, it must be assured that a minimum number of idle workers exist. As workers consume resources, there should be a strategy to adapt the number of idle workers and therefore the resource usage to the server load, without reducing server response time.

Solution   Provide a *Worker Pool Manager* who creates and terminates the workers and controls their status using shared worker pool management data.

To save resources, the Worker Pool Manager can adapt the number of workers to the server load. If the number of idle workers is too low or no idle worker is

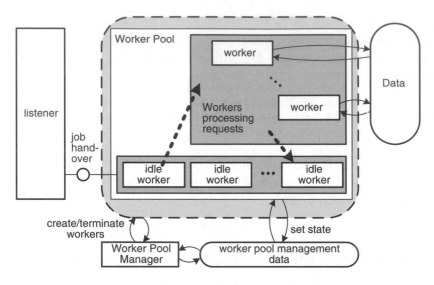

Figure 11.7:   The WORKER POOL MANAGER pattern

available, he creates new workers. If the number of idle workers is too high, he terminates some idle workers.

Figure 11.7 shows a worker pool and its manager. The worker pool manager creates all tasks in the pool. For every task in the pool, it creates an entry in the worker pool management data. This storage is shared by the workers in the pool. Whenever an idle worker is activated or a worker becomes idle, it changes its state entry in the worker pool management data. The worker pool manager can count the number of idle and busy tasks and create new tasks or terminate idle tasks, depending on the server load. Additionally, it can observe the 'sanity' of the workers. If one no longer shows any signs of life, or terminates due to a crash, the manager can replace it with a new one.

Figure 11.8 shows the behavior of the worker pool manager and the workers. After creating the workers, the worker pool manager enters the maintenance loop where he counts the number of idle workers and terminates or creates workers, depending on the limits. The workers set their current state information in the worker pool management data.

Do not implement the WORKER POOL MANAGER in the same task as the listener, or you will get the same problems as with the Forking Server because creating a new process may take some time which may increase the listener latency time dramatically.

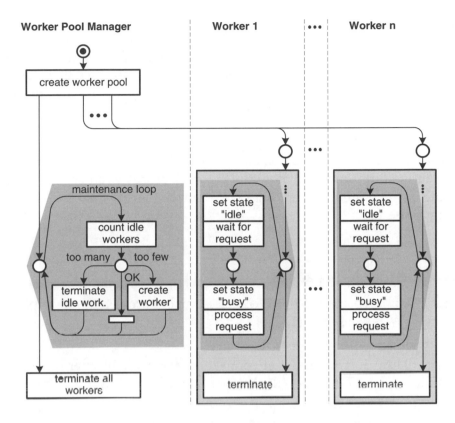

Figure 11.8: The WORKER POOL MANAGER pattern: behavior

Consequences

Benefits The WORKER POOL MANAGER takes care of the workers and makes it easier to shut-down a server in a well–defined way. By constantly monitoring the status of the workers, it helps to increase the stability of the server. If it controls the number of workers, depending on the current server load, it helps to react to sudden changes in the server load and still keeps resource usage low.

Liabilities A worker now has to update its state entry in the worker pool management data storage whenever it enters another phase. This storage should be a shared memory. It is important to avoid blocking the workers while they update their state.

The Worker Pool Manager is an additional task which consumes resources as it has to run continuously.

Known uses

Apache HTTP server   All variants of Apache have a dedicated process for worker pool management. Only the Windows version has a static worker pool while all other variants let the worker pool manager adapt the number of workers in the pool to the current server load.

SAP R/3 Dispatcher   The Dispatcher in an R/3 system manages the worker pool. It starts, shuts down and monitors the work processes and can even change their role in the system, depending on the current server load and the type of pending requests.

11.2.8   The JOB QUEUE pattern

Context   You have applied the WORKER POOL pattern (11.2.6) to implement a LISTENER / WORKER server (11.2.4) .

Problem   How do you handover connection data from listener to worker in a WORKER POOL server and keep the listener latency time low?

Forces

- To decrease $t_{latency}$, the listener should not have to wait for a worker to fetch a new job. This happens when the listener has just established a connection to the client and needs to handover the connection data to a worker.

- Switching tasks takes some time.

- Handing over connection handles or sockets is not possible with operating system processes.

Solution   Provide a *Job Queue* between the listener and the idle worker. The listener pushes a new job, the connection data, into the queue. The idle worker next in line fetches a job from the queue, reads the service request using the connection, processes it and sends a response back to the client.

One or many listeners have access to the network sockets, either one listener per socket or one for all, as shown in Figure 11.9. Instead of creating a worker task

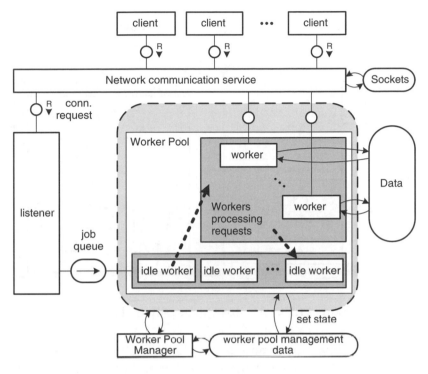

Figure 11.9: The JOB QUEUE pattern

(like the FORKING SERVER), he puts the connection data into the job queue and waits for the next connection request, see Figure 11.10. All idle workers wait for a job in the queue. The first one to fetch a job waits for and processes service requests on that connection. After that, it becomes idle again and waits for the next job in the queue.

Consequences

Benefits

- The listener just has to push a job into a queue and then return to listen again. The listener latency time $t_{latency}$ is therefore low.

- The queue allows for a static number of workers in the pool. If all workers are busy, the listener still can handle connection requests and put new jobs into the queue.

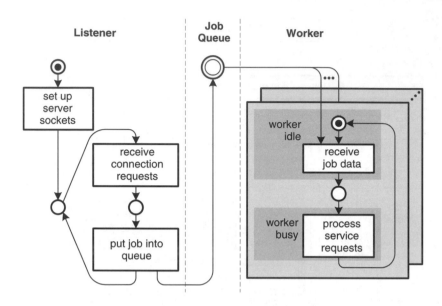

Figure 11.10:   The JOB QUEUE pattern: behavior

Liabilities   The job handover time $t_{handover}$ is not optimal as the operating system has to switch tasks between listener, worker and queue mutex. When using operating system processes, the JOB QUEUE is not applicable, as there is no way to transfer a socket file descriptor (corresponding to the connection to the client) between two processes. In both cases, use the LEADER / FOLLOWERS pattern.

Known uses

Apache web server   The Windows version (since Apache 1.3) and the WinNT variant, implement the JOB QUEUE with a fixed number of worker threads. The worker variant uses a Job Queue on thread level (inside each process) while the processes concurrently apply for the server sockets using a mutex (Section 11.2.1).

SAP R/3   On each application server of an R/3 system, requests are placed into a queue. These requests are removed from the queue by the work processes for job processing, see Section 11.3.3.

Related patterns   JOB QUEUE is applicable as a consecutive pattern to the WORKER POOL pattern (11.2.6) . LEADER / FOLLOWERS (11.2.9) is an alternative pattern which does not introduce a queue and avoids the transfer of job–related data between tasks.

The HALF-SYNC / HALF REACTIVE pattern in [SSRB00, p. 440] describes the mechanism to decouple the listener (asynchronous service, reacting to network events) from the workers (synchronous services) using a message queue combined with the thread pool variant of the ACTIVE OBJECT pattern [SSRB00, p. 393]. A description of the Thread Pool with JOB QUEUE can be found in [SV96a, SV96b, SV96c], including an evaluation of some implementation variants (C, C++ and CORBA).

Example code

This example only shows the code executed in the listener and worker threads. The creation of the threads and the queue is not shown here. The job queue transports the file descriptor of the connection socket to the workers and servers as a means of selecting the next worker.

Listener thread

```
while(TRUE) {
  [...]
  /* wait for connection request  */
  NewSocket = accept(ServerSocket,...);
  /* put job into job queue */
  queue_push(job_queue,~NewSocket);
  }
```

Worker thread

```
while (TRUE) {
  /* idle worker: wait for job */
  scoreboard[myslot].status = IDLE;
  [...]
  ConnSocket = queue_pop(job_queue);
  /* worker: process request */
  scoreboard[myslot].status = BUSY;
  process_request(ConnSocket);
  }
```

11.2.9 The LEADER / FOLLOWERS pattern

Context You have applied the WORKER POOL pattern (11.2.6) to implement a LISTENER / WORKER server (11.2.4) .

Problem How do you handover connection data from listener to worker in a WORKER POOL server using operating system processes? How do you keep the handover time low?

Forces

- To access a new connection to the client, a task has to use a file descriptor which is bound to the process. It is not possible to transfer a file descriptor between processes.

- Switching tasks (processes or threads) between listener and worker increases $t_{handover}$.

Solution Let the listener process the service request himself by changing his role to 'worker' after receiving a connection request. The idle worker next in line becomes the new listener while the old listener reads the service request, processes it and sends a response back to the client.

All tasks in the worker pool transmute from listener to worker to idle worker, eliminating the need for a job queue. Using a mutex, the idle workers (the *followers*) try to become the listener (the *leader*). After receiving a connection request, the listener establishes the connection, releases the mutex and becomes a worker, processing the service request he then receives. Afterwards, he becomes an idle worker and tries to get the mutex to become the leader again. Hence, there is no need to transport information about the connection as the listener transmutes into a worker task, keeping this information.

Figure 11.11 shows the structure. The processes or threads in the Worker Pool have three different states: worker, idle worker and listener. The listener is the one to react to connection requests, while workers and idle workers process service requests or wait for new jobs, respectively.

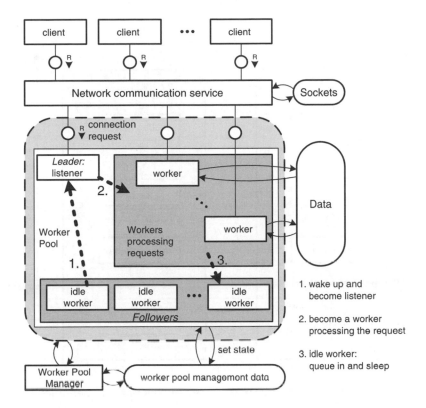

Figure 11.11: The LEADER / FOLLOWERS pattern

The corresponding dynamics are shown in Figure 11.12. Initially, all tasks of the pool are idle workers. Listener selection is done by a task acquiring the mutex which is released as soon as the listener changes his role to become a worker.

Consequences

Benefits   The listener changes his role just by executing the worker's code. This keeps $t_{handover}$ very low as all information remains in this task. As the file descriptors needed to get access to the connection to the clients do not leave the task, the LEADER / FOLLOWERS pattern enables the use of operating system processes to implement the WORKER POOL pattern.

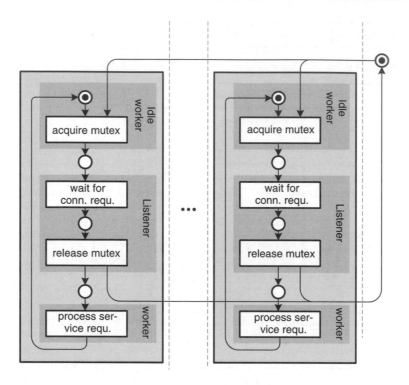

Figure 11.12:   The LEADER / FOLLOWERS pattern: behavior

Liabilities   The election of the next listener is handled via a mutex or a similar mechanism. This requires a task switch and leads to a non-optimal $t_{latency}$. The LEADER / FOLLOWERS pattern avoids transferring job-related data, but introduces the problem of dynamically changing the role of a process or thread. For example, the server sockets must be accessible to all workers to allow each of them to be the listener. Both listener and worker functionality must be implemented inside one task.

Known uses

Apache web server   A very prominent user of the LEADER / FOLLOWERS pattern is the preforking variant of the Apache HTTP server (see Section 11.3.2).

Call center   In a customer support center, an employee has to respond to customers' support requests. The customer's call will be received by the next available employee.

Taxi stands   Taxis form a queue at an airport or a train station. The taxi at the top of the queue gets the next customers, while the others have to wait.

Related patterns   LEADER / FOLLOWERS is applicable as consecutive pattern to the WORKER POOL pattern (11.2.6). JOB QUEUE (11.2.8) is an alternative pattern which uses a queue for job transfer between tasks with static roles.

The LEADER / FOLLOWERS pattern was originally described in [SSRB00, p. 447].

Example code

```
while (1) {
  /* Become idle worker */
  scoreboard[myslot].status = IDLE;
  [...]
  acquire_mutex(accept_mutex);
  /*  Got mutex! Now I'm Listener! */
  scoreboard[myslot].status = LISTENING;
  newSocket = accept(ServerSocket,...);
  [...]
  /* Become worker ... */
  release_mutex(accept_mutex);
  /* ... and process request */
  scoreboard[myslot].status = BUSY;
  process_request(NewSocket);
  }
```

11.2.10   The SESSION CONTEXT MANAGER pattern

Context   You implement a LISTENER / WORKER server (11.2.4) for multiple-request sessions.

Problem   If a worker processes service requests from different clients and a session can contain multiple requests, how does a worker get the session context data for his current service request?

Forces

Keeping session context data within a worker can be a problem:

- If a worker task is assigned exclusively for one session, it is unable to handle requests from other clients. This is usually a waste of resources and interferes with the goal of limiting the number of workers.

- You have to consider that the connection to the client may be interrupted during the session, without terminating the session. The same applies to the worker task which can die unexpectedly. Therefore you might need to save and resume a session state.

Solution   Introduce a *session context manager*. Identify the session by the connection or by a session ID sent with the request. The session identifier is used by the session context manager to store and retrieve the session context as needed.

This is a specialized variant of the MEMENTO pattern [GHJV95]. Figure 11.13(a) shows a solution using a central session context manager. Each worker has a local storage for a session context. Before he processes a request, he asks the context manager to retrieve the session context corresponding to the client's session, using the session ID extracted from the request. After processing the request, he asks the context manager to store the altered session context. In the

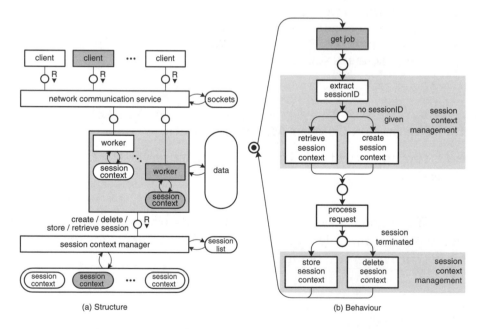

Figure 11.13:   The Session Context Manager pattern

case of a new session, he has to create a new session context and assign a session ID to it. In the case of the last request of a session, the worker has to delete the session context. The session context shaded grey in Figure 11.13(a) belongs to the grey client. The grey worker currently processes a request of this client and works on a copy of its session context. Figure 11.13(b) shows how to extend the behavior of the worker to support session context management.

Variants CENTRAL SESSION CONTEXT MANAGER. There is a single context manager for all tasks. If, for example, the session is bound to the connection, the listener not only reacts to connection requests but also to requests on open connections. The functionality of the session context manager can then be included in the listener.

LOCAL SESSION CONTEXT MANAGER. Each worker manages the sessions and the session list. The functionality of the session context manager in Figure 11.13(a) is then included in every worker task. The storage for the session contexts is shared between all workers.

Consequences

Benefits

- Any worker can process a request in its session context. This enables an efficient usage of workers, especially in a WORKER POOL server.

- If the session ID is sent with every request, the connection can be interrupted during the session. This is useful for long sessions (from a few minutes to several days).

- Using a dedicated context manager helps to separate the request-related and context-related aspects of request processing. For each request to be processed, session context management requires a sequence of: (1) retrieving (creating) a session context; (2) job processing; and (3) saving (deleting) the context.

Liabilities

- A client must store its session ID and send it with every service request.

- A garbage collection strategy might be needed to remove session contexts of 'orphan' sessions.

- Session context storage and retrieval increases the response time.

Known uses

SAP R/3   Each application server of an SAP R/3 system contains workers, each of them having their own local session context manager (the so-called taskhandler, see Section 11.3.2).

CORBA portable object adapter   CORBA–based servers can use objects (not tasks) as workers similar to a WORKER POOL. In such configurations the so-called object adapters play the role of session context managers, see Section 11.3.4.

CGI applications   An HTTP server starts a new CGI program for every request, like the FORKING SERVER. The CGI program extracts the session ID from the request (for example by reading a cookie) and then gets the session context from a file or database.

Related patterns   The pattern is consecutive to FORKING SERVER (11.2.5) or WORKER POOL (11.2.6). To realize access to session contexts of workers, the MEMENTO pattern [GHJV95] could be used. In the case of local context management, the TEMPLATE METHOD [GHJV95] could be applied to enforce the retrieve–process–save sequence for each request. The KEEP SESSION DATA IN SERVER and SESSION SCOPE Patterns [Sø02], describe session management in a more general context.

11.3   Example applications

11.3.1   Internet Daemon

The Internet Daemon (inetd) is a typical representative of the FORKING SERVER without SESSION CONTEXT MANAGER.

Figure 11.14 shows the structure of the inetd server. It waits for requests on a set of TCP ports defined in the configuration file /etc/inetd.conf. Whenever it receives a connection request, it starts the server program defined for this port in the configuration file which handles the request(s) of this connection. The inetd starts a server program by the fork() -exec() sequence which creates a new process and then loads the server program into the process. The file descriptor

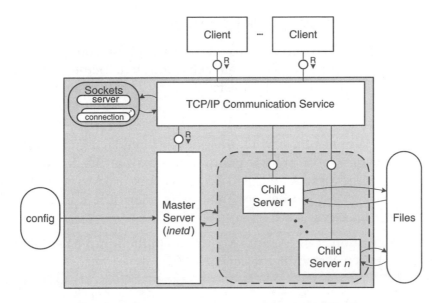

Figure 11.14: The Inetd: a typical FORKING SERVER

table is the only data which will not be deleted by exec(). A server program to be started by the inetd must therefore use the first file descriptor entry (#0) to access the connection socket.

11.3.2 Apache HTTP server

The Apache HTTP server [Apa] is a typical request processing server, which has been ported to many platforms. The early versions use the preforking server strategy as described below. Since version 1.3, Apache supports the Windows platform using threads which forced another server strategy (JOB QUEUE).

Apache 2 now offers a variety of server strategies called MPMs (Multi–Processing Modules) which adapt Apache to the multitasking capabilities of the platform and may offer different server strategies on one platform. The most interesting MPMs are:

- Preforking: LEADER / FOLLOWERS using processes with dynamic worker pool management. The promotion of the followers is done with a mutex (results in a FIFO order).

- WinNT: JOB QUEUE using a static thread pool.

- Worker MPM: Each process provides a JOB QUEUE using a static thread pool. The process pool is dynamically adapted to the server load by a WORKER POOL MANAGER (Master Server). The listener threads of the processes use a mutex to become a listener. (see Section 11.2.1)

All MPMs use a WORKER POOL with processes or threads, or even nest a thread pool in each process of a process pool. They separate the listener from the WORKER POOL MANAGER. A so-called Scoreboard is used to note the state of each worker task. Most worker pool managers adapt the number of worker tasks to the current server load.

A detailed description of the Apache MPMs and of their implementation can be found in the Apache Modeling Project [GKKS04].

The Preforking variant of Apache

Since its early versions in 1995, Apache uses the so-called *Preforking* strategy – a LEADER / FOLLOWERS pattern. A master server starts (forks) a set of child server processes doing the actual server tasks: listen for connection requests, process service requests. The master server is responsible for adjusting the number of child servers to the server load by assuring that the number of idle child servers will remain within a given interval.

Figure 11.15 shows the conceptual architecture of a preforking Apache server. At the top we see the clients, usually web browsers, sending HTTP requests via a TCP connection. HTTP is a stateless protocol, therefore there is no need to keep a session context. On the right-hand side we see the data to be served: documents to be sent to the client, or scripts to be executed, which produce data to be sent to the client. The Scoreboard at the bottom keeps the Worker Pool management data as mentioned in the WORKER POOL pattern.

The master server is not involved in listening or request processing. Instead, it creates, controls and terminates the child server processes and reacts to the commands of the administrator (the agent on the left side). The master server also processes the configuration files and compiles the configuration data. Whenever it creates a child server process, the new process gets a copy of this configuration data. After the administrator has changed a configuration

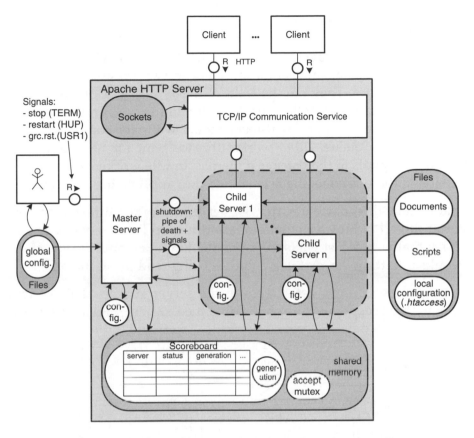

Figure 11.15: The Apache server using the preforking MPM

file, he has to advise the master server to re-read the configuration and re-place the existing child servers with new ones, including a copy of the new configuration data. It is possible to do this without interrupting busy child servers. The master server just terminates idle child servers and increments the generation number on the scoreboard. As every child server has an entry including its generation in the scoreboard, it checks after each request whether its generation is equal to the current generation and terminates otherwise.

The child servers use a mutex to assign the next listener, according to the LEADER / FOLLOWERS pattern. In contrast to Figure 11.11, the different roles of the workers in the pool are not shown.

The worker variant of Apache

Figure 11.16 shows the system structure of the Apache HTTP server using the worker MPM. The center shows multiple child server processes which all have an identical structure. They are the tasks of the WORKER POOL on the process level, as in the preforking MPM. Inside each child server process we find an extended job queue structure: A listener thread waits for connection requests and supplies a job queue. (Idle) worker threads wait for new jobs. The idle worker queue signals to the listener if there is an idle worker ready to process the next job. If there is none, the listener does not apply to the accept mutex.

The child_main thread creates the listener and worker threads by creating the starter thread (which terminates after setting up listener, workers and the queues) and after that just waits for a termination token on the 'pipe of death'. This results in setting the 'exit flag' which is being read by all threads.

Only one process listener gets access to the server sockets. This is done by applying for the accept mutex. In contrast to the LEADER / FOLLOWERS pattern,

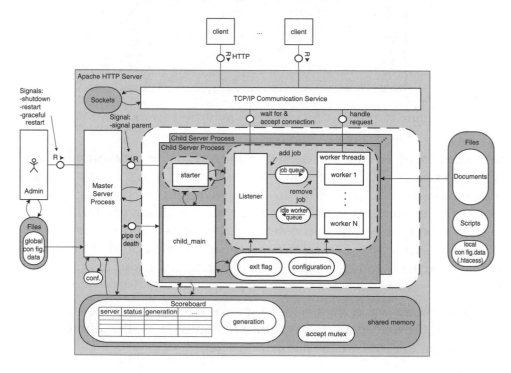

Figure 11.16: The Apache server using the worker MPM

the listener task does not change its role and processes the request. Instead, it checks if there is another idle worker waiting and applies for the accept mutex again.

11.3.3   SAP R/3

SAP's System R/3 [SAP94] is a scalable ERP system with an overall three-tier architecture as shown in Figure 11.17. The diagram also shows the inner architecture of an R/3 application server. (In practice, R/3 installations often include additional applications servers – these are omitted here for reasons of simplicity.) In the application server three of the patterns discussed above are actually applied.

The server's basic architecture is designed after the WORKER POOL pattern. The so-called dispatcher (a process) plays the role of the listener and forwards requests (sent by the SAP GUI clients) to worker tasks called *dialog work processes*. (There are further types of work processes, but these are of no interest here.)

Besides other purposes, the request queue is used for forwarding requests from the dispatcher to the work processes, i.e., it represents a *Job Queue*. While the

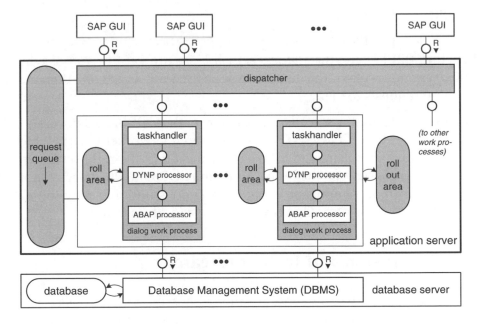

Figure 11.17:   The SAP R/3 application server architecture

work processes read request data from the queue by themselves, initial worker selection is actually done by the dispatcher.

As an R/3 session (called a transaction in SAP terms) spans multiple requests, a local SESSION CONTEXT MANAGER called a taskhandler is included in each work process. Before a request can be processed by the DYNP processor and the ABAP processor, the taskhandler retrieves the appropriate context from the roll out area (or creates a new one) and stores it in the work process' roll area. Afterwards, the taskhandler saves the context to the roll out area (at the session end, it would be deleted).

11.3.4   Related applications at object level

All of the above patterns have been discussed under the assumption that processes or threads are the building blocks for server implementation. However, some of the patterns are even applicable if we look at a system at the level of objects instead of tasks. When realizing a server's request-processing capabilities by a set of objects, these objects can be pooled in a similar way to a WORKER POOL. Instead of creating objects for the duration of a session or a single request, *worker objects* are kept in a pool and activated on demand. This helps to control resource consumption and avoids (potentially) expensive operations for creating or deleting objects.

For example, this idea has been put into practice with Sun's J2EE server architecture [J2E]. Here, the *stateless session beans* are kept in a pool while the so-called *container* plays the listener role, activating beans on demand and forwarding requests to them.

Another example are the so-called *servants* from the CORBA 3.0 portable object adapter specification [COR03]. These are server-side worker objects which can also be kept in a pool managed by the *object adapter* (if the right *server retention policy* has been chosen, see the POA section in [COR03]). The object adapter (in cooperation with an optional *servant manager*) does not only play the listener role – it also acts as SESSION CONTEXT MANAGER for the servants.

11.4   Conclusion and further research

Design patterns in the narrow sense are often discussed in a pure object–oriented context. Hence, they often present object–oriented code structures as a solution, typically classes, interfaces or fragments of methods. In contrast, the patterns presented here are conceptual patterns which deliberately leave open most of the coding problem. This initially seems to be a drawback, but it also widens the applicability of a pattern and increases the possibility of identifying a pattern within a given system. In fact, most of the industrial applications (known uses) examined in this paper are not implemented using an object–oriented language (although some OO concepts can be found). Furthermore, central ideas and topics (e.g., scheduling, task and session management) behind the patterns, have already been described in the literature about transaction processing systems [GR93].

Designing a good code structure is often a secondary problem with additional forces such as given languages, frameworks or legacy code. In order to remain 'paradigm–neutral', conceptual architecture patterns should be presented using appropriate notations like FMC. Object–oriented implementation of conceptual architecture models is an important research topic in this context [TG03, TG05].

Epilogue

Now that you have read the book, you may wonder where to go next. Perhaps you are wondering whether or not FMC might improve your development process. As for any new approach, the evaluation requires one to set up up some initial trial projects and gather experience in practice. For instance, you might occasionally include block diagrams in presentations or meetings when it serves to illustrate some idea. Convince people with results and avoid ideological discussions. Another starting point can be to analyze and document the architecture of a legacy system. It is important to get as much as feedback as possible. This does not mean that you have to walk around and ask people whether they like your diagrams. Feedback may come in the form of questions from people working with your presentations. What do they ask, what do they understand, what confuses them? The answer will help to improve your understanding of systems as well as the way in which you talk about systems.

Of course, discussing with other people using FMC can also be very useful, for instance, when addressing a new domain with specific modeling problems. For this reason, the discussion forum on the FMC website provides a meeting place for people to share their experiences about modeling, discuss problems and ask questions which are primarily, but not only, about FMC. It can be found at the following URL:

http://www.f-m-c.org

This website also provides access to the FMC Visio™ stencils which ease the creation of clear-layout FMC diagrams. A syntax checker, a PDF generator and a Petri net simulator complement this software package.

Once you have had your own experience of FMC and feel confident about its advantages, you might want to share your knowledge and convince others. We have found that the best way to achieve this is not to argue about FMC but simply to use it in projects. Other people will see how your simple but concise models improve their system understanding and communication.

Appendix A

Solutions

Exercise 2.1: Basic communication scenarios: television broadcast

The solution in Figure A.1 shows that the TV station transmits its program using one broadcast channel to which all TV receivers are connected. There are no individual channels between TV station and receivers!

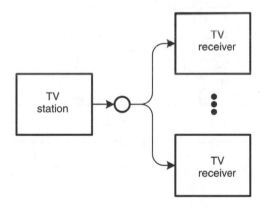

Figure A.1: **Exercise 2.1:** Television broadcast

Exercise 2.2: Basic communication scenarios: publish/subscribe

Figure A.2 shows a solution in two possible layouts. In either case, the wake-up service needs to maintain a storage for subscriptions. Each time a client subscribes or unsubscribes for a wake-up call, it is registered in this storage. A different channel is used for the wake-up calls. The extensive layout of alternative 1 emphasizes this aspect of the system. The reduced layout of

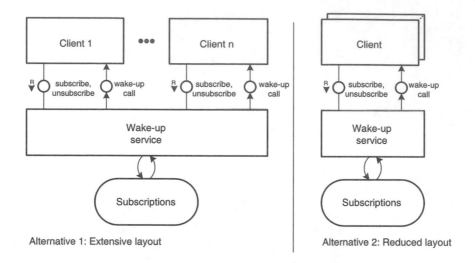

Figure A.2: Exercise 2.2: Wake-up service

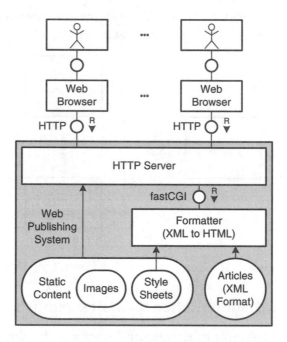

Figure A.3: Exercise 2.3: Block diagram of newspaper system

alternative 2 represents the same model. However, a trade-off has been made between visual complexity and conciseness in expression. The labeling provides the context which is necessary in order to understand that the second alternative does not show any broadcast channel either.

Exercise 2.3: Block diagram: newspaper system 1

The solution in Figure A.3 shows the HTTP Server accessing static content and using a fastCGI communication channel to request dynamic content from the Formatter. The protocol on the channel between Web Browser and HTTP Server is HTTP.

Exercise 2.4: Block diagram: newspaper system 2

The solution in Figure A.4 extends the block diagram of Figure A.3 and slightly adapts the layout: The editorial department of the print version uses their specific DTP tool and article storage, while the editorial department of the online version works on the same data as the HTTP Server reads.

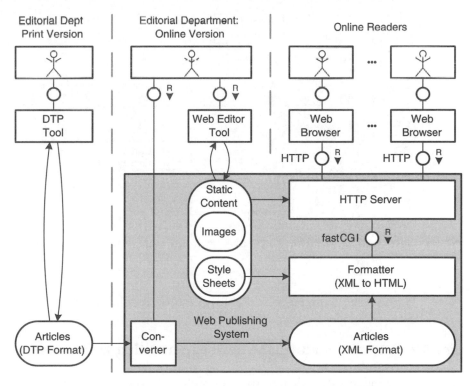

Figure A.4:   Exercise 2.4:   Block diagram of newspaper system, complete view

Exercise 3.1: Petri net: publisher/subscriber interaction

The two swimlanes in Figure A.5 show the activities of the model (publisher) and the views (subscribers), the Petri net shows their interaction. The central component is the update loop: The publisher browses through his subscriber list and sends an update request to each subscriber. A subscriber performs his update method. Not shown here are the details of the "Examine model" transition. Please note that, for simplicity reasons, only one view is shown although many view agents can subscribe to change events!

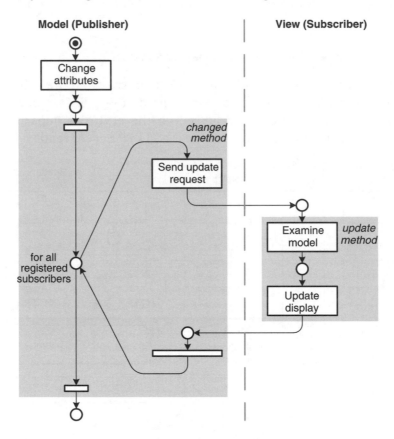

Figure A.5:   Exercise 3.1:   Publisher/subscriber interaction

Exercise 3.2: Petri net: reading the newspaper with a web browser

The Petri net in Figure A.6 shows the interaction between web browser and HTTP server when accessing resources that may require authorization. It is

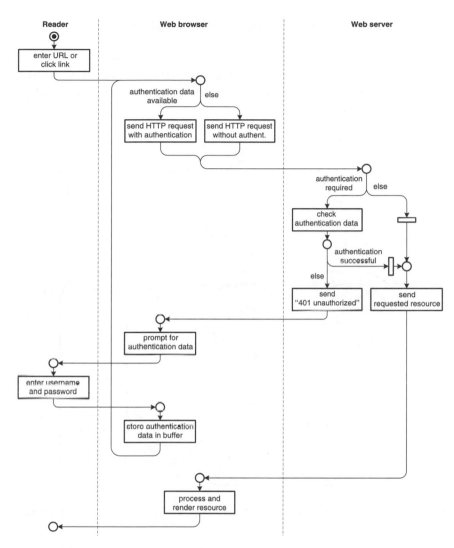

Figure A.6:   Exercise 3.2:   Interaction between the human reader, Web browser and
Web server

important to note that in case the resource requires authorization, the first
request fails. The browser requests authentication data from the user and then
sends the same request with additional authentication data to the server again.
For all further requests to this server, the browser adds the authentication data.
This method is called *Basic Authentication*. Using this method, an HTTP server
doesn't have to store session data for authenticated users.

Exercise 4.1: Data stored in the newspaper system

The E/R-diagram in Figure A.7 focuses on the sections to which articles are assigned. Only authenticated registered readers are allowed to access the restricted section. Not shown here is the fact that articles in the public section can be accessed by everyone.

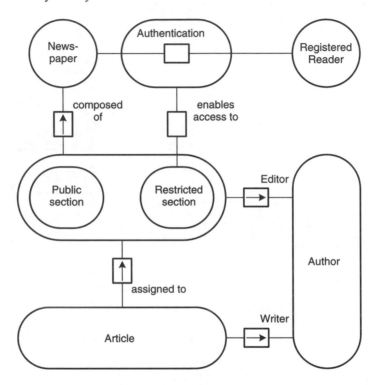

Figure A.7:   Exercise 4.1:   E/R diagram of the newspaper system's data

Exercise 4.2: Min/max notation

Following the min/max notation, the cardinality number denotes the number or range of relations in which an entity of a certain type participates. This applies to the solution in Figure A.8: since each child has a father, who is a male, and a mother, who is a female, we may say that each child participates in exactly one relation defining its biological parents: more mathematically, each child is assigned to exactly one binary tupel (male, female).

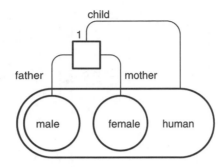

Figure A.8:   **Exercise 4.2:**   E/R diagram – Typical example of the min/max notation

Exercise 4.3: Cardinality number

Figure A.9 shows the cardinality numbers for relationship nodes with a uni-directed and a bi-directed arrow.

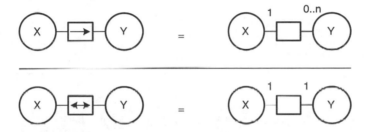

Figure A.9:   **Exercise 4.3:**   E/R diagram: short form for cardinality numbers denoting a functional relationship

Exercise 6.3: Dashboard device: operational versus control state

In the solution shown in Figure A.10, the number of the current source is the only state variable of the dashboard device. It is an operational variable: It can be specified without itemizing each transition between the possible values explicitly. There is also no need to itemize the different values explicitly. If *MAXSOURCENR* denotes the number of sources which can be displayed, the following expression describes the behavior of the selection mechanism:

$$
srcNumber(n+1) = \begin{cases}
srcNumber(n) + 1 & \text{IF userInput(n) = NEXT} \quad\text{AND srcNumber(n) < MAXSOURCENR} \\
1 & \text{IF userInput(n) = NEXT} \quad\text{AND srcNumber(n) = MAXSOURCENR} \\
srcNumber(n) - 1 & \text{IF userInput(n) = PREVIOUS AND srcNumber(n) > 1} \\
MAXSOURCENR & \text{IF userInput(n) = PREVIOUS AND srcNumber(n) = 1}
\end{cases}
$$

A Petri net is neither necessary nor appropriate to visualize this structure.

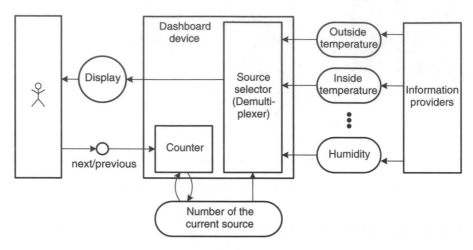

Figure A.10:   **Exercise 6.3:**   Dashboard device with its environment: compositional structure

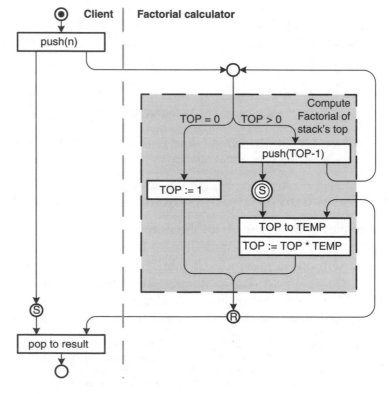

Figure A.11:   **Exercise 6.4:**   Recursive computation factorials: the Petri net

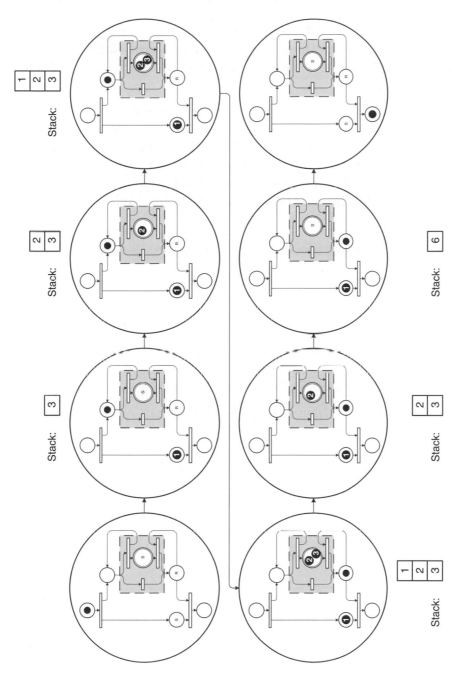

Figure A.12:   Exercise 6.4:   Reachability graph of the preceeding Petri net

Exercise 6.4: Recursive Petri nets and marking of stack places

Figure A.11 shows one possible solution for recursively computing factorials by using a stack and an additional storage to temporarily buffer intermediate results (TEMP). TOP refers to the top element of the stack. In this solution, it may be modified directly.

A reachability graph is used to illustrate the sequence of markings that is passed when computing the factorial of 3 (see Figure A.12). The particular content of the stack is shown beside each single marking. This recursive processing may be useful to understand the concept of recursive Petri nets. In general, recursively entering a recursive sub-net is not required for understanding. Instead, you should traverse the sub-net only once and consider any recursive re-entrance as an indivisible step.

Appendix B

Reference Sheets

Many thanks to Rémy Apfelbacher and Anne Rozinat, who did a great job in preparing this summary. (The layout was slightly changed in order to include the reference sheets into this book.)

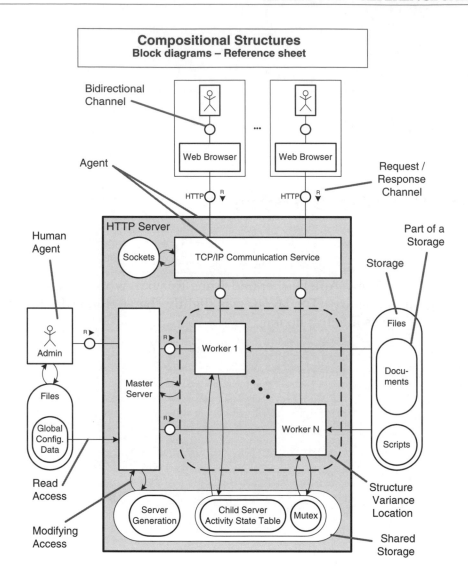

Compositional Structures
Block diagrams – Reference sheet

FMC Block diagrams show the compositional structures as a composition of collaborating system components.
There are active system components called agents and passive system components called locations. Each agent processes information and thus serves a well-defined purpose. Therefore an agent stores information in storages and communicates via channels or shared storages with other agents. Channels and storages are (virtual) locations where information can be observed.

Basic elements

[diagram: box "A" and stick figure]	active system component: agent, human agent	Serves a well-defined purpose and therefore has access to adjacent passive system components and only those may be connected to it. A human agent is an active system component exactly like an agent but the only difference is that it depicts a human. (Note 1: nouns should be used for identifier "A" Note 2: do not need to be depicted as rectangle or square but has to be angular)
[diagram: ellipse "S" and circle]	passive system component (location): storage, channel	A storage is used by agents to store data. (Note: do not need to be depicted as ellipse or circle but has to be rounded) A channel is used for communication purposes between at least two active system components. (Note: channels are usually depicted as smaller circles but may also vary like the graphical representation of storage places)
[diagram: arrow]	access type	Directed and undirected edges represent the kind of access an active system component has to a passive system component. The types of access are read access, write access and a combination of both. (Note: usually undirected edges depicting read/write access are used on channels, whereas two directed edges also depicting read/write access are used on storages)

common structures

[diagram: A ◄ S]	read access	Agent A has read access to storage S.
[diagram: A ► S]	write access	Agent A has write access to storage S. In the case when all information stored in S is overwritten
[diagram: A ⇄ S]	read/write access (modifying access)	Agent A has modifying access to storage S. That means that some particular information of S can be changed.
[diagram: A1 →O→ A2]	unidirectional communication channel	Information can only be passed from agent A1 to agent A2.
[diagram: A1 —O— A2]	bidirectional communication channel	Information can be exchanged in both directions (from agent A1 to agent A2 and vice versa).
[diagram: A1 ⇄ A2 REQ/RES; A1 —O— A2 R]	request/response communication channel (detailed and abbreviation)	Agent A1 can request information from agent A2 which in turn responds (e.g., function calls or http request/responses). Because it is very common, the lower figure shows an abbreviation of the request/response channel.
[diagram: A1 ⇄ S ⇄ A2]	shared storage	Agent A1 and agent A2 can communicate via the shared storage S, much like bidirectional communication channels.

advanced

[diagram: A1 with dotted A2]	structure variance	Structure variance deals with the creation and disappearance of system components. An agent (A1) changes the system structure (creation/deletion of A2) at a location depicted as dotted storage. System structure change is depicted as modifying access. After creation, agent A1 can communicate with agent A2, or vice versa.

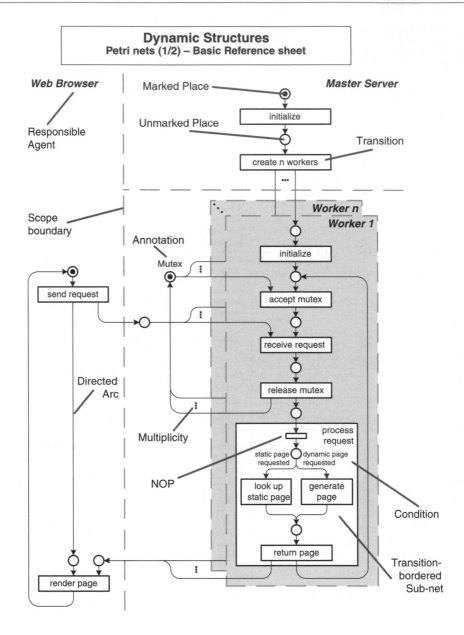

Dynamic Structures
Petri nets (1/2) – Basic Reference sheet

Web Browser

Marked Place

Master Server

Responsible
Agent

initialize

Unmarked Place

Transition

create n workers

Scope
boundary

Worker n
Worker 1

initialize

Annotation

Mutex

accept mutex

send request

receive request

Directed
Arc

release mutex

Multiplicity

process
request

NOP

static page   dynamic page
requested   requested

look up   generate
static page   page

Condition

return page

render page

Transition-
bordered
Sub-net

FMC diagrams for dynamic structures are based on transition-place Petri nets. They are used to express system behavior over time, depicting the actions performed by the agents, so they clarify how a system is working and how communication takes place between different agents. Here only the basic notational elements are covered, whereas the rest is located on another–more advanced–reference sheet (2/2).

Basic elements

T	transition	Stands for an operation, an event or an activity. (Note: verb should be used for identifier "T")
◯ ◎	place	Represents a control state or an additional condition. (Note: capacity = 1)
↓	directed arc	Connects a place and a transition.

further elements

▭	NOP	A transition meaning No OPeration. (Note: often used to keep the bipartiteness)
┊	swimlane divider	Distinguishes competences of agents.

common structures

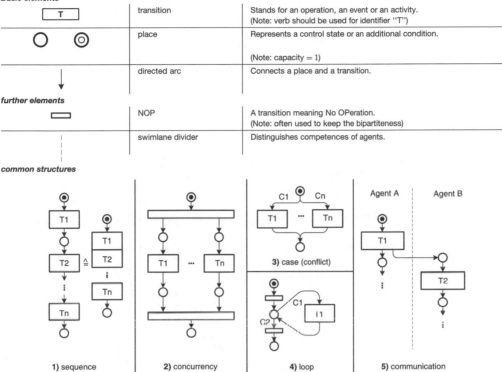

1) sequence   2) concurrency   4) loop   5) communication

1) Defines that transition T1 fires first, followed by transition T2, followed by transition T3 ....

2) Means that transitions have no causal ordering. The transitions T1, ..., Tn are concurrent, the firing of T1, ..., Tn has no special order.

3) Is used to choose one transition from among others. Only one of the transitions T1, ..., Tn will fire, depending on the conditions C1, ..., Cn associated to the arcs.

4) Is used to repeat the firing. Transition T1 will be repeated as long as condition C1 is fulfilled. Often C2 is not mentioned as it is assumed to be "else".

5) Whenever a swimlane divider is crossed, communication takes place. Upon this structure all possible communication types can be expressed (synchronous, asynchronous, etc.).

Dynamic Structures
Petri nets (2/2) – Advanced Reference sheet

Users

Print Spooler

Print Filter

create print job

load next job of
print queue

determine type
of print data

Multi-Token
Place

type=post-
script

else

transform to
postscript

printer is
postscript
printer

else

send data to
printer

create printer-
specific data

*Multitoken Place
Example–Processing
Print Jobs (UNIX)*

*Recursive Example–
Fibonacci Series*

PUSH (arg)

else

TOP > 1

arg := TOP
PUSH (arg -1)

Multitoken
Stack
Place

Stack
Place

res := POP
arg := POP -2
PUSH (res)
PUSH (arg)

TOP := 1

res := POP
return res

res := POP
TOP := res+TOP

$$\text{Fib(arg)} = \begin{cases} 1 & \text{if arg = 1} \\ 1 & \text{if arg = 2} \\ \text{Fib (arg -1) + Fib (arg -2) else} \end{cases}$$

Return Place

FMC diagrams for dynamic structures are based on transition-place Petri nets. They are used to express system behavior over time, depicting the actions performed by the agents. So they clarify how a system is working and how communication takes place between different agents. Here only the advanced notational elements are covered whereas the rest is located on the basic reference sheet (1/2).

Extended elements

	multitoken place	Places which can hold multiple tokens, but not an infinite number, are indicated as enlarged places with an annotation specifying the capacity (n > 1). Places with an infinite capacity are indicated by a double circle.
cap. n (cap. ∞)		
↓ [n]	arc	The arc weight n determines how many tokens will be consumed or produced when the connected transition fires. An arc weight of 1 is assumed, if there is no one specified.

recursion elements

	stack place (cap. 1, cap. infinite)	Is a place to store information about return positions using stack tokens. All stack places with the same name are strongly coupled with each other as the stack tokens, although placed on several stack places, are managed in a single stack. So all the stack places together constitute the return stack.
Ⓢ Ⓢ		
	return place	Is used like a normal place. But there is always a conflict to solve, as a return place is an input place for at least two transitions that also have stack places as input places.
Ⓡ		When a return place gets a token and more than one associated stack places have a stack token, the conflict is always solved in the same manner: the newest token on the stack must be consumed first. The newest token belongs to exactly one stack place and so the transition, where this stack place is an input place, will fire.

general recursion scheme

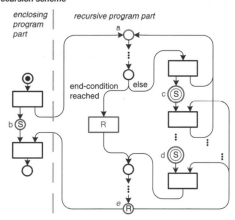

Each recursive diagram shows the following characteristics:
1) There is an entry point of the recursion (place a). Initially called by the enclosing program part, it is called afterwards several times by the recursive program part itself.
2) Transition R represents the reaching of the end-condition, which is always present to finish the recursion by determining the function value of at least one argument without calling the recursive part again.
3) Stack places like b, c and d are always input places for transitions that additionally have a return place (e) as input. All the stack places together constitute the return stack, which is used to store information about return positions.
4) A return place (e) is always an input place for at least two transitions that also have stack places (b, c, d) as input places.
5) Be aware that the return stack's only task is to guide the recursion handling. In addition all the necessary data stack modifications like PUSH, POP and TOP have to be done to remember values such as intermediate results.

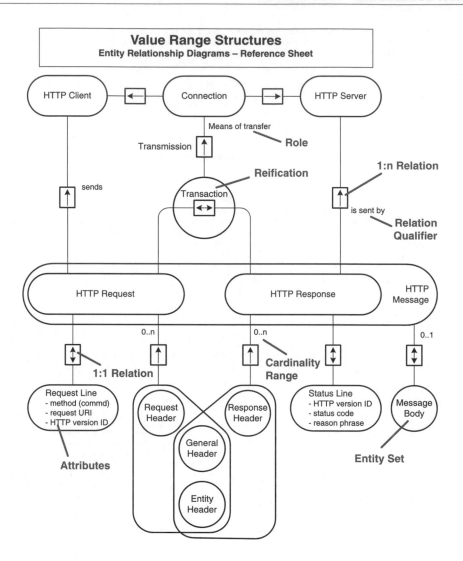

Value Range Structures
Entity Relationship Diagrams – Reference Sheet

FMC Entity Relationship Diagrams are used to depict value range structures or topics as mathematical structures.
Value range structures describe observable values at locations within the system, whereas topic diagrams allow a much wider usage in order to cover all correlation between interesting points.

Basic elements

	entity set	Consists of classified entities. Sets of entities participate in relations. Furthermore attributes (A1 ... An) might be specified. (Note: singular nouns should be used for identifier "E")

E
- A1
- ...

		Is a subset of the cross-product of all entities from the participating entity sets.
[R] [R] [R]	relation (n:m, 1:n, 1:1)	If the relation qualifier "R" is aligned with one of the entity set symbols it should be read from this direction (a sentence can be built up as aligned entity set identifier + relation identifier + entity set identifier.).
		If the relation qualifier "R" is aligned in the middle of the relation symbol there is no reading direction (usually nouns are used in this case).
		Connects a relation and an entity set.
[cardinality range] [role]	arc	A cardinality range may specify the minimum and maximum number of participation of all entities from the respective entity set in the relation just like the *(min,max)*-notation.
		Furthermore, a role might clarify the kind of participation of an entity in the relation.
		(Note: singular nouns should be used for identifier "role")

further elements

	orthogonal partitioning	Additional partitioning of an entity set which is independent of any previous partitioning.
	structure entity set	Is used to create an entity set from a structure (entity sets and relations).

common structures

	n:m relation	Each element of E1 occurs I to n times in the relation with E2 while each element of E2 occurs j to m times in the relation.

E1 i .. n   j   m E2

	1:n relation	Is like a unique function f(x ∈ E1) = y ∈ E2. Each element of E1 is associated with exactly one element of E2. (Note: the cardinality ranges should be omitted due to the arrow symbol inside the relation. Deviant cardinality ranges must be mentioned explicitly.)

E1 (1)   (1..n) E2

	1:1 relation	Is like an one-to-one function. One element of E1 is associated to exactly one element of E2 and vice versa. (Note: the cardinality ranges should be omitted due to the arrow symbol inside the relation. Deviant cardinality ranges must be mentioned explicitly.)

E1 (1)   (1) E2

advanced

1) n 'ary' relation (e.g., ternary)   **2)** reification   **3)** orthogonal partitioning

1) Sometimes it is necessary to correlate more than two entity sets to each other via n 'ary' relations. The example shows a ternary relation.

2) Elements of a relation constitute the elements of a new entity set, which in turn can participate in other relations. The example shows the relation C being reificated.

3) Partitioning of entity set E into the entity sets X, Y and additional independent partitioning of entity set E into the entity sets A, B. e.g., let entity set E be "Human Being" then entity set X may stand for "Man", Y for "Woman" and t here, of independent entity sets A and B, could mean "European" and "Non-European".

Appendix C

Glossary

Term	Definition
Access (read/write/modify)	Access of agents to locations. Can be categorized into read, write, or modifying access. With read access the information flows from location to agent, with write access the information flows from agent to location, and with modifying access it flows in both directions. → location; agent
Activity	Any sequence of operations → operation; processed–oriented activity; result–oriented activity
Agent	Active system component serving a specific purpose. The behavior of an agent can be observed in the locations connected with it as it processes the data stored there. → system component, active; location
Arc weight	The weight of a directed arc which connects a place and a transition in a Petri net defines the number of tokens that, in the case of firing of the transition, are taken from the place, if it is an input place; or are put into the place, if it is an output place. An arc weight is assigned to each arc, if it is not specified the default arc weight is one. → place; transition; Petri net; token; firing; input place; output place

Term	Definition
Block diagram	Bipartite diagram type showing the compositional structure of a system. The node types are angular and rounded shapes. Angular shapes represent agents (active system components), rounded shapes represent locations (passive system components). → compositional structure; node; agent; location; system component, active; system component, passive
Capacity	Maximum number of tokens a place can hold. → token; place; Petri net
Cardinality	The number or range of relations of a certain type that an entity may be engaged in. For instance, each identity card participates exactly once in a 'belongs to' relationship with its owner.
Channel	Passive system component connected to at least two agents which can communicate through it. Information transported over a channel is volatile. → agent; system component, passive
Class	A class is a set of entities which are of the same type, i.e., which have similar characteristics in terms of attributes and relations. A class of objects in terms of a programming language is only a special case. For instance, any eagle on this planet belongs to the class of 'birds' which is a subclass of 'animals', etc.
Compositional structure	The network of active and passive system components constituting a dynamic system, which performs the foundation for any observable behavior. Block diagrams are used to depict compositional structures. → system component, active; system component, passive

Term	Definition
Concurrency, degree of	Number of transitions in a Petri net which are independently enabled. → transition; Petri net; enabled transition
Concurrency	Two activities, or operations, are concurrent when they are causally independent of each other. They can therefore occur simultaneously or in arbitrary order. → activity; operation
Condition–event net (C/E net)	A Petri net whose places all have a capacity of one. The places of a condition–event net can be seen as statements which are either true or false according to their marking state. The firing of a transition is called an event because it makes some statements false (places lose their marking) and others true (places get marked). For a transition to be enabled, certain statements have to be true (corresponding places are marked), hence these are called conditions. → Petri net; place; firing; transition; enabled
Conflict	Marking of a Petri net in which the firing of one transition disables another transition. Arc predicate may be specified to determine the conflict resolution. → firing rules; marking Petri net; firing; enabled
Control unit	→ discrete control loop
Control state	To reduce the complexity of systems with a large set of possible states, state variables may be separated into those for control state and those for operational state. The value range of a control state can only be defined by explicitly listing all values and all value transitions. Nevertheless, when compared with operational variables the domain of control variables is usually relatively small. → discrete control loop; operational state

Term	Definition
Directed arc	One way connection between two nodes in a graph → node
Discrete control loop (Steuerkreis)	A system pattern which is often applied to reduce the complexity of systems with large sets of possible states. The basic idea is the separation of variables for control state and those for operational state. Accordingly, the system structure of a discrete control loop consists of a control unit and a connected operational unit. The control unit is that component of a discrete control loop which coordinates the sequence of actions of the operational unit. The state of the control unit reflects the control state of the discrete control loop. The operation unit is that part of a discrete control loop which provides the components to operate on and store the operational state and which connects the discrete control loop with its environment. It also provides the feedback to the control unit for further decisions. → control state; operational state
Dynamic structure	Summarizes the causal dependencies between the different types of operations, activities and events that determine the behavior of the system. The dynamic structure is represented using Petri nets. → operation; activity; event; Petri net
Entity relationship diagram E/R diagram	Bipartite graph used to describe value range structures and topic diagrams. The node types are both angular and rounded shapes. Rounded shapes represent entity sets and angular shapes represent the relationships between them. E/R diagrams whose entities are values describe value range structures. The entities in E/R diagrams that are topic plans can be of any type. → value range structure; topic diagram; entity.

Term	Definition
Enabled transition	A transition in a Petri net is enabled (ready to fire), if it meets two requirements: 1. Each input place of the transition contains as many tokens as the arc weight specifies. 2. Each output place of the transition can still accept as many tokens as the arc weight specifies. → transition; Petri net; marking; firing rule; input place; output place
Entity	Anything that constitutes a definable object, an individual. Each entity has an identity and entities are countable. Sets of entities and their relationships are represented using entity relationship diagrams. → Entity relationship diagram
Environment	Systems which have interfaces to interact with other components are called open systems. The components interacting with an open system are called the environment of that system. Since IT systems are always open systems, most FMC descriptions consider the system itself as well as its environment, to illustrate the purpose. Example: Describing an interactive system, a corresponding FMC model usually also refers to the user.
Event	The change from pre–value to post–value at some location which an observer may assign to a specific point in time. → location; Petri net
Event communication	Communication where the relevant information is not its content but the time of occurrence. Event communication between agents in a Petri net is represented by a flow of tokens between the agents swimlanes. → agent; Petri net; swimlane
Firing	The firing of a transition implies that this transition is enabled. Then, as many tokens as the arc weight specifies are taken from each input place; to each output place the number of tokens specified by its arc weight is added.

Term	Definition
	→ transition; enabled; token; arc weight; input place; output place
Firing rule	Defines the valid changes of the marking of a Petri net. It is used to transform the initial marking into other markings. The firing rule consists of two parts, the definition of firing and the definition of enabledness. → Petri net; place; transition; firing; enabled
Initial marking	The initial marking of a Petri net defines how many tokens each place contains at the beginning of the processing. The number of tokens per place may not exceed the place's capacity. → marking; Petri net; place; token; processing; capacity
Input place	The input place of a transition in a Petri net is a place which is connected to the transition by a directed arc that points towards the transition. Transitions can have any number of input places. → Petri net; place; transition; directed arc; enabled; firing; firing rule; output place
Layer diagram	Used to illustrate layerings, i.e., quadratic relations. Members of the basic set thus appear in two different, usually hierarchically distinct, roles in the relation. For instance, if the basic set consists of procedures in a computer program and the relation is that A calls B procedures can assume the role of the caller or the callee. Example: Procedure A calls B and C, procedure C calls D, procedure D calls itself (recursion).
Location	Storage or channel on which values can be observed. → channel; storage; system component, passive

Term	Definition
Location–bordered sub-net	A sub-net of a block diagram is location–bordered, if any node which belongs to the sub-net and that is connected with a node in the environment of the sub-net is a channel or storage. The identification of meaningful location–bordered sub-nets enables non–hierarchical transformations between abstract passive components and active implementations. → simplification
Marking	The marking of a place is equivalent to the number of tokens being put on that place. The marking of a Petri net follows from the markings of all its places. → place; Petri net; token
Node	Graphs consist of nodes and arcs. Nodes are generally represented as circles or squares, arcs as lines connecting the nodes.
Operation	Elementary activity which an agent can perform. It includes at least one write access to a location and an arbitrary number of read accesses. → activity; agent
Operational unit	→ discrete control loop
Operational state	To reduce the complexity of systems with a large set of possible states, state variables may be separated into those for control state and those for operational state. The domain of an operational variable can be specified without itemizing each transition between the possible values, explicitly. If compared with control variables, the domain of operational variables is usually very large. → control state; discrete control loop

Term	Definition
Output place	The output place of a transition in a Petri net is a place which is connected to the transition by a directed arc that points towards the place. Transitions can have multiple output places. → transition; Petri net; place; directed arc; input place; enabled; firing; firing rule
Partition	A partition of the set A is a set B whose elements are disjoint, non-null subsets of A. Each element of A has to be contained in exactly one element of B.
Partitions, orthogonal	Different partitions of an entity are orthogonal to each other if the criteria by which they have been classified are independent. Example: orthogonal partition of the entity Human Being by criteria gender and age. → partition
Petri net	A directed bipartite graph used with regard to FMC to describe the causal dependencies between events and activities, and thus to define a process type. Transitions–visualized by rectangular nodes–represent activities. Places–visualized by circles–refer to the control state and event communication. Applying firing–rules, a discrete order of sequences representing a causal ordering of events and activities is generated. → firing; event; operation; activity
Place	Node in a Petri net representing a possible state of a control variable or another condition, e.g., a communication event. → Petri net; marking; place-transition net; transition; capacity
Place–bordered sub-net	A sub-net of a Petri net is place–bordered, if any node which belongs to the sub-net and that is connected with a node in the environment of the sub-net is a place. → simplification

Term	Definition
Place–transition net	Place-transition nets are condition-event nets extended by 1. assigning an individual capacity to each place, 2. assigning a weight to each arc, and 3. defining a firing rule. Note: In the Context of FMC the term 'place-transition net' is rarely used. The term 'Petri net', however, always refers to graphs being place-transition nets. → transition; marking; firing rule; arc weight; capacity
Platform	System consisting of hard and software components that, by installing and executing an application software, becomes the application system which conforms to a domain specific role system model. → program processor
Process-oriented activity	The purpose of a process–oriented activity is its process and not a calculated result, e.g., a computer game. → result–oriented
Processing/executing	The task of a (program) processor. → program processor
Program net	Petri net associated with a corresponding program text making it possible to identify each place in the net with a line of code in the text. → Petri net
Program processor	An agent (usually part of a platform model) which executes a program. The platform thereby becomes the system specified in the program. → agent; platform
Refinement	Relation between models of the same type, which does not have to be formal. Refinements show more information and a more detailed depiction of structures, respectively, and represent a step towards implementation.

Term	Definition
Reification	A statement about the relation among some given entities that provides the foundation for a new entity with its own attributes and relations to other objects. Example: Given a 'married to' relationship between a man and a woman 'might', one can reify the relation and introduce the entity 'marriage' with an attribute 'date' and a relation to the wedding location.
Result–oriented activity	The purpose of a result–oriented activity is a calculation of some final state and output value. The process of determining the result is not of interest. → process–oriented
Return place	Return places, besides stack places and stack tokens, are used to model recursion in Petri nets. A return place is always an input place for at least two transitions which also have stack places as input places. This results in potential conflicts because the token in the return place can only be used for one transition. This conflict is solved by the token that was put on the stack places last. → stack place; stack token; input place
Simplification	The opposite of refinement → refinement
Stack place	Multitoken place used besides return places and stack tokens to model recursion in Petri nets. Stack places are marked by stack tokens and are always input places for transitions that additionally have a return place as an input place. → return place; stack token; Petri net; input place

Term	Definition
Stack token	Tokens of a stack place used, besides stack and return places, to model recursion in Petri nets. They are called stack tokens because, although placed on several stack places, their order of placement is managed in a single stack. If there is a conflict involving a return place, the stack token on top of the (placement) stack is released and the associated transition is fired. → stack place; return place; Petri net; token; transition
Storage	Persistent information storage available to at least one agent. → system component, passive
Structure	A structure is a construct of sets and relations linking the elements of the sets with each other, which contains at least one set and one relation.
Structure variation	A change in the compositional structure of the system implying the creation/activation or removal/deactivation of agents and locations. A part of the system structure which constitutes the content of a structure variance storage is modified by some agent performing a structure variance operation on that storage. → system component, active; system component, passive; agent
Swim lane	A sub-net of a Petri net delimited by a scope boundary to emphasize the responsibility of a specific agent or a group of agents for the behavior defined by that sub-net. → transition; Petri net; agent
System component, active	System components which act on storages and channels, i.e., which perform operations. → operation; system component, passive; agent
System component, passive	Passive system components are storages and channels. → system component, active

Term	Definition
System, continuous	A continuous system is characterized by a model according to which the values which may be observed on the different system locations may change continuously. → system, informational
System, discrete	A discrete system is characterized by a model according to which the values which may be observed on the different system locations may not change continuously – they are elements of a set of discrete values. → system, informational; location
System, dynamic	A concrete thing showing observable behavior. This behavior can be seen as the result of inter-acting system components. → system component, active; system component, passive
System, informational	A system is called informational if the essential point of the issues, which are observed in different places in the system, is not their material or energetic appearance, but their interpretation.
Token	Basic element of a Petri nets marking. The readiness to fire a transition requires that the transitions input places contain sufficient tokens. → Petri net; marking; transition; firing
Topic diagram/mind map	Diagram describing relationships between entities of arbitrary type using E/R diagram notation. → Entity relationship diagram/E/R diagram
Transition	A transition is a node in a Petri net and represents an event, operation, or activity. → place; place-transition net; event; operation; activity
Transition–bordered sub-net	A sub-net of a Petri net is transition–bordered, if any node which belongs to the sub-net and that is connected with a node in the environment of the sub-net is a transition.

Term	Definition
Transition–like sub-net	Transition–like sub-nets are transition–bordered sub-nets, such that we may think of describing the refinement of a determined, indivisible operation – an operation that may be represented by a single transition.
Value communication	Communication where the relevant information is the content and not the time of occurrence.
Value range	The value range of some channel or storage defines the set of (informational) values that can be written and read from that location during operation of the system. Values can be structured or unstructured. Well-known ranges of unstructured values are BOOLEAN and INTEGER.
Value structure, range of	Many operational values are structured values. This refers to the structure of the information, not the structure of the form which encodes the information and which also usually has its own structure. Whenever the range of structured values is quite large, which is quite common in practice, entity relationship diagrams are an appropriate means of characterizing the range. → structure; Entity relationship diagram/E/R diagram.

References

[Apa]   Apache HTTP Server Project. Web site. Available from: http://httpd.apache.org.

[BMW94]   Ted J. Biggerstaff, Bharat G. Mitbander, and Dallas E. Webster. Program Understanding and the Concept Assignment Problem. *Communications of the ACM*, 37(5):72–83, May 1994.

[Boo94]   Grady Booch. *Object-Oriented Analysis and Design with Applications*. Benjamin Cummings, 1994.

[BRJ05]   Grady Booch, James Rumbaugh, and Ivar Jacobson. *The Unified Modeling Language User Guide*. Addison Wesley, 2005.

[CDK94]   George Coulouris, Jean Dollimore, and Tim Kindberg. *Distributed Systems - Concepts and Design*. Addison Wesley, 1994.

[Che76]   Peter Pin-Shan S. Chen. The Entity-Relationship Model: Toward a Unified View of Data. *ACM Transactions on Database Systems*, 1(1):9–36, 1976.

[Cle96]   Paul C. Clements. A survey of architecture description languages. In *IWSSD '96: Proceedings of the 8th International Workshop on Software Specification and Design*, p. 16. IEEE Computer Society, March 1996.

[COR03]   The Common Object Request Broker Architecture, 2003. version 3.02.

[DeM78]   Tom DeMarco. *Structured Analysis and System Specification*. Yourdon Press, 1978.

[DeM95]   Tom DeMarco, ''Why does software cost so much?: and other puzzles of the information age.'', Dorset House Publishing, 1995.''

[DIN92]   DIN. DIN66200 - Betrieb von Rechensystemen - Begriffe, Auftrags-
             beziehungen. Deutsche norm, Deutsches Institut für Normung e.V.,
             Maerz 1992.

[Fra03]   David S. Frankel. *Model Driven Architecture −Applying MDA to En-
             terprise Computing*. John Wiley & Sons, 2003.

[Gal98]   Frank Gales. *Ein Beitrag zur Begriffswelt der Schaffung Programmierter
             Systeme*. Shaker Verlag, 1998.

[GHJV95]   Erich Gamma, Richard Helm, Ralph Johnson, and John Vlissides.
             Design Patterns. Addison Wesley, 1995.

[GKKS04]   Bernhard Gröne, Andreas Knöpfel, Rudolf Kugel, and Oliver
             Schmidt. The Apache Modelling Project. Technical Report 5, Hasso-
             Plattner-Institute, Potsdam, 2004.   Available from: http://www.
             f-m-c.org.

[Gla02]   Robert L. Glass. The Naturalness of Object Orientation: Beating a
             Dead Horse? *IEEE Software*, 19(3):104, 103, May/June 2002.

[Glu65]   V.M. Glushkow. Automata Theory and Structural Design Problems
             of Digital Machines. *Kibernetika*, 1(1):3−11, 1965.

[GR89]   Adele Goldberg and David Robson. *Smalltalk-80, the Language*. Ad-
             dison Wesley, 1989.

[GR93]   J. Gray and A. Reuter. *Transaction Processing: Concepts and Techniques*.
             Morgan Kaufmann, 1993.

[Grö04]   Bernhard Gröne. Konzeptionelle Patterns und ihre Darstellung.
             Phd. thesis, Hasso-Plattner-Institut, Universität Potsdam, 2004.
             http://pub.ub.uni-potsdam.de/volltexte/2005/230/ (urn:nbn:de:
             kobv:517-opus-2302).

[Grö05]   Bernhard Gröne. Architekturmodelle als zentrales Kommunikations-
             mittel - Erfahrungen aus einem SAP-Projekt. In NetObjectDays 2005
             Proceedings, pages 381−390, September 2005.

[GT03]   Bernhard Gröne and Peter Tabeling. A System of Conceptual
             Architecture Patterns for Concurrent Request Processing Servers.
             In *Proceedings of the Second Nordic Conference on Pattern Languages of
             Programs (VikingPLoP 2003)*, Bergen, Norway, 2003.

[Hab01]   Naji Habra. Separation of Concerns in Software Engineering Education. In *Proceedings for Advanced Separation of Concerns Workshop, 23rd International Conference on Software Engineering, ICSE2001*, May 2001.

[HC70]   Anatol W. Holt and Frederic Commoner. Events and Conditions. In *Record of the Project MAC Conference on Concurrent Systems and Parallel Computation*, pages 3–52. ACM, 1970.

[HNS00]   Christine Hofmeister, Robert Nord, and Dilip Soni. *Applied Software Architecture*. Addison-Wesley, 2000.

[Hoa78]   C.A.R. Hoare. Communicating Sequential Processes. *Communications of the ACM*, 21(8):666–677, August 1978.

[HR82]   Theo Härder and Andreas Reuter. Principles of Transaction Oriented Database Recovery – A Taxonomy. Technical report, University of Kaiserslautern, Germany, 1982.

[J2E]   Java 2 Platform: Enterprise Edition. Web site. Available from: `http://java.sun.com/j2ee`.

[Jac95]   Michael Jackson. The World and the Machine. In *Proceedings of the 17th International Conference on Software Engineering*, pages 283–292, April 1995.

[JCJ92]   Ivar Jacobson, Magnus Christerson, and Patrik Jonsson. *Object-Oriented Software Engineering*. Addison-Wesley, 1992.

[Kai99]   Hermann Kaindl. Difficulties in the Transition from OO Analysis to Design. *IEEE Software*, 16(5):94–102, September/October 1999.

[Kel03]   Frank Keller. Über die Rolle von Architekturbeschreibungen im Software-Entwicklungsprozess. Phd. thesis, Hasso-Plattner Institute Potsdam, 2003.

[KJ02a]   Michael Kircher and Prashant Jain. Eager Acquisition. In *Proceedings of EuroPLoP 2002*.

[KJ02b]   Michael Kircher and Prashant Jain. Pooling. In *Proceedings of EuroPLoP 2002*.

[Kle99]   Wolfram Kleis. *Konzepte zur Verständlichen Beschreibung Objektorientierter Frameworks*. Shaker Verlag, 1999.

[Knö04]   Andreas Knöpfel. Konzepte der Beschreibung interaktiver Systeme (Concepts of Describing Interactive Systems). Phd. thesis, Hasso-Plattner-Institut, Universität Potsdam, 2004. http://pub.ub.uni-potsdam.de/volltexte/2005/289/ (urn:nbn:de:kobv:517-opus-2898).

[KTA+02]   Frank Keller, Peter Tabeling, Rémy Apfelbacher, Bernhard Gröne, Andreas Knöpfel, Rudolf Kugel, and Oliver Schmidt. Improving Knowledge Transfer at the Architectural Level: Concepts and Notations. In *Proceedings of The 2002 International Conference on Software Engineering Research and Practice*, June 2002.

[Mey97]   Bertrand Meyer. *Object-oriented Software Construction*. Prentice Hall, 1997.

[Mil02]   Joaquin Miller. What UML 2.0 Should Be – Article Series. *Communications of the ACM*, 45(11):67–85, 2002.

[MT00]   Nenad Medvidovic and Richard N. Taylor. A Classification and Comparison Framework for Software Architecture Description Languages. *IEEE Transactions on Software Engineering*, 16(1):70–93, 2000.

[Mur89]   Tadao Murata. Petri nets: Properties, Analysis and Applications. *Proceedings of the IEEE*, 77(4):541–580, September/October 1989.

[OMG03]   OMG. UML 2.0 Superstructure Specification, 2003. http://www.omg.org/.

[PAC01]   Helen C. Purchase, Jo-Anne Allder, and David A. Carrington. User preference of graph layout aesthetics: A UML study. In *GD '00: Proceedings of the 8th International Symposium on Graph Drawing*, p. 5–18. Springer-Verlag, London, UK, 2001.

[Par72]   David L. Parnas. On the criteria to be used in decomposing systems into modules. *Communications of the ACM*, 15(12):1053–8, December 1972.

[Pet61]   Carl Adam Petri. Kommunikation mit Automaten (Communicating with automata). Phd. thesis, Technical University of Darmstadt, July 1961.

[Pet77]   James L. Peterson. Petri Nets. *ACM Computing Surveys*, 9(3):223–252, September 1977.

[Pet95]   Marian Petre. Why looking isn't always seeing. *Readership Skills and Graphical Programming*. 36(6):33–44, 1995.

[PS97]   Dorina Petriu and Gurudas Somadder. A pattern language for improving the capacity of layered client/server systems with multi–threaded servers. In *Proceedings of EuroPLoP 1997*, 1997.

[RBP+91]   James Rumbaugh, Michael Blaha, William Permerlani, Frederick Eddy, and William Lorensen. *Object-oriented Modeling and Design*. Prentice Hall, 1991.

[SAP94]   SAP Basis Modeling Group. SAP technical documentation (blue books). Technical report, SAP AG, Walldorf, 1994.

[Sch98]   Douglas C. Schmidt. Evaluating architectures for multithreaded object request brokers. *Communications of the ACM*, 41(10):54–60, 1998.

[SDK+95]   Mary Shaw, Robert DeLine, Daniel V. Klein, Theodore L. Ross, David M. Young, and Gregory Zelesnik. Abstractions for Software Architecture and Tools to Support Them. *IEEE Transactions on Software Engineering*, 21(4):314–335, 1995.

[Sø02]   Kristian Elof Sørensen. Session Patterns. In *Proceedings of EuroPLoP 2002*. EuroPLOP 2002 Web Site, 2002. Available from: http://hillside.net/patterns/EuroPLoP2002/papers. html.

[SSRB00]   Douglas Schmidt, Michael Stal, Hans Rohnert, and Frank Buschmann. *Pattern-oriented Software Architecture Vol. 2 – Patterns for Concurrent and Networked Objects*. Series in Software Design Patterns. John Wiley & Sons, 2000.

[SV96a]   Douglas C. Schmidt and Steve Vinoski. Object Interconnections: Comparing Alternative Programming Techniques for Multi-threaded Servers (Column 5). *SIGS C++ Report Magazine*, February 1996.

[SV96b]   Douglas C. Schmidt and Steve Vinoski. Object Interconnections: Comparing Alternative Programming Techniques for Multi-threaded Servers (Column 6). *SIGS C++ Report Magazine*, April 1996.

[SV96c]   Douglas C. Schmidt and Steve Vinoski. Object Interconnec-
            tions: Comparing Alternative Programming Techniques for Multi-
            threaded Servers (Column 7). *SIGS C++ Report Magazine*, July
            1996.

[Tab02]   Peter Tabeling. Multi Level Modeling of Concurrent and Distributed
            Systems. In *Proceedings of the International Conference on Software
            Engineering Research and Practice*. CSREA Press, June 2002.

[Tab04]   Peter Tabeling. Architectural Description with Integrated Data Con-
            sistency Models. In *Proceedings of the IEEE International Conference
            and Workshop on the Engineering of Computer-Based Systems*. IEEE
            Computer Society, May 2004.

[Tel94]   Gerard Tel. *Introduction to Distributed Algorithms*. Cambridge Uni-
            versity Press, 1994.

[TG03]   Peter Tabeling and Bernhard Gröne. Mappings between object-
            oriented technology and architecture-based models. In *Proceedings
            of the International Conference on Software Engineering Research and
            Practice, SERP '03*, p. 568–74, June 2003.

[TG05]   Peter Tabeling and Bernhard Gröne. Integrative architecture elicita-
            tion for large computer based systems. In *Proceedings of the 12th IEEE
            Symposium and Workshops on Engineering of Computer Based Systems
            (ECBS 2005)*, pages 51–61. IEEE Computer Society, April 2005.

[VKZ02]   Markus Völter, Michael Kircher, and Uwe Zdun. Object-oriented
            remoting – basic infrastructure patterns. *Proceedings of VikingPLoP
            2002*, 2002.

[War89]   Paul T. Ward. How to Integrate Object Orientation with Structured
            Analysis and Design. *IEEE Software*, 6(2):74–82, 1989.

[Wen70]   Siegfried Wendt. Eine Methode zum Entwurf komplexer
            Schaltwerke unter Verwendung spezieller Ablaufdiagramme. *Digi-
            tal Processes*, 5(3-4):213–22, 1970.

[Wen79]   Siegfried Wendt. The programmed action module: An element for
            system modelling. *Digital Processes*, 5(3-4):213–22, 1979.

[Wen80]   Siegfried Wendt. Modified Petri Nets as flowcharts for recursive
            programs. *Software – Practice and Experience*, 10:935–42, 1980.

[Wen91]   Siegfried Wendt. *Nichtphysikalische Grundlagen der Informationstechnik*. Springer-Verlag, Berlin, 1991.

[Wen98a]   Siegfried Wendt. The Concept of State in System Theory. Technical report, Universität Kaiserslautern, 1998. http://www.f-m-c.org/.

[Wen98b]   Siegfried Wendt. Operationszustand versus Steuerzustand – eine äußerst zweckmäßige Unterscheidung. Technical report, Universität Kaiserslautern, 1998. http://www.f-m-c.org/.

[Wen01]   Siegfried Wendt. Ein grundlegender Begriffsrahmen für das Wissensmanagement im Software-Engineering. In *Proceedings of the KnowTech (Dresden, 2001)*, November 2001. http://www.community-of-knowledge.de.

[WK03]   Siegfried Wendt and Frank Keller. FMC: An Approach Towards Architecture-Centric System Development. In *Proceedings of the 10th IEEE Symposium and Workshops on Engineering of Computer Based Systems (ECBS 2003)*, pages 173–182, April 2003.

[YC79]   Edward Yourdon and Larry L. Constantine. *Structured Design – Fundamentals of a Discipline of Computer Program and Systems Design*. Prentice-Hall, 1979.

Index